HOW TO OPEN & OPERATE
A FINANCIALLY SUCCESSFUL

IMPORT EXPORT
BUSINESS:

WITH COMPANION CD-ROM

BY MARITZA MANRESA

HOW TO OPEN & OPERATE A FINANCIALLY SUCCESSFUL IMPORT
EXPORT BUSINESS: WITH COMPANION CD-ROM

Copyright © 2010 Atlantic Publishing Group, Inc.
1405 SW 6th Avenue • Ocala, Florida 34471 • Phone 800-814-1132 • Fax 352-622-1875
Web site: www.atlantic-pub.com • E-mail: sales@atlantic-pub.com
SAN Number: 268-1250

Library of Congress Cataloging-in-Publication Data

Manresa, Maritza.
  How to open & operate a financially successful import export business : with companion
CD-ROM / by Maritza Manresa.
      p. cm.
  Includes bibliographical references and index.
  ISBN-13: 978-1-60138-226-9 (alk. paper)
  ISBN-10: 1-60138-226-X (alk. paper)
  1. Trading companies--United States--Management. 2. Imports--United States. 3.
Exports--United States. 4. New business enterprises--United States--Management. I. Title. II.
Title: How to open and operate a financially successful import export business.
  HF1416.5.M355 2010
  658.8'4--dc22
                        2010005093

Printed in the United States

PROJECT MANAGER: Nicole Orr • norr@atlantic-pub.com
PEER REVIEWER: Marilee Griffin • mgriffin@atlantic-pub.com
INTERIOR DESIGN: Samantha Martin • smartin@atlantic-pub.com
INTERIOR LAYOUT: Harrison Kuo • hkuo@atlantic-pub.com
ASSISTANT EDITOR: Angela Pham • apham@atlantic-pub.com
COVER DESIGN: Meg Buchner • meg@megbuchner.com
BACK COVER DESIGN: Jackie Miller • millerjackiej@gmail.com

Printed on Recycled Paper

We recently lost our beloved pet "Bear," who was not only our best and dearest friend but also the "Vice President of Sunshine" here at Atlantic Publishing. He did not receive a salary but worked tirelessly 24 hours a day to please his parents. Bear was a rescue dog that turned around and showered myself, my wife, Sherri, his grandparents Jean, Bob, and Nancy, and every person and animal he met (maybe not rabbits) with friendship and love. He made a lot of people smile every day.

We wanted you to know that a portion of the profits of this book will be donated to The Humane Society of the United States. *—Douglas & Sherri Brown*

The human-animal bond is as old as human history. We cherish our animal companions for their unconditional affection and acceptance. We feel a thrill when we glimpse wild creatures in their natural habitat or in our own backyard.

Unfortunately, the human-animal bond has at times been weakened. Humans have exploited some animal species to the point of extinction.

The Humane Society of the United States makes a difference in the lives of animals here at home and worldwide. The HSUS is dedicated to creating a world where our relationship with animals is guided by compassion. We seek a truly humane society in which animals are respected for their intrinsic value, and where the human-animal bond is strong.

Want to help animals? We have plenty of suggestions. Adopt a pet from a local shelter, join The Humane Society and be a part of our work to help companion animals and wildlife. You will be funding our educational, legislative, investigative and outreach projects in the U.S. and across the globe.

Or perhaps you'd like to make a memorial donation in honor of a pet, friend or relative? You can through our Kindred Spirits program. And if you'd like to contribute in a more structured way, our Planned Giving Office has suggestions about estate planning, annuities, and even gifts of stock that avoid capital gains taxes.

Maybe you have land that you would like to preserve as a lasting habitat for wildlife. Our Wildlife Land Trust can help you. Perhaps the land you want to share is a backyard— that's enough. Our Urban Wildlife Sanctuary Program will show you how to create a habitat for your wild neighbors.

So you see, it's easy to help animals. And The HSUS is here to help.

THE HUMANE SOCIETY
OF THE UNITED STATES.

2100 L Street NW • Washington, DC 20037 • 202-452-1100
www.hsus.org

Trademarks

All trademarks, trade names, or logos mentioned or used are the property of their respective owners and are used only to directly describe the products being provided. Every effort has been made to properly capitalize, punctuate, identify, and attribute trademarks and trade names to their respective owners, including the use of ® and ™ wherever possible and practical. Atlantic Publishing Group, Inc. is not a partner, affiliate, or licensee with the holders of said trademarks.

Dedication

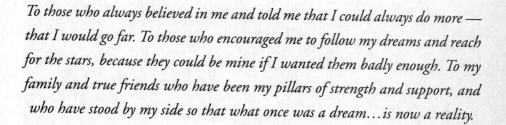

*To those who always believed in me and told me that I could always do more —
that I would go far. To those who encouraged me to follow my dreams and reach
for the stars, because they could be mine if I wanted them badly enough. To my
family and true friends who have been my pillars of strength and support, and
who have stood by my side so that what once was a dream…is now a reality.*

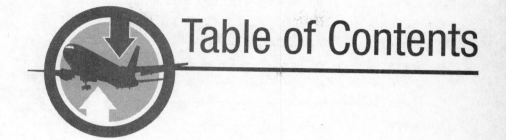

Table of Contents

Chapter 3: Determining the Legal Structure of Your Business   45

Chapter 4: Prepare a Business Plan   53

Chapter 5: Effective Financial Management for a Profitable Business — Budgeting & Financing   65

Chapter 6: Product Classification — Understanding the Harmonized Tariff Schedule 89

Chapter 7: Importing 99

Chapter 12: Government Regulations, Free Trade Agreements, and Other International Trade Issues 231

Chapter 13: Managing an Ethical and Environmentally Responsible Business 247

# Introduction

S tarting a business, regardless of its nature, is always very exciting. How
could it not be? It is the realization of the American dream. However,
the dream is not to simply start your own business, but to successfully operate it for as long as you wish. To accomplish this, it will take more than the
initial enthusiasm and excitement of starting a new venture — it will take
a positive outlook, commitment, and the willingness to learn new things.
The purpose of this book is to provide you with the knowledge and tools
to successfully compete in the global market. Looking at it as a whole, the
information may seem a bit overwhelming; it is my intention, however, to
take you through this process step by step. Each step is essential and plays a
part in the ultimate outcome: establishing and operating a financially successful import export business.

Your potential for success in the import export business is immense —
95.5 percent of the world's population exists outside the United States,
and 67 percent of the global purchasing power is also generated from outside the U.S. Regardless of fluctuations in the world economy, the international trade industry continues to flow. There will always be demand
for goods not available locally, but that can be obtained from another part
of the world. Also, the possibilities for importation and exportation are

practically endless. During the years I was involved in international trade as a foreign-trade zone manager, I worked with many companies that were exporting goods that you would have never imagined had a market abroad. Patented inventions that might have seemed useless to us turned out to be a great hit when exported abroad. In other words, there is no such thing as a bad idea when it comes to a possible product to import or export. Be creative. Look around you as you walk around the great city in which you live, or the small town you call home, and pay attention to all of the things that were probably imported being consumed in your area. These are things that you could be importing as part of your business.

As you make your way through the book, putting into action the recommended steps, you will see your business unfold and materialize into a thriving, prosperous international trade operation. The first few chapters of the book have been designed to take you step by step through the process of establishing your business — starting with the inception of your idea to enter the import export industry, then going through the moment you are ready to begin operations. You will be exposed to every form of a business's legal structures, allowing you to make educated decisions as to how you want your business to operate. You will also learn about the Internal Revenue Service's requirements, as well as each individual state's filing requirements. Most importantly, you will learn about the different capacities in which you can operate as you become involved in international trade. Choosing one of these roles will determine the course of your business operations in the import and export industry. I have included, for your use and reference, an outline of a business plan, which is critical in the successful operation of any business. Every significant detail is addressed in order to take you through the process of establishing your new business as smoothly as possible.

Toward the middle part of the book, you will find the knowledge and the tools you will need to actually operate your import export business successfully. I discuss the intricacies of importing and exporting separately in an effort to more clearly explain the concepts individually affecting each operation. The Harmonized Tariff Schedule, which is critical to understand in the international trade business, is discussed at length, as well as topics such as the process of selecting suppliers from foreign countries. U.S. Customs and Border Protection requirements and regulations are also addressed in this part of the book, including the benefits of using Customs bonded warehouses, as well as operating under foreign-trade zone status.

Finally, in the last few chapters of the book, I address key elements essential to operating successfully throughout the life of your business. It also takes a look at the importance of managing your business ethically and dealing with countries that have unfair labor practices. Lastly, because it is so important to seek the advice of experts in unfamiliar matters, there are references for professional trade organizations and international trade business resources to assist you in staying current with changes in the industry. From experience, I can honestly say that while I was involved in international trade, I saw many changes take place in the industry that affected the way importers and exporters conducted their business. That is why it is so important to stay on top of any changes in laws and regulations affecting the international trade industry, as it will directly impact the way you do business.

At any given time, your import or export arrangements may be impacted by changing political or economic conditions in any of the countries with which you are doing business. Therefore, this book includes references to a comprehensive list of resources, both through the Internet and personal contacts to whom you can refer for assistance, guidance, and support. The Internet has proved to be a live source of information, as it is continuously updated, but oftentimes what is gained from personal contact cannot be compared to anything we may get online. The networking and information exchange that results from joining professional organizations or seeking the assistance of professionals in the trades associated with importing and exporting is extremely valuable.

I hope you keep this book within arm's reach and turn to it whenever you have a question about what is the appropriate document for a particular transaction, whom to contact regarding an issue at hand, or simply to refresh your memory about a particular subject. Make this book your import export business partner. Together, you will move from a start-up company to a business with increasing profit margins. Going global truly is as exciting as it sounds — the possibilities are truly endless. Good luck!

Chapter 1

The World of International Trade

What an exciting world that is! Starting up your own business is quite exciting in itself, but when you are talking about an import export business, you are really in for quite an adventure. Before I start getting into the "nuts and bolts" of how to set up your business and start discussing the details of what you need to know to run your business, I would like to first start with a little bit of history of the international trade industry. Also, I will briefly touch on some basic information that will get you acclimated to the world of international trade.

A Little Bit of History

International trade has been around for centuries, and it continues to grow as trading across international borders has become easier and faster due to constantly evolving technology. The development and continued proliferation of the World Wide Web, the speed and accuracy in which goods can be mass produced around the world, and the speed in which these goods can be transported to and from anywhere globally has opened the doors for even the smallest import export business to take part of this ever-expanding industry. International trade has definitely come a long way when you consider how trading has evolved from when the Arabs traveled by camel to trade spices and silk to the highly automated way in which international trade takes place today.

As civilizations evolved, so did trading among countries. However, it can also be said that as trading expanded among countries, civilizations and countries continued to expand. The expansion of many thriving civilizations can be attributed to trade because the search for goods and necessities not available in local markets inspired many civilizations to look for those goods somewhere else, resulting in the trade of goods with others. Although in the early Middle Ages trading was somewhat restricted because of transportation issues, by the early modern era it was starting to evolve even more. For example, in the late 1500s to prevent piracy and smuggling, Japan began to require a system of licenses to conduct foreign trade. By the 1800s, Japan was trading with Portugal, and Britain and China went to war over the trade of opium. The first free trade agreement, between Britain and France, was established as a result.

As far as the United States' involvement in international trade is concerned, for most of its early history, the U.S. imposed barriers on foreign importers in the form of steep tariffs in an effort to protect the U.S. manufacturers from foreign producers. However, that policy later changed, and for many years the United States has maintained an open market policy more conducive to open trading. As industrialization continued to the develop in the 1900s, so did international trade. In 1947, the General Agreement on Tariffs and Trade (GATT) was established, with 23 countries participating from throughout the world. This was a major event of significant impact in the international trade industry. GATT became a multilateral international agreement that would regulate world trade. Although it went through many modifications throughout the years, GATT remained in place until 1995, when the World Trade Organization was created by GATT to take over as the agency responsible for facilitating trade around the world.

In a global effort to encourage fair free trade, numerous free trade agreements have entered among countries throughout the years. These agreements are entered into by members of the World Trade Organization (WTO) in an effort to promote trade among its members and stimulate the economy in participating countries. There are multiple international free trade agreements currently in effect throughout the world. These agreements can be amended while in effect, and they can also be terminated. Currently, the U.S. has free trade agreements in effect with 17 countries throughout the world. One of the most well-known free trade agreements is the North American Free Trade Agreement (NAFTA) between the United States, Canada, and Mexico, which became effective in January 1994 and has resulted in the world's largest free trade area, producing over 17 trillion dollars worth of products and services.

In recent years, most specifically after the events of September 11, we have seen organizational changes in governing and administrative agencies regulating international trade domestically. What used to be U.S. Customs is now U.S. Customs and Border Protection. Security of the transportation of goods across borders has been heightened and requirements are stricter. There has also been significant advancements made in technology, making the movement of goods across borders smoother. It is an industry that, although highly regulated and document-intensive, can now be managed with ease since so much of it has been automated. It used to be that all Customs and Border Protection forms had to be in paper form with multiple copies, all signed. Now, much of the "paperwork" can be done electronically, speeding up the process of importing and exporting.

Although Customs is at the center of it all, they are not the only agency involved in the import and export industry. There are other agencies and organizations, both private and public, as well as industry-related service providers that play an intricate role in the overall activities of international trade.

Some of the Players:
The Game of International Trade

In addition to the expected individuals and agencies that you have to deal with in the establishment of a business, you will also be interacting with those directly involved in the international trade part of your business. The players in the international trading game are many. It is not a simple relationship between the importer and supplier or exporter and buyer abroad. There are also government agency representatives, such as Customs agents, freight forwards, Customs brokers, and many others, which will be discussed throughout the book. Just to give you an idea of whom these "players" are so that they fall into place better as you work your way through the book, I will introduce them and briefly touch on whom they are for your future reference.

Get to know your U.S. Customs and Border Protection agents. In general, this agency is charged with the duty of protecting and facilitating international trade. They are also responsible for assessing and collecting duties, taxes, and other fees associated with the importation and exportation of goods. In addition, Customs law enforcement activities also include detecting and investigating any illegal international trade activity, such as unlawful importation of arms and other fraudulent transactions intended to avoid paying appropriate duties and other fees. You will be working with Customs representatives from the various areas within the agency. For instance, you will work with Customs agents from the port of entry where you will bring your goods in, if you are importing. You will interact with these agents in different ways as you conduct your import export business. There are also classification specialists, whom you will need in case there is a question as to the classification of your products (which determines the duty rate you will pay on that product). These specialists review your product's information and make a determination as to the duty rate it will pay.

You will also be working with suppliers and buyers. Suppliers, who can also be manufacturers, could be located in the United States, from whom you would acquire the goods you intend to export. However, suppliers can also be located abroad, from whom you would purchase merchandise to import into the U.S. You can also expect to work with governmental agencies abroad, as well as the occasional middleman in the countries where you will be conducting business. In some of the less developed countries, sometimes it is to your advantage to work with a middleman who is familiar with the area and who can serve as an intermediary between you and the supplier.

In addition, there will be times when it will be in your best interest to secure the services of individuals or companies who specialize in the various trades of the import export industry and will be of great assistance to you. For example, Customs brokers are an excellent source to go to when processing importation documents. These individuals may work independently or as part of a company; they have the expertise necessary to make sure your documentation is accurate and that it has been sent through the appropriate channels to ensure the proper processing of your merchandise, thereby avoiding costly fees and penalties. Another service provider in the industry is the freight forwarder. Freight forwarders work out the logistics of shipping your goods, making sure your cargo reaches its destination safely, on time, and in the most cost-effective manner.

How about your local chamber of commerce or economic development council (or agency)? These agencies can be invaluable sources of information that can connect you with possible suppliers or buyers. They often also provide informational sessions regarding business start-ups, and some even have international business development divisions that would be even more helpful. These agencies can also put you in touch with statewide or regional agencies that specialize in assisting businesses involved in international trade.

The players list, as mentioned, is not all-inclusive of all those you will come in contact with as you conduct your business. However, the list does provide you with the key roles people play in the industry that you should know before you get started. All these individuals and agencies are all trying to make it work for a collective goal, but yet each is guided by their own country's rules, regulations, and cultural differences (for those located abroad). Because of these differences between the local players, which include you, and those across the borders, common ground rules have been established and are amended from time to time, with the objective of promoting fair trade across the borders and ultimately having a positive economic impact on the countries involved.

Industry Basics — What You Need to Know to Get Your Feet Wet

I wish I could tell you that the business you are about to embark in is going to be easy, but the truth is that it is not. However, the rewards will make it worth every bit of effort you put into it. Without going into a lot of detail to avoid confusing you, I will give you a general overview of what the business of importing and exporting is all about. The details are addressed in the various parts of the book. Every aspect of the import export business has been discussed in full in the chapters that follow. It has been laid out in such a way that each chapter will provide you with the knowledge and information you will need to understand (and make sense) of the chapter that follows.

As intricate as the industry is, the most basic and critical aspect to keep in mind at all times about international trade is that it is very volatile — volatile in every aspect. Laws and regulations affecting international trade in one way or another are amended from time to time; they could be domestic laws or the laws of the countries in which you are conducting business.

Therefore, staying well informed of international news and events is of great importance.

Also, thoroughly researching and familiarizing yourself with the products you will be trading is a must. Make sure it is something that you want to import or export and that you feel comfortable making available to the general population, in the U.S. or abroad. Be mindful that because of the nature of the industry, it lends itself to corrupt practices, especially in the less developed countries. Make sure you stay away from that, because it will eventually come back to you and hurt your business.

Never be afraid to ask questions. In the import and export world, there truly is not such a thing as a "dumb question." Every question is relevant and of equal importance to your success. There are experts in the various areas of the industry who are excellent sources of information. There are also professional organizations directly related to international trade that are worth joining. These organizations are constantly sponsoring educational training sessions that will help you successfully operate your business. In addition, the networking opportunities are immense, providing you with a venue where you can make contacts for future business opportunities, which is what this business is all about.

The international trade business is for those who are always looking at expanding their horizons with new products to import and export, and new territories to penetrate. Taking educated chances and following through with new ideas and opportunities that will take you places across the globe — that is what lies within the heart of the import and export business.

Chapter 2

Materialize Your Business

Now that you have familiarized yourself with the industry basics and lingo about importing and exporting, and you have decided what products you are going to import or export, it is time to take a look at the steps necessary to make your business a reality. Start with the most basic step, which is finding a place from where you can start working to begin operations.

Setting Up a Temporary Office

A temporary office is a location from where you can conduct all the preliminary research of determining exactly what kind of business you want to establish — whether you will be importing, exporting, or doing both — as well as what type of legal structure will best fit your operation. This preliminary work will then provide you with the information you need to select an appropriate name for your business, especially if you think you may eventually want to add an LLC or Inc. at the end of your business name. It will determine the extent of the paperwork that will be involved and give you a better idea as to what kind of location you will ultimately need to operate your business.

To do all this preliminary work, a home office works great. Start by setting aside room in your office for all the basic equipment you will need, as well as enough room to spread out your research material. In addition, if you are establishing this operation with partners, you are going to want to have a setting available where private discussions can be held, rather than at the local coffee shop.

Items that you absolutely must have include:

- A desk with a comfortable chair

- A filing cabinet

- A printer/copier/scanner combination, or one of each

- A telephone with fax and answering machine capabilities

- A laptop computer, allowing you the flexibility to take the information with you should you need to travel as you work toward getting your business started

- Internet access

Having Internet access from day one is essential. As there are still rural areas in the country where high speed Internet is not available through the telephone service provider or cable network, investing in a USB broadband connection device is worth the expense. These devices are available through your cellular phone service provider and are billed as if it were another cellular phone line. Another alternative is to acquire service through a satellite receiver; however, in addition to your monthly fees, there is an initial set-up cost.

If you are going to initially set up your office at home, it would be a good idea to install a separate business telephone line. It will be more professional to have your business answering machine answer when you are not available rather than have a family member take a message for you. Remember that first impressions, even through telephone contact, are critical, and you will be conducting business with people from all around the world who have no idea the extent of your operation. An answering machine will give the caller a visual impression of a professional office, whereas a family member says loud and clear "small home office," which — unfortunately — is not always perceived as professional.

There is nothing wrong with purchasing pre-owned office furniture and equipment, as neither usually shows much wear. Keep in mind that your purpose is to establish and operate a business that will be financially successful. Therefore, it is important to spend your start-up money wisely, as you will be building your company from there.

Creating an Image for Your Company

Selecting an appropriate name for your new business should not be taken lightly. You want to give it a name that will clearly state what it is about — a name that is unique, different, and easy for people to remember. Regardless of what industry you are in, there is always going to be plenty of competition. The goal is to make yourself stand out from the crowd, starting with a company name that will help create an image for your company that represents professionalism — something that will appeal to potential customers. When all you have is a list of company names, all of which provide the same service, you will most likely call the first company whose name appeals to you the most and, in your opinion, reflects professionalism. Choosing just the right name can result in new business opportunities.

Another factor to consider when selecting a name for your company is the nature of the industry you are about to enter. In the import export business, your business partners will be located all around the world. Therefore, make sure that the name of your company is not so complicated and long that it will make it difficult for people who are not native English speakers to pronounce, let alone remember. Additionally, if the laws or regulations of various governmental agencies requires it, make sure to add LLC, Inc., or Co. at the end of the name when applicable. *Chapter 3 will address the various forms of legal structures in which you can set up your business, such as limited liability companies (LLCs), S corporations, and other options.*

Trademarks

An option to consider in regard to the name of your business is to have it certified as a registered trademark through the U.S. Patent and Trademark Office, an agency of the U.S. Department of Commerce. Registering your name with the secretary of state's office in your state alone will not prevent another business owner from using the same name. However, having your business name trademarked will prevent other companies from using the same name. Filing your request to have your business name trademarked can be done online through the U.S. Patent and Trademark Office Web site at **www.uspto.gov**. The application fee for filing electronically is $275 and $375 if filing by mail. After receiving confirmation from the Patent and Trademark Office that they have received your application, it may take several months before the trademark is granted. Through this user-friendly Web site, you are also able to conduct an initial search to make sure no one else is using the same name you want trademarked.

Fictitious name registration

If your business name is different from your real name, most states require that you file a fictitious name registration, a "doing business as" (DBA) registration, or some form of similar registration that specifies that the name you are using to conduct business is not your own. For example, a fictitious name would be calling your company IMPORTS Trading Company. The agency with which the fictitious name or DBA name is filed varies from state to state. In some states, the registration is done with the city or county in which the company has its principal place of business; however, the majority of states require the registration to be done with the state's secretary of state office. Of all 50 states, the only ones that specifically do not require any type of filing when conducting business with a name other than your personal name are Alabama, Arizona, Kansas, Mississippi, New Mexico, and South Carolina. Washington, D.C., makes it optional, and Tennessee does not require such filing for sole proprietorships or general partnerships.

Once you have determined what the perfect name for your company is, then create an image for your business. Creating an image of how you want your company to be perceived by the general public, customers, and suppliers is quite significant, as people will identify with it and relate with what your company is truly all about. Part of creating and developing your image as your business grows is cultivating your company's professional attitude, culture, and business ethics.

An integral part of this image is your business logo. The logo must be unique and different from anyone else's, because the last thing you want is to have your company mistaken for another. Graphic artists, marketing agencies, and print shops are excellent places to go to for the design of your logo — make sure to ask them for a high-resolution digital copy so that you can reproduce it for all your business stationery and marketing needs. In addition to being able to find an abundance of graphic artists on the Internet, marketing agencies and print shops usually have graphic artists as part of their staff. You will also be able to find marketing agencies and printing companies on the Internet; however, tapping into your local talent by using local professionals is always a good idea, and for that there is no better source of information than your local phone book.

Obtain an employer identification number

As you get more involved in the start-up and operation of your import export business, you will notice that it is a highly regulated industry with multiple forms to fill out and submit to the appropriate governmental agencies. One of these agencies is the IRS. Keeping up with all the requirements of the IRS by filling out and returning the appropriate forms on time will keep you out of a lot of trouble. Any required forms that are submitted late, or neglected and not submitted at all, can result in stiff penalties.

Therefore, when starting a business, one of the first things that needs to be done before you actually conduct business transactions or hire any employees is to obtain an employer identification number (EIN) from the IRS. The EIN is used by the IRS to identify the tax accounts of employers, certain sole proprietors, corporations, and partnerships. The IRS uses the following criteria to determine if you need to secure an FEIN:

- If you have employees
- If you established a qualified retirement account
  (per IRS standards)
- If you operate your business as a corporation or a partnership
- If you file alcohol, tobacco, firearms, employment, or excise
  tax returns
- If you have a Keogh plan

The EIN can be obtained by filling out and submitting Form SS-4. This form can be submitted online (**www.irs.gov/businesses/small/ article/0,,id=102767,00.htm**), or you can print the form and mail it in to the address provided on the Web site.

The IRS has developed a Web site called the Small Business Resource Guide, specifically designed to better assist the small business owner and those just starting new business ventures. This guide can be accessed at **www.sbrg.irs.gov**, where new business owners can access and download any number of the necessary forms and publications required by the IRS.

Open a bank account

Establishing a strong working relationship from the beginning with a well-established financial institution is essential in ensuring your financial success. When you are starting up a business venture, it is sound practice to seek the advice of business professionals in their fields of expertise, such as in the banking industry. Taking the time to meet with a bank representative when you open a business checking account is time well spent; you might be surprised as to the many services available and the sound financial advice you can receive from bank officials. Discuss your plans with a representative specializing in international business, not only for starting up your business, but also for where you foresee your business to be in the future. This information will allow the representative to better advise you. He or she can also provide you with information regarding services provided by the bank, which can benefit you during the early stages of your business and in the future. This is also a good time to find out about the bank's policy on a business line of credit account. A line of credit account is an arrangement through a financial institution whereby the bank extends a specified amount of unsecured credit to the borrower.

To establish a business checking account, most financial institutions will require a copy of the state's certificate of fictitious name filing from a partnership or sole proprietor, or an affidavit, which is a written declaration sworn under oath before someone legally authorized to administer an oath. To open a business checking account for a corporation, most banks will require a copy of the articles of incorporation, an affidavit attesting to the actual existence of the company, and the EIN acquired from the IRS.

Now that you are entering into the international market, the foremost element you need to look for is a bank with a strong international department. A banking institution with an international department, such as Bank of America, Wachovia-Global Connect, and Regions Bank, will be able to handle and process specialized transactions, such as foreign exchange payments and letters of credit, which are used by financial institutions to guarantee payments on behalf of its customers — the buyer of the goods — thereby facilitating the business transactions between to parties. *Letters of credit are discussed at length in Chapter 5.* In addition, you would want the bank to provide other services, such as speed in handling transactions, electronic banking, a strong but flexible credit policy, and a good, solid relationship with other financial institutions overseas.

Secure an accountant or purchase accounting software

Deciding whether to secure an accountant or purchase financial software for your business accounting needs will ultimately be up to you. It all depends on the size of your operation, as well as your knowledge of accounting principles. If you feel comfortable enough to keep your accounting records, then purchasing good accounting software should suffice. However, it is recommended you still have an accountant look over the business records at the end of the year to ensure accuracy. There are several accounting software packages available, but you have to be careful which one you choose — some are very limited and only include payroll, invoicing, and general recordkeeping. One of the most widely used packages, known for its all-encompassing versatility, is QuickBooks financial software. The basic version of this program, QuickBooks Pro, sells for $159.95 and has the capability of doing everything from invoicing, keeping track of sales tax and all income and expenses, and even printing checks. QuickBooks' Premier Edition is a complete accounting system for your business and more. You can create forecasts, a business plan, and even do your budgeting, and it sells for $249.99.

If your strengths are not in accounting and recordkeeping, you should secure the services of an accountant, at least during the first year of operation, or until you are comfortable enough to do the recordkeeping yourself. Accurate recordkeeping is essential in maintaining your company's finances, and sometimes this is something that only an accountant can do.

Knowing exactly where you stand financially at any given time will influence a number of business decisions that must be made on short notice.

Get a post office box

Regardless of whether you started by establishing a temporary office at home or elected to go ahead and acquire a location for your business, securing a post office box is a good idea. As a convenience to its customers, the United States Postal Service has now made it even easier to secure a post office box by providing this service online. Enter the U.S. Postal Service Web site, at **www.usps.com**, and you will find the "P.O. Boxes Online" function, which will walk you through the process of setting one up.

Having a post office box for your company helps keep your business's correspondence separate from your personal correspondence. Most importantly, it will prevent you from having to reprint any business stationery should you decide to relocate your office later. Continuity in any business means stability, which is what business partners across the borders (as well as those in the United States) look for when establishing long-term business relationships.

Print stationery

Now you are ready to print stationery for your new business. Your business stationery, letterhead, and business cards should be designed to reflect the image you want to project. Avoid the temptation to save some of the start-up costs by printing your own stationery. Some of the best-spent dollars when establishing your new business will be for the design and printing of your stationery. Choose the design and colors wisely, keeping in mind that the same theme will be followed throughout the rest of your printed material and digital products, such as your company's Web site.

Determining Your Role: Agent, Distributor, or Manufacturer

Before you move further into the planning and organizing of your business, evaluate the different areas of importing and exporting with which you might get involved. As you learn more about the import export industry, you will likely expand your operations. Identifying the different roles will give you an idea as to what is really involved in operating at the different capacities within the international trade industry. As you will see, you can get involved as little or as much as you want, allowing you to get into the business slowly if you so desire. You can start as an agent and, as you gain more confidence and knowledge about the international trade industry, you can be more involved, becoming a distributor or even a manufacturer.

Agent

Acting as an import export agent is the simplest form of involvement in international trade. As an agent, you simply bring two parties together — one being the party needing certain goods, and the other being the party that supplies those goods. Even though as an agent you actively participate in negotiations for the sale and purchase of the goods and receive a commission on the transaction, you never actually take title to the goods, meaning you never take ownership of the merchandise. The import agent would be the agent arranging for the goods to be received for consumption, and the export agent would be the agent working in the country from where the goods would be originating.

For example, Dave, owner of IMPORTS Import and Export Company, is an import/export agent in Miami and learns that Colombia Rica, Inc., located in Bogota, Colombia, is interested in importing peaches. IMPORTS has a customer, Fruiti, Inc., which produces peaches and exports its products. Dave brings the two parties together, negotiating with Colombia Rica, Inc., on behalf of Fruiti, Inc., for the sale and exportation of the peaches.

Once the sale is completed, IMPORTS gets paid a commission for the transaction, even though the actual product being imported and exported had nothing to do with IMPORTS.

Acting as an agent requires the least amount of start-up capital and working capital; however, your revenues will be based on commission only, which can be limiting. You also run the risk of the supplier and the vendor coming together and leaving you out of the loop. Should you decide to operate as an agent, you will likely be able to operate your business from a home office for the entirety of your business, and it should not affect your potential for growth in the industry.

Distributor

As a distributor, you take title to the goods by purchasing them from a manufacturer overseas and then looking for customers to purchase these goods at a higher price. As a distributor, you will incur more expenses and higher risks, meaning you are investing a large sum of money on products and getting stuck with products if your prospective buyers back out. However, you would have more control over the process than an agent does.

Distributors can be divided into two categories:

Full-service distributor: A full-service distributor purchases a variety of goods in bulk from several different suppliers, takes title to the goods, then sells these goods to the end customers at a higher price. Therefore, if you choose to start up your import export business by operating as a full-service distributor, then you may consider leasing warehouse space with a small office. For example, IMPORTS brings in a whole shipment of ladies and children's shoes, purchased from various suppliers in Brazil. IMPORTS clears the shipment through Customs, stores them in its warehouse, then sells the shoes for a profit to various wholesalers in the U.S. IMPORTS has acted as a distributor because it purchased the goods in bulk and then sold (distributed) the goods among several wholesalers locally. When a shipment is said to have "cleared Customs," it means that all the regulatory paperwork for the goods to enter into U.S. territory have been inspected and approved by U.S. Customs and Border Protection, and all duties (taxes imposed by the government on products imported from abroad) have been paid.

Drop ship distributor: The drop ship distributor purchases goods in bulk, taking title of the goods; however, rather than having the goods delivered to a central warehouse and redistributed, the goods are shipped directly from the supplier to the end customer. Using the same scenario from above but with IMPORTS acting as a drop ship distributor, instead of bringing the shipment to a warehouse for distribution after clearing Customs, IMPORTS has the shoes delivered directly to the wholesale company that purchased the shipment of shoes.

Manufacturer

If your choice is to enter the international trade business as a manufacturer, then export your products, your start-up costs will be quite significant. For such an operation, you will need significant start-up capital just to get the business going. At the very least, you will need the manufacturing plant, some employees, and manufacturing and office equipment before you see any money come in. Should you decide to start as a manufacturer, consider the following steps:

- Secure enough financing to assist you with the start-up costs as well as to carry you through the beginning stages of your operation, should you start running short of working capital.

- Conduct research to ensure the product will be market-worthy upon completion (e.g., look into product safety issues).

- Research the market to ensure there is a demand for this product.

If you already are a manufacturer, you may be considering importing components for use in the manufacturing process or expanding your market by exporting products already manufactured across the borders. If you are currently a manufacturer, you would not need to expand, other than possibly your shipping and receiving department, as you can expect an increase of activity there. *As a manufacturer, there are several money-saving opportunities in regard to the payment of duties, which will be addressed in Chapter 10.*

CASE STUDY: GLOBAL SOURCING AND IMPORTING

Michelle Bonn, Owner
Expedient Trade, LLC, New York
www.expedienttrade.com
(716) 276-1255

Previously in the manufacturing quality control and financial analysis arenas, Michelle Bonn experienced first-hand the importance of assisting small- to medium-sized companies in sourcing abroad. Not only does she find sourcing and importing to be an arena where she can use her sales and leadership skills, but she also finds it to be a rewarding career that impacts companies worldwide. Bonn's idea to leave her previous employer and start a business in the international trade industry sparked from a quality control assignment in Singapore where, as she said, "I could see that U.S.-based companies were interested in expanding operations offshore (to partake in the cost savings) but had very little experience or knowledge as to how to manage the offshore manufacturing or sourcing process."

Aware of the demand for Italian leather by the American market and familiar with the Italian language, Bonn chose Italy as her first country from which to import. She started her business importing products from Italy in 2006, with intentions to learn about importing, international business costs, foreign payment, and the manufacturing process. Her business was successful, and as her customer base grew, so did the demand for similar products at lower prices. Seeing the potential for growth, Bonn started sourcing in Asia, learning the process of managing multiple possible vendors while at the same time trying to understand cultural differences.

With help from experienced people in both the U.S. and China, Bonn assembled a team of companies and individuals who assisted her with the manufacturing of products, international delivery issues, and foreign payment practices. Along the way, she learned about many important aspects of sourcing and importing, such as quality control issues.

To avoid quality control problems, she recommends developing a description of material specifications, production methods, and directions about how the end product should look and work in the final state, giving the factory and outside inspectors a "blueprint" or checklist to follow when the inspection or manufacturing process takes place. Bonn also advises having third-party inspectors review the goods ready to be shipped to ensure the products are what was actually ordered.

Bond was the recipient of the 2008 Entrepreneur of the Year Award by the YWCA of Western New York for excellence in helping women domestically and internationally expand their business practices into foreign markets. She is the U.S. Ambassador for a women's business organization based in Iceland, and she has also been appointed to the Board of Directors for the National Association for Women Business Owners, as well as the Buffalo World Trade Association.

Establish Your Place of Business — Selecting a Location

After doing so much preliminary work setting up your import export business, you now come to a major crossroad in the process: Where are you going to permanently set up shop? At this point, you should have fulfilled all of the legal requirements and given your business a name that will serve as a roadmap for your success. Most importantly, by this point you should have determined the type of business you will operate and your role in the international trade industry. Therefore, you are now ready to commence operations at the most appropriate location for your business.

If you decide that the best way to enter the international trade industry is to start-up as an agent, then the location from where you conduct business is not that critical. You can successfully operate an import export business acting as an agent from a home office. Working from home has many advantages, but also disadvantages, such as not having the capability of easily expanding your work area, having a lack of a meeting room to bring customers to, and falling behind schedule on tasks due to distractions and interruptions. The greatest advantages, however, are not having to spend additional money on rent, travel, or any other expenses associated with an office, as well as the ability to have flexible hours of operation.

To operate as a full-service distributor or manufacturer, you will need to secure a warehouse facility with office space that will be conducive to your operations. The type of goods and volume you anticipate moving through your facility will dictate what size of warehousing space you will need, including ceiling height (for stacking purposes) and number of docks for truck deliveries. Another consideration is whether refrigerated or air-conditioned space will be required for the type of goods that will be handled in the warehouse. In addition, where you locate your operation — such as an industrial park, an airport facility, a seaport, or near railroad tracks — can prove to be of considerable advantage, both financially as well as in the logistics of your shipments.

Industrial parks

Industrial parks are areas zoned by the local government specifically for industrial and business use, thus making them great settings for warehousing operation. The parks are already set up to accommodate heavy equipment traffic and meet zoning and other code regulations that allow you to store and move your imported goods. Normally, warehouses located in industrial parks also contain a small office. When you are shopping for a facility, take into consideration its geographic location in relation to main highways and interstate roads. It is advantageous for your facility to be easily accessed from major thoroughfares.

Airports

Another option is establishing your operations in an industrial park within an airport. A large number of airports throughout the United States have opted to build industrial parks within their facilities in order to offset operational costs. In addition to airports' usually being located where they are easily accessed, industrial parks located in airports can offer benefits such as easy access to air-delivered goods, as well as the capability of shipping goods by air with ease. If you are importing goods from overseas and they can be transported by air from the port of entry, flying them into the airport where you are operating can cut back on delivery time and may eliminate the need for ground transportation. Some airports are also designated foreign-trade zone areas, which, depending on the status of your shipments, could be financially viable. Foreign-trade zones are designated areas considered to be outside Customs territory; therefore, duties are not due until the time that the goods leave the foreign-trade zone. *There are a lot of advantages to operating an import export business under foreign-trade zone status, which will be discussed further in Chapter 10.*

Seaports

Some seaports also offer warehousing facilities to operate from. The advantages of being located on seaport grounds are significant, especially if you import in bulk from abroad and your goods arrive by ocean freight. The same holds true for exporting. You will save the cost of transporting goods from a distant warehouse to the port from where the goods would be shipped. The greatest advantage is that you drastically cut back the amount of time that would normally transpire between the goods' arrival at the port and accessing those goods once the Bureau of Customs and Border Protection (CBP) has cleared them. In addition, there is the benefit of having Customs offices nearby for support, as seaports are considered ports of entry.

Rail access

Should you import in bulk using containers but do not have access to a seaport facility, your next best choice would be a facility with rail access. Due to the nature of the operations at seaports, most of them have rail corridors running through their site, therefore making it easy and cost-effective to have the containers transported directly from the seaport to your facility by rail. This process enables you to avoid ground transportation costs and also cuts back on the number of times your shipment is handled from loading and unloading, which is when most cargo damage occurs.

Public warehousing as an alternative

An alternative to leasing warehouse space is securing the services of a public warehouse, an operation that provides short- or long-term storage on a month-to-month basis. The charge is based on storage fees, either per pallet or per square foot, and on the number of transactions involving your merchandise — that is, the number of inbound and outbound warehouse transactions. This is a great alternative if your business requires warehousing facilities but you are not necessarily prepared to invest capital into leasing the space and purchasing the equipment needed to run it. In a public warehousing situation, they even provide the manual labor if your operations involve importing, repackaging, and distributing to the domestic market. Public warehouses are actually run and operated by private enterprises that own the large facilities and provide a multitude of services relating to warehousing and distribution. The prices they charge for their services are based on usage factor — you pay for the space you rent and the labor provided. They provide services such as inventory control, packaging, labeling, local trucking, shrink-wrapping of boxes on pallets, containerization, and import export handling. This can seem pricey, but when considering all the other costs associated with leasing and paying for the labor yourself, it may be worth it.

When deciding which leasing arrangement will be best, consider all the factors involved, such as how much you plan to ship by air or steam ship, how often, and whether you plan to do bulk shipping.

Leasing Space

Wherever it may be that you are looking to establishing your business, make sure that you have taken everything into consideration before signing a lease. Review the following checklist and address every item. This is not to say you cannot purchase a warehouse facility to conduct business. However, it is a significant investment, and as a start-up business, you must decide whether it would be wise to invest so much capital in a facility at such an early stage:

Item	Availability	Value
Location		
Proximity to port of entry		
Road accessibility		
Railroad access		
Office space		
Availability of high speed Internet		
Party responsible for utilities		
If part of a complex, insurance included		
Warehouse space		
Manufacturing space		
Number of drive — in doors		
Number of dock — high doors		
Outside storage space		
Criminal activity in the area		

Please see the accompanying CD-ROM for a template of this form

Chapter 3

Determining the Legal Structure of Your Business

Now that you have determined your business location and started to make your mark on the import export industry, you will need to decide the legal structure of your business. The legal structure of your business will set the platform for your everyday operations, as it will influence the way you proceed with financial, tax, and legal issues — just to name a few. Remember when you were choosing the name of your company, and you had visions of adding Inc., Co., or LLC to the end of its name? Now is the time to make that vision a reality. It will dictate what type of documents need to filed with which governmental agencies, what type of documentation you will need to make accessible for public scrutiny, and how you will actually operate your business. To assist you, a description of the different legal structures is provided as follows, along with a sample of documents you may need to file with state and federal agencies.

Sole Proprietorship

Sole proprietorship is the most prevalent type of legal structure adopted by start-up or small businesses, and it is the easiest to put into operation. It is a type of business that is owned and operated by one owner and not set up as any kind of corporation. Therefore, you will have absolute control of all import and export operations. Under a sole proprietorship, you own 100 percent of the business, its assets, and its liabilities. Some of the disadvantages are that you are wholly responsible for securing all monetary backing, and you are ultimately responsible for any legal actions against your business. However, it has some great advantages, such as being relatively inexpensive to set up and, with the exception of a couple of extra tax forms, there is no requirement to file complicated tax returns in addition to your own. Also, as a sole proprietor, you can operate under your own name or a fictitious one. Most importers and exporters that start small begin their operations as sole proprietors.

General Partnership

A partnership is almost as easy to establish as a sole proprietorship, with a few exceptions. In a partnership, all profits and losses are shared among the partners. But not all partners necessarily have equal ownership of the business. Normally, the extent of financial contributions toward the business will determine the percentage of each partner's ownership. This percentage relates to sharing the organization's revenues, as well as its financial and legal liabilities. One key difference between a partnership and a sole proprietorship is that the business does not cease to exist with the death of a partner. Under such circumstances, the deceased partner's share can be taken over by a new partner, or the partnership can be reorganized to accommodate the change. In either case, the business is able to continue without much disruption.

Although not all entrepreneurs benefit from turning their sole proprietorship businesses to partnerships, some thrive when incorporating partners into the business. In such instances, the business benefits from the knowledge and expertise each partner contributes toward overall operations. As your import export business grows, it may be advantageous for you to come together with someone knowledgeable about international trade and potential expansion. Sometimes as a sole proprietorship grows, the needs of the company outgrow the knowledge and capabilities of the single owner.

When establishing a partnership, it is in the best interest of all partners involved to have an attorney develop a partnership agreement. Partnership agreements are simple, legal documents that normally include information such as the name and purpose of the partnership, its legal address, how long the partnership is intended to last, and the names of the partners. It also addresses each partner's contribution, both professionally and financially, and how profits and losses will be distributed. A partnership agreement needs to disclose how changes in the organization will be addressed, such as the death of a partner, the addition of a new partner, or the selling of one partner's interest to another individual.

Limited Liability Company

A limited liability company (LLC), often wrongly referred to as a limited liability corporation, is not quite a corporation, yet much more than a partnership. An LLC encompasses features found in the legal structure of corporations and partnerships, which allows the owners — called members in an LLC — to enjoy the same liability protection of a corporation and the recordkeeping flexibility of a partnership. Some of the perks include not having to keep meeting minutes or records. In an LLC, the members are not personally liable for the debts incurred for and by the company, and profits can be distributed as deemed appropriate by its members. In addition, all expenses, losses, and profits of the company flow through the business to each member, who would ultimately pay either business taxes or personal taxes — not both on the same income.

LLCs are a recent type of legal structure, with the first one established in Wyoming in 1977. It was not until 1988, when the IRS ruled that the LLC business structure would be treated as a partnership for tax purposes, that other states followed by enacting their own statutes establishing the LLC form of business. These companies are now allowed in all 50 states, and although they are easier to establish than a corporation, they require a little more legal paperwork than a sole proprietorship.

An LLC structure would be most appropriate for an import export business that is not quite large enough to warrant assuming the expenses incurred in becoming a corporation or being responsible for the recordkeeping involved in operating as such. But the extent of its operations requires a better legal and financial shelter for its members.

Regulations and procedures affecting the formation of LLCs differ from state to state; they can be found in your state's "corporations" section of the secretary of state office's Web site.

There are two main documents normally filed when establishing an LLC. One is an operating agreement, which addresses issues such as the management and structure of the business, the distribution of profit and loss, the method of how members will vote, and how changes in the organizational structure will be handled. The operating agreement is not required by every state.

Articles of organization, however, are required by every state, and the form is generally available for download from your state's Web site. The purpose of this second document is to legally establish your business by registering with your state. It must contain, at a minimum, the following information:

- The LLC's name and the address of the primary place of business

- The purpose of the LLC

- The name and address of the LLC's registered agent (the person authorized to physically accept delivery of legal documents for the company)

- The name of the manager, or managing members, of the company

- An effective date for the company and signature

Corporation

Corporations are the most formal type of all the legal business structures discussed so far. A corporation can be established as a public or private corporation. A public corporation, with which most of us are familiar, is owned by its shareholders (also known as stockholders) and is public because anyone can buy stocks in the company through public stock exchanges. Shareholders are owners of the corporation through the ownership of shares, or stocks, which represent a financial interest in the company and gives them voting rights. Not all corporations start up as corporations, selling shares in the open market. They may actually start up as individually owned businesses that grow to the point where selling its stocks in the open market is the most financially feasible business move for the organization. However, openly trading your company's shares diminishes your control over it by spreading the decision-making to stockholders or shareholders and a board of directors. Some of the most familiar household names, like Tupperware Corporation and The Sports Authority, Inc., are public corporations.

A private corporation is owned and managed by a few individuals who are normally involved in the day-to-day decision-making and operations of the company. If you own a relatively small business but still wish to run it as a corporation, a private corporation legal structure would be the most beneficial form for you as a business owner because it allows you to stay closely involved in the operation and management. Even as your business grows, you can continue to operate as a private corporation. There are no rules for having to change over to a public corporation once your business reaches a certain size. The key is in the retention of your ability to closely manage and operate the corporation. For instance, some of the large companies that are often assumed to be public corporations happen to be private corporations — companies such as Publix Super Markets, L.L. Bean, and Mary Kay cosmetics.

Whether private or public, a corporation is its own legal entity, capable of entering into binding contracts and being held directly liable in any legal issues. Its finances are not directly tied to anyone's personal finances, and taxes are addressed completely separately from its owners. These are only some of the many advantages to operating your business in the form of a corporation. However, forming a corporation is no easy task, and not all business operations lend themselves to this type of setup. The process can be lengthy and put a strain on your budget due to all the legwork and legal paperwork involved. In addition to the start-up costs, there are additional maintenance costs, as well as legal and financial reporting requirements not found in partnerships or sole proprietorships.

S Corporation

An S corporation is a form of legal structure, under IRS regulations designed for the small businesses — "S corporation," meaning small business corporation. Until the inception of the limited liability company form of business structure, forming S corporations was the only choice available to small business owners that offered some form of limited liability protection from creditors, but yet afforded them with the benefits that a partnership provides. Operating under S corporation status results in the company's being taxed close to how a partnership or sole proprietor would be, rather than like a corporation.

Operating under the S corporation legal structure, the shareholders' taxes are directly impacted by the business' profit or loss. Any profits or losses the company may experience in any one year are passed through to the shareholders, who in turn must report them as part of their own income tax returns. According to the IRS, shareholders must pay taxes on the profits the business realized for that year in proportion to the stock they own.

In order to organize as an S corporation and qualify as such under the IRS regulations, the following requirements must be met:

- It cannot have more than 100 shareholders.
- Shareholders must be U.S. citizens or residents.
- All shareholders must approve operating under the S corporation legal structure.
- It must be able to meet the requirements for an S corporation the entire year.

Additionally, Form 253, "Election of Small Business Corporation," must be filed with the IRS within the first 75 days of the corporation's fiscal year.

Electing to operate under S corporation status is not effective for every business; however, it has proved to be beneficial for a number of companies through many years of operation.

Deciding under which legal structure you want to operate your business should not be taken lightly. Dedicate as much time as it takes to this task and make a well-educated decision. Although having LLC or Inc., as part of your business name may seem more prestigious, it may not be in your best interest to operate as such. Think of what your goals are for your company and work your way from there. As your company grows, you may have to move from one type of legal structure to another that will better fit your needs.

Chapter 4

Prepare a Business Plan

Business plans are your roadmap to success. The only way you can reach your goal of succeeding with your business is by having a plan. It is difficult at best to establish and operate a business when you do not quite know how to go about it — let alone to try to accomplish it without a thorough assessment of what you want to accomplish, how you plan to go about it, and what financial support you have to do so. As you prepare to undertake the enormous task of starting a new business, evaluate your situation as it stands and visualize where you want to be three to five years from now.

But before you constrain yourself to any one business plan format, consider that the business plan should be as unique as the business for which it is being written. Even though it is recommended that you follow the basic structure of commonly used templates, you should customize your business plan to fit your needs. There are a number of Web sites that provide you with a variety of samples and templates that can also be used as reference, such as **www.bplans.com**, **www.nebs.com/nebsEcat/business_tools/bptemplate**, and **www.planmagic.com**, to name a few.

When writing your business plan, stay focused on its ultimate purpose and take into consideration the many reasons why the plan is developed and its possible applications. For instance, if you do not have a loan proposal — essentially a condensed version of the business plan and used by businesses to request financing — when trying to secure financing for your business, business plans are great supporting documentation to attach to a loan application. Plans are also used as a means of introducing your business to a new market or presenting your business to a prospective business partner or investor. *A template of the following business plan, which follows the basic structure and incorporates key elements of an import export business, is included on the accompanying CD-ROM.*

The Business Plan

Cover page

The cover page should be evenly laid out with all the information centered on the page. Always write the name of your company in all capital letters in the upper half of the page. Several line spaces down, write the title "Business Plan." Lastly, write your company's address, the contact person's name, and the current date.

Table of contents

Mission statement

    I.   Executive summary

    II.   Description of proposed business

    III.   Management and staffing

    IV.   Market analysis

         a. Industry background

         b. Target market

Body of the business plan

MISSION STATEMENT

It is important that you present your business and what it is all about from the beginning of your plan. A mission statement is only as significant as you intend for it be. It can be written somewhere and then disregarded as unimportant. However, it should ideally be used as a beacon that will always guide you in the right direction. When writing your mission statement, three key elements must be taken into consideration: the purpose of your business, the goods or services you provide, and a statement as to your company's attitude toward employees and customers. A well-written mission statement could be as short as one paragraph but should not be longer than two.

I. EXECUTIVE SUMMARY

The executive summary should be about one to two pages in length and should actually be written last, as it is a summary of all the information you would have included in the plan. It should address what your market is; the purpose of the business — if you plan to import, export, or both — where will it be located, and how it will be managed. Write the executive summary in such a way that will prompt the reader to look deeper into the plan. Discuss the various elements of your business plan in the order you address them in the rest of the document.

II. DESCRIPTION OF PROPOSED BUSINESS

Describe in detail the purpose for which the business plan is being written. State what is it that you intend to accomplish. Describe your goods, services, and the role your business will play in the overall global market. Explain what makes your business different from all the rest in the same arena. Identify clearly the goals and objectives of your business. The average length for the proposed business description section should be one to two pages. However, the number of goods you anticipate importing or exporting, as well as whether you will operate as an agent, distributor, or manufacturer, will also dictate the length of this section. A more detailed description may be necessary.

III. MANAGEMENT AND STAFFING

Clearly identifying the management team and any other staff who may be part of the everyday operations of the business will strengthen your business viability by demonstrating that the business will be well managed. Keep in mind that a company's greatest asset is its employees. State whom the owners of the business are, as well as other key employees with backgrounds in the international trade industry. Identify the management talent you have on board (this may even include yourself), as well as any others you may need in the future to expand your business. For instance, it may just be yourself when starting up; however, in your plans for expansion, you might think about incorporating someone well-versed in U.S. Customs forms and documents to accommodate additional volume. The management and staffing section of the plan could be as short as one paragraph if you are the only employee or as long as a page or two.

IV. MARKET ANALYSIS

The market analysis section should clearly demonstrate your knowledge of the international trade business. If you are new to the industry, do your research and include information that you have acquired through research and data collection. There are numerous sources of information available, both online and through printed media, that can provide you with a wealth of knowledge about international trade. This process will add validity to your presentation, and you will be better prepared to answer any questions that may be presented to you. Essential elements to include in this section include a general description of the international trade industry as it relates to your specific business, a description of the targeted customer and possible needs, a description of your products or services, an overview of your competition, and what your planned approach to the market is. The market analysis element of your business plan should be one of the most comprehensive sections of the plan.

Industry background

The international trade industry is vast, thus providing a comprehensive description of trading business in the global market would be overwhelming. Instead, focus on the segment of the market that you will be a part of. Include trends and statistics that reflect the direction the market is going and how you will fit into that movement. Discuss major changes that have taken place in the industry recently that affect how you will conduct business. Provide a general overview of your projected customer base, such as wholesalers or domestic consumers. Great sources to research, which are easily accessible online, are the Web sites for the U.S. Customs and Border Protection (**www.cpb.gov**), the World Trade Organization (**www.wto.org**), the U.S. International Trade Commission (**www.usitc.gov**), and the International Trade Administration (**www.trade.gov**).

Target market

This is one of the largest sections of the business plan because you will be addressing key issues that will determine the volume of sales, and ultimately, the revenue that you will be able to generate for your business. The target market is who your customer, or groups of customers, will be. These are the companies that would use your services and buy your goods domestically or abroad, depending on whether you are importing or exporting. Since by this point you would have already decided on the role you will take on in the industry — that of importer or an exporter — then it is a good idea to narrow down your proposed customer base to a reasonable volume. If you try to spread your possibilities too thin, you may be wasting your time on efforts that will not pay off and end up missing out on some real possibilities. Identify the characteristics of the principal market you intend to target, such as demographics, market trends, and geographic location of the market. The international trade business will include numerous locations over seas.

Discuss what resources you used to find the information you needed on your target market. For example, state whether you used the World Trade Organization's Web site or U.S. Customs' statistical data. Elaborate on the size of your primary target market — your potential customers — by indicating the possible number of prospective customers, what their purchasing tendencies are in relation to the product or services your anticipate providing, their geographical location, and the forecasted market growth for that particular market segment. Expand your discussion to include the avenues you will use to reach your market. Whether you plan to use the Internet, printed media, trade shows, and such. Trade shows are exhibitions organized with the purpose of providing a venue where companies, in this case, involved in international trade can showcase their products and services. Explain the reasons why you feel confident that your company will be able to effectively compete in such a vast industry. Discuss your pricing strategies to be able to compete in the global market, such as discount structures in the form of bulk discounts or prompt payment discounts. Finally, you must address potential changes in trends that may favorably or negatively impact your target market.

Product description

Do not just describe your product or service — describe it as it will benefit or fill the needs of potential customers, and center your attention on where you have a clear advantage. Elaborate on what your products or services are; for instance, as you start your operation are you going to be importing footwear products to be distributed and sold domestically? If this is the case, then explain who you anticipate your suppliers will be and their location, as well as your customers. State what you anticipate the cost of the goods will be when you import them from your supplier abroad, and then what you estimate the cost would be to sell the goods to a domestic market distributor.

Market approach strategy

How do you anticipate entering such a vast market? Do you anticipate carving out a niche in the import export business? Determining how to enter the market and what strategy to use will be critical for breaking into the international trade market. There are new importers and exporters entering the market every day. Therefore, a good strategy to use which will be key to your success is entering the market cautiously by finding the right product to import, or choosing to start as an agent, thereby limiting your financial involvement. You may even limit yourself to exporting components to be used in the manufacturing process abroad.

V. MARKETING STRATEGY

In order to operate a financially successful business, you must not only maintain a constant flow of income, but also boost your profits by increased sales. The best way to accomplish this is through an effective marketing program, such as promoting your products and services by advertising, attending trade shows, and establishing a presence on the Internet. *The marketing of your business is discussed at length in Chapter 11.* The marketing strategy element of the business plan identifies your current and potential customers, as well as the means you will use to advertise your business directly to them. The marketing strategy portion of your business plan is likely to be several pages long. The marketing strategy section should include the following elements: products and services, pricing strategy, sales/distribution plan; and advertising and promotions plan.

Products and services

This section will focus on the uniqueness of your products or services and how your potential customers will benefit from them. Detail the services and products your business provides and what makes them superior to and unique from other similar businesses in the industry.

Pricing strategy

The pricing strategy segment is about determining how to price your products or services in such a way that it will allow you to remain competitive while still able to make a reasonable profit. You would be better off making a reasonable profit rather than pricing yourself out of the market and losing money by pricing your goods or services too high. Therefore, you must take extreme care when pricing your goods and services. The most effective method of doing this is by gauging your costs, estimating the tangible, measurable benefits to your customers, and making a comparison of your goods, services, and prices to similar ones on the market.

A good rule of thumb to follow is to set your price by taking into consideration how much the goods or services cost you and adding what you think would be a fair price for the benefits the goods or services will provide to the end customer. Take all costs into consideration, such as freight costs, the cost of labor and materials, selling costs, and administrative costs. Also look into similar products available in the market that could be comparable to yours and set your price up or down from that based on how much more or less the customer will benefit from your product when compared to others. For example, when pricing shoes imported from Brazil, leather shoes would be priced higher than shoes that look about the same that were manufactured with man-made materials.

Address why you feel the pricing of your goods and services is so competitive in comparison to others. If your price is slightly higher than that of the competition, then explain why even though it is higher than the rest, you can still move the product in the marketplace. In addition, it is noteworthy to point out the kind of return on investment (ROI) you anticipate generating. ROI is a return ratio that compares the net benefits — in this case, your products and services versus their total cost.

Sales and distribution

Now that you have determined how to price your goods and services, it is time to think about how you are going to sell and distribute your products and services. Describe the system you will use for processing orders, shipping the goods, and billing your customers. Also, address what methods of payment will be acceptable from your customers, including credit terms and discounts. In regard to the actual distribution of the goods, discuss the methods of distribution you anticipate using, as well as the anticipated costs associated with it. Remember that if you are going to be sourcing from a manufacturer abroad to then import into the domestic market, there will be a lot of variables involved, making it a little difficult to come up with exact terms. Hence, it will be acceptable to use standard terms for the sake of the business plan.

In addition, if you anticipate importing products that will undergo some form of manipulation, such as re-labeling or re-packaging before being shipped to the end consumer, packaging requirements must be specified.

Advertising and promotion

Discuss how you plan to advertise your products and services through market-specific channels, such as international trade magazines and periodicals. Promoting your import export business has to be market-specific. One of your goals in this section is to break down what percentage of your advertising budget will be spent in which media.

VI. OPERATIONS

Under the operations section, all aspects of management and manufacturing operations, distribution of goods, and logistics services provided will be discussed. Logistics refers to the storage and movement of goods from its original location to its final destination. Concentrate your discussion on how to improve resources in operations and production, which will facilitate the success of the company. The length of this section will be determined by what aspect of importing and exporting your business focuses on. Remember that all of the information outlined in this section needs to be backed by realistic numbers, such as the cost of buildings, machinery and equipment, and salaries.

Discuss the business's current and proposed location, describing in detail any existing facilities. If you are in the manufacturing end of international trade, include discussion of any equipment you currently have or require in order to expand, as well as the methods you anticipate using in your manufacturing and distribution operation. If you have employees, give a brief description of the tasks the employees will perform.

VII. STRENGTHS AND WEAKNESSES

As it is the case in most industries, the competition is tough with numerous business owners in the import export market all competing for the same prospects. Getting ahead of the game is a matter of who can take better advantage of company strengths and work in overcoming their weaknesses. In this section of the plan, elaborate on the particulars of your business that enable you to be successful. Discuss those factors that set you apart and give you an advantage over your competitors, such as your particular geographic location, a supplier you found overseas that manufactures unique products, or maybe the fact that you are skilled in multiple languages.

As hard as it may be to face the weaknesses that could be holding you back, addressing them will actually help you to either overcome or deal with them better. Some weaknesses you may be dealing with at the time you are writing the business plan may be due to inexperience and limited exposure to the market, both of which can be overcome. However, some weaknesses that cannot be overcome but must be dealt with head on are issues such as threats to your products caused by environmental concerns and other regulatory issues. Each of the weaknesses identified must be discussed in detail in terms of how you plan to overcome the particular weakness or how foresee ultimately eliminating it. Keep this section relatively short — no more than one page in length.

VIII. FINANCIAL PROJECTIONS

Financial projections are normally derived from already existing historical financial information. Therefore, even though your goal in this section is to address financial projections for your business, you should include some historical financial data that will help support your projections. If you are preparing a business plan as part of your business start-up process, then historical financial data will not be available, and working with estimates based on other similar business's performances can be acceptable. If you are using the business plan as part of the application process for a loan, then be sure to match your financial projections to the loan amount being requested.

Think of every possible expense, expected and unexpected, but be conservative in your revenues. It is not critical that your actual revenues exceed the estimated amount; however, it is not a good situation when expenses are more than expected. Your projections should be addressed for the next three to five years, breaking down each year with forecasted income statements, cash flow statements, balance sheets, and capital expenditure budgets. You can anticipate its taking up several pages of your business plan, as you might want to include graphs in addition to the budget forms.

IX. CONCLUSION

The conclusion is the last written element of the business plan. Make use of this last opportunity to state your case wisely, highlighting key issues discussed in the plan. Then wrap it up and close with a summary of your future plans for the expansion and progress of your business, using language that will help the reader visualize what you will be able to accomplish.

X. SUPPORTING DOCUMENTS

Attaching supporting documentation to your business plan will strengthen it and make it more valuable. However, you do not want to over-burden it with too many attachments. Before you start attaching documents, ask yourself if that particular piece of information will make a difference; if the answer is no, then leave it out. Documents that you want to attach include copies of the business principals' résumés; tax returns and personal financial statements of the principals for the last three years; a copy of licenses, certifications, and other relevant legal documents; a copy of the lease or purchase agreement, if you are leasing or buying space; and copies of letters of intent from suppliers (if applicable).

Chapter 5

Effective Financial Management
for a Profitable Business —
Budgeting & Financing

You would not be a typical entrepreneur if your vision were not larger than the depth of your pocket. When entering the international trade industry, it is easy to get caught up in the excitement and go beyond your financial means. This is where establishing a sound budget — and adhering to it — comes into play. Remember, a budget is only as good as your ability to operate within it. In addition, it is important that you become familiar with the various sources of financing that will provide you with the capital to successfully operate your import export business.

Business Start-up and Operating Budget

The only way to prepare a sound, realistic budget is by researching current market costs for start-up and normal operating expenses. When you are developing a budget to start your company, your numbers can be quite accurate because you are looking at concrete expenses for items such as office equipment, stationery, and filing fees. *See the accompanying CD-ROM for an example business start-up budget costs chart.*

For all of those expenditures, you can get hard numbers; however, when developing your first operating budget — where, in addition to anticipated operating expenses, you also have to include anticipated revenues — this may be a bit of a challenge. Start by listing all your anticipated operating expenses, and do a little bit of legwork to come up with good estimates. For example, if you lease an office space or warehouse space, contacting the previous tenant may be helpful in estimating what your utility bills may look like. The same holds true for budgeting anticipated revenue, in that you can only base your figures on what business transactions you anticipate may come to fruition. A way to forecast your possible revenue is to look into published reports issued by various international trade associations and agencies. These reports provide information such as what products are being imported and exported, as well as quantities.

The World Trade Organization has international trade statistics available at their Web site, **www.wto/english/res_e/statis_e.htm**, subdivided by product and country. USA Trade Online is a Web site supported by the Foreign Trade Division of the U.S. Census Bureau and STAT-USA, which is part of the Department of Commerce. This site, **www.usatradeonline.gov**, contains a wealth of import and export data regarding prices, countries of origin, and other import and export related information for over 42,000 commodities — import and export combined. Another good source of import export market research data can be found in the Export.gov Web site, **www.export.gov/mrktresearch/index.asp**. The following example uses the fictitious company IMPORTS Import and Export Company and serves as a good guideline for preparing an operating budget. *See the accompanying CD-ROM for a template of this form:*

IMPORTS Import and Export Company Operating Budget Year 2008 to 2009	
INCOME	
Sales	$257,000.00
Commissions	$55,875.00
Miscellaneous Revenues	$187,750.00
TOTAL INCOME	**$500,625.00**
EXPENSES	
Personnel	$75,000.00
Salaries	$50,000.00
Benefits	$15,000.00
Operating Expenses	$72,470.00
Rent	$38,770.00
Utilities	$5,200.00
Cellular Phones	$3,400.00
Office Supplies	$3,000.00
Professional Services	$150.00
Marketing & Advertising	$5,500.00
Dues & Subscriptions	$1,200.00
Repair & Maintenance	$1,600.00
Travel	$9,300.00
Miscellaneous Expenses	$4,350.00
TOTAL EXPENSES	**$147,470.00**
TOTAL PROFIT	**$353,155.00**

The truth is that figures in a business's first operating budget are rarely concrete because you are only using numbers that are estimated as to what the actual expenses or revenue may end up being. However, there is light at the end of the budgeting tunnel, because it gets easier as you move forward from year to year. Just make sure that as the year ends, you file your financial records in an organized fashion so that you can access them the following year during the budgeting process. That way, with each year that passes you will have better financial history to work with, and you can actually get close to budgeting your revenues and expenses more accurately.

Obtaining Financing for Your Operation

Obtaining financing for your new business can be accomplished by requesting financing through banks, commercial lenders, finance companies, and government agencies designed to assist start-up business and small business owners. However, before you start looking at what your options are when considering requesting a loan for your business, you should first be familiar with the types of financing available, which are equity financing, debt financing, secured financing, and banker's acceptance (BA). By knowing the difference between these types of financing, you will be in a better position to decide what will best fit your needs.

Types of Financing Available

Equity financing

Equity financing is when private investors trade owning a specific amount of funds for a percentage of a business. There are various sources for equity financing, which include family, friends, and even employees. However, equity financing can also be attained through professional investors (also known as venture capitalists). For instance, in the case of a corporation, it would entail selling a certain number of shares to venture capitalists to immediately inject that much capital into the business. One of the advantages of equity financing is that it allows the business to secure the funds it needs without having to incur additional debt, therefore having more cash available. In addition, the business assets do not have to be used as guarantee to obtain financing, and most importantly, investors do not have to be paid back if your company goes bankrupt. On the other hand, the disadvantage to equity financing is that part of your business is now owned by investors who will have some form of control over the operation of your business, and you will have to accept and work with ideas that you do not really agree with on how to run your business.

Debt financing

Debt financing is when funds are secured to be paid with interest over a designated period of time. Debt financing can be short-term, which means it would have to be repaid in less than a year or long term — meaning any specified period of time over a year. An example of debt financing would be a company applying to a lending institution for a long-term loan to purchase and install new manufacturing equipment. Due to the high dollar value of manufacturing equipment, the bank will more than likely require the business to use the title to the property to secure the loan. The biggest advantage with this type of financing is that the lending institution does not take ownership in any way of your business or any part thereof, and your responsibility is limited to simply repaying the loan. Other advantages of debt financing are that this type of loan can be used to buy business assets, and any interest paid on the loan is usually tax-deductible. There are also disadvantages to debt financing, one of them being that the bank will require the loan to be secured with a company asset of the same value as the loan, and some banks may even require some form of personal guarantee in order to secure the loan. In addition, with debt financing, the business is obligated to pay that debt monthly, even at times when the company is losing money.

Secured financing

Secured financing is similar to debt financing; however, in this type of financing, the banks and lending institutions loan the funds against the business's payment obligations, storage documents, or shipment documents. The most commonly used form, of all these, is that of securing funds against payment obligations, whereby the business owner commits the goods being imported or exported as collateral for the loan and the bank retains the documents that convey title to those goods as security for the loan. When using storage documents for securing financing, most of the times the financial institution will accept documents such as inventory control records. If you are using shipment documents as guarantee, the bank will accept a copy of the bill of lading, which is the contractual agreement between the supplier and the carrier who will be transporting the goods.

The main advantage of secured financing is that these loans can be either long-term or short-term, and you can benefit from fixed interest rates through the life of the loan. A disadvantage of this form of financing is that depending on the term of the loan, you will have a monthly debt obligation that, during slow times, may actually erode at your profits.

Banker's acceptance (BA)

A banker's acceptance is a form of secured financing. A banker's acceptance is a negotiable instrument, also called a draft, drawn on and accepted by a bank. Before the document is actually accepted by the bank, it is simply an order by the drawer to the bank to pay a specified amount of money to a specific individual or firm, and by a certain date, which is normally within six months. At this point, the document serves the same purpose as a postdated check. Once the bank accepts the document, which is done by signing it and stamping it "accepted," it becomes a liability of the bank, thus assuming responsibility for total payment on behalf of the drawer. An advantage of using a banker's acceptance is that they allow importers and exporters to substitute the financial institution's credit standing for their own. Another advantage, and the reason why they are predominantly used in for international trade transactions, is that they provide a safe avenue for collection and payment when one of the parties to the transaction does not know the creditworthiness of the other. On the other hand, one of the disadvantages of using a banker's note is that the amount paid to the drawer is less than the face value of the draft, thus the draft has to be done for more than the required amount to pay for the shipment. In addition, the money obtained from the bank under a banker's acceptance can only be used to pay for the specific shipment it was drawn for — it cannot be used for working capital, even if it is for expenses related to that particular shipment.

For example, IMPORTS is importing a shipment of children's shoes from a new trading partner in Brazil. Because IMPORTS has never done business with this shoe manufacturer before, the manufacturer will not sell IMPORTS the goods on credit. Consequently, IMPORTS secures a banker's acceptance agreement from the bank, in which the bank agrees to accept a draft for IMPORTS to pay for the shipment, and IMPORTS agrees to repay the bank the value of the draft. The bank gives IMPORTS the amount requested, which is used to pay the manufacturer in Brazil within 180 days from shipment of the goods.

Government-Sponsored Financing

In addition to obtaining financing from traditional private sector banks and lending institutions, there are also public sources of funding available through government-assisted programs, which assist small and start-up businesses. These agencies are the Small Business Administration, the Export-Import (EXIM) Bank, the Agency for International Development (AID), and the International Development Corporation Agency (IDCA).

Small Business Administration loans (SBA)

The Small Business Administration is one of the executive branches of the federal government, established with the purpose of providing assistance and overseeing the growth and development of small businesses. The SBA not only provides financial assistance for small businesses, but also the knowledge for planning and properly managing the funds. Unlike loans obtained from traditional financial institutions that are often short-term and with temporary lines of credit, the SBA has programs for long-term loans.

The SBA in itself does not loan money. The SBA guarantees the loans, which are awarded to small business owners by banks and other private financial institutions, with funds assigned to them by the federal government for the specific purpose of being used as loan guarantees. The SBA has three different types of loans for exporters: Export Express, the Export Working Capital Loan Program (EWCP), and International Trade Loans. All these types of loans are explained as follows; however, for any additional information, you can visit the SBA's International Trade Web site at **www. sba.gov/international**.

Export Express

The Export Express loan program combines the technical and financial assistance necessary to help the small business owner who has difficulties obtaining adequate export financing. SBA's Export Express is the most flexible export loan program available because of its versatility. The advantage of Export Express loans is that funds can be used to pay for any activity intended to increase exports, such as financial assistance to be able to fund the export of an order, standby letters of credit, lines of credit to assist with exporting efforts, trade shows participation, and even translation of product-specific documents to be used in overseas markets. In addition, the application process can be done at an SBA-approved lending institution in your area.

Export Express loans provide exporters with the capability of obtaining SBA-sponsored financing for loans and lines of credit up to $250,000, with the SBA guaranteeing the loan for 85 percent of its value. The actual lenders use their own loan documentation and procedures, making it more feasible for them to process, and the business owner can access their funds faster. The terms of maturity (the length of the loan) for SBA's Export

Express loans vary depending on the purpose of the loan, starting with five to ten years for working capital loans and up to 25 years for loans expressly geared toward the purchase of real estate.

To apply for an Export Express loan, you must contact your financial institution and determine if they are an SBA Express lender. If they are, then you can submit an application directly to your lender, where it will be processed. Should your application be approved by your lender, formation on your application is then submitted to the SBA for final approval. To qualify for an Export Express loan, you must demonstrate that funds obtained from the loan will help you enter new export markets or expand your existing market. In addition, you have to have been in business for at least a year.

Export Working Capital Loan Program (EWCP)

Oftentimes, the small exporting business owner invests time and money in developing prospective export sales leads — only to realize later that it will be impossible to secure funding through conventional means to complete the transaction. To fill that gap and to help exporters to not lose those sales, the SBA implemented the Export Working Capital Loan Program (EWCP). The purpose of the EWCP loan is to provide funding for businesses that are capable of generating export sales, but do not have the necessary working capital to support these sales. In general, funds secured under this loan program can be used to purchase inventory to be exported, to finance export working capital during long payment cycles, pay for preexportation expenses — such as the cost of components to be used in the manufacturing process of the exported product — and pay for labor and other general expenses incurred by the exporting company. The maximum loan amount, or line of credit, is $2 million dollars, and the lending institution receives a 90 percent guarantee for the loan from the SBDC. As far as collateral for this loan, the SBDC will accept the revenue generated by the export funded by the EWCP and the export-related inventory.

One of the major advantages of the EWCP is that you can apply for this type of loan even in advance of finalizing an export contract. In addition, EWCP loans can be used as short-term loans for a one-time transaction, or they can be extended to a 12-month line of credit for multiple export transactions. But in addition to your business-related guarantees, the SBDC also requires the personal guarantee of the business owners for this loan program. There are export eligibility restrictions, such as to where the products are being exported. The terms of maturity for the EWCP loans are normally one year, and the SBA fee for a 12-month EWCP loan is 25 percent of the part of the loan, which is guaranteed.

To be eligible for a EWCP loan, you must be a manufacturer, wholesaler, or an export company. In addition, you must meet the SBA eligibility size standard of having fewer than 100 employees for wholesalers, or fewer than 500 employees for manufacturers. Applications for EWCP loans are submitted to your local SBA-approved lending institution and forwarded to the SBA for final approval.

International Trade Loan program

This program is designed to finance funds required by export businesses for them to be able to continue to operate, as well as for those exporters who want to continue exporting, but are in financial distress as a result of increased competition from imported products. Small businesses that are capable of expanding their export markets — or even developing new ones — and are able to show that the funds loaned will increase their ability to compete in the global market are eligible for this program. Funds can be used to purchase property, build a new facility, expand an existing one, purchase or rebuild machinery, and make any other improvements of long-term fixed assets associated with exporting activities. An advantage of this loan is that it can also be used to refinance an existing loan that was obtained for one of the above-stated purposes. The maximum loan amount for an International Trade Loan is $2 million dollars with an SBA guarantee of $1.5 million dollars. A disadvantage of this type of loan is that as collateral for this type of loan program, the SBA requires their holding the first mortgage on the equipment or the property for which financing is being secured.

To apply for an International Trade Loan, you must go through an SBA-approved lender in your area who will process the application, then forward it to the SBA for final approval.

The Export-Import (EX-IM) Bank of the United States

The Export-Import Bank of the United States is a federal agency that acts as the export credit agency of the U.S. The EX-IM Bank is part of the executive branch of the federal government and was established for the purpose of helping finance exports of U.S. goods by issuing loans, guarantees, and insurance for companies involved in international trade. By financing sales transactions of exported goods that otherwise would have not taken effect due to the lack of the exporter's credit, the EX-IM Bank helps create and sustain jobs associated with the export industry. In addition, one of the main functions of the EX-IM Bank is issuing credit to international buyers of U.S.-made products, making the sale of goods from the U.S. a possibility. The EX-IM Bank has a number of programs available to these foreign buyers that ultimately have had a favorable impact on the sale of U.S.-made goods. Although the EX-IM Bank provides products and services to large and small local exporters as well as foreign investors, the vast majority of its loans are for small businesses. As a governmental agency, the purpose of the EX-IM Bank is to finance those business transactions that would have otherwise not taken place because of the inability or unwillingness of the private commercial lenders to take the risk.

The EX-IM Bank's working capital loans are fully backed by its guarantee but are actually made by commercial lenders such as Union Bank, City National Bank, and the First National Bank of Omaha, to name a few.

These loans make it possible for the business owner to increase the export of U.S. manufactured goods by providing the exporter with the additional cash flow needed to expand the business and increase international sales. Funds originating from this type of loan can be used by the exporter to purchase finished goods for export; cover the cost of raw materials, equipment, supplies, and labor to manufacture the goods; fund standby letters of credit; and finance the payment of invoices received from foreign suppliers. The requirements for the exporter to quality for this type of loan are to have been operational for 12 months or longer; to have a strong net worth; and to be located in the U.S. Also, the goods must contain a minimum of 50 percent of U.S.-manufactured components and must be shipped from the United States. Typically, the terms of the loans are for one to three years and can be transaction-specific or revolving. In addition, 90 percent of the total loan, including principal and interest, is guaranteed by the EX-IM Bank. As collateral for loans, the EX-IM Bank accepts export-related accounts receivables such as bills the exporter is expecting to collect as well as the inventory tied the export order, if the loan is to pay for goods being shipped to a buyer. However, for letters of credit issued under this type of loan, the required collateral is 25 percent of its face value.

The Export-Import Bank also issues short-term insurance policies to the small business owner (in this case, the exporter) to protect them from default from foreign buyers, whether it is due to bankruptcy or political issues, such as wars. To be qualified as a small business under the EX-IM Bank's guidelines, the business must meet the qualifications specified by the SBA that define a small business and have annual export credit sales for the previous two years of less than $5 million dollars. The EX-IM Bank has single-buyer short-term insurance policies that cover single or multiple sales to the same buyer, and multi-buyer short-term policies that cover all the shipments of the exporter requesting the insurance.

The EX-IM Bank provides assistance to small businesses at a local level through one of the five regional offices located throughout the United

States. Information and assistance on products and services provided by the EX-IM Bank is also available through a network of organizations and agencies in 48 states and the District of Columbia. To locate a member of the EX-IM Bank's network nearest you, visit the Export-Import Bank's Web site at **www.exim.gov**.

Writing a Loan Proposal

Successfully securing a loan for your business takes some work on your part because the more prepared you are, the better the chances are of a favorable outcome. When you approach a lending institution to request a loan for your business, you need to state your need clearly and provide all the required supporting documentation as to the financial situation of your business. Therefore, the best and most professional way to present your request is by preparing a loan proposal.

A loan proposal is virtually a condensed version of your business plan, as you want to provide the lending institution enough information for them to make an informed decision on your loan. Therefore, the information must be concise, yet adequate in presenting a full picture of your business, containing all the critical information. It must be a professional document with up-to-date information on your operation, including any possible changes in the company in the near future. In addition, because not all of individuals who are going to be reviewing your loan proposal will be knowledgeable about the international trade business, you should explain any terms or technical information that may not be common to someone not involved in this industry.

When working on your financial projections for your loan proposal, try to be conservative in developing your revenue estimates. Extremely high revenues may be assumed to be unrealistic and out of reach. On the other hand, when estimating expenses, make sure you consider all possible costs and avoid underestimating because you do not want to run short of funds earlier than anticipated. To avoid any questions as to the validity of your numbers, it is good practice to include a narrative explaining how you arrived at the figures for both your revenues and your expenditures.

A solid loan proposal will include a written narrative of the fundamental aspects of the project for which you are seeking the loan, relevant financial information, and all necessary supporting documentation. Each lending institution may have different requirements when submitting an application for a loan; however, as a general rule, the outline in this chapter will provide the prospective lender with all the information they need in order to evaluate and process your loan request favorably.

Although the information included in loan proposals varies, the format and key elements remain the same. The following loan proposal outline will serve as a guide as to what you should include in the document. Be precise and to the point — remember, it is supposed to be something like a condensed version of a business plan. Address each section, keeping in mind your audience and the purpose of the document. When in doubt as to how much information you should provide in any one section, remember there is no right or wrong to it; just include what you feel is necessary to bring your point across:

Loan Proposal

General Information
    Name of business
    Business address
    Name of owners or principals (whichever is applicable)
    Owner's social security number or EIN
Loan Information
    State the purpose of your loan
    State amount of funds requested
    State the requested terms of the loan, such as length and interest rate

List the collateral you will use to secure the loan, using current market values

State how much equity you will be contributing

Business Description

State the history and nature of your business

State the business legal structure

Describe any future plans for the business and how the loan will benefit the business

Market Information

Clearly define the services provided by your company

Discuss your business's market; describe your target customer base

Demonstrate that there is a demand for your products or services

Identify your competitors and explain how you are able to compete in the global marketplace

Identify your customers and how you are able to serve them

Discuss your marketing plan and identify costs associated with it

Business Financial Information

Demonstrate your ability to pay the loan through financial projections

For a start-up business loan, provide a projected balance sheet and income statement

For sole proprietors or partnerships, provide your and the other owners' financial statements

For other loans:

- Provide balance sheets, financial, and income statements for the past three years
- Provide tax returns for the past three years

Other Supporting Documentation

Provide copies of important legal documents related to your business such as articles of incorporation, fictitious name registration, etc.

Please see the accompanying CD-ROM for a template of this form.

Become Familiar with Methods of Payment

In the process of globalization, it is imperative to promote and facilitate international commerce. However, in the importing and exporting business — where the buyers of the goods can very well be across the globe from the seller of those goods — insuring payment for a sales transaction is reason for serious concern. There are too many variables involved, such as not knowing the parties involved, the internal politics of that country or region, and dealing with fluctuating exchange rate. Therefore, whether you are importing, exporting, or both, being familiar with the different methods of payment available in the international trade industry will allow you to better negotiate the terms of your sale. If you are on the exporting side of the transaction, you want to negotiate payment terms, which will allow you to collect as soon as possible after the sale and with the highest guarantee for collection on your part. You want to negotiate terms that will make it financially feasible and attractive for your customer, thus ensuring future sales. However, if you are on the importing side of the transaction, it is then in your best interests to negotiate terms that will delay paying for the goods as long as possible, as well as use a method of payment that will carry the lowest interest rate in the market at that particular time.

Negotiating terms that are acceptable to both parties in an international sales transaction is only part of the deal. Ensuring the safety and integrity of the sale by having some form of guarantee that the goods will be paid for is the other part. Throughout the years, various forms of payment have been developed and are commonly used in the international trade industry. These methods will give you an idea of what is available to you, the importer or the exporter.

Commercial documentary letter of credit

The most commonly used form of payment when importing and exporting is a commercial documentary letter of credit. More often referred to as a letter of credit, it is "commercial" in this case because it is used for commercial purposes and is payable upon producing specific documents. A letter of credit is the legal instrument whereby the issuing bank, working on behalf of the client (the buyer), makes a payment to a third party (the seller) based on the purchase agreement between the parties, which states the terms of the transaction — as long as the credit terms have been met. It is the written commitment by the bank to pay the seller, up to the total amount stated and within a determined amount of time, once confirmation has been received that the merchandise has been shipped. Letters of credit are a well-known and trusted form of payment used in the international trade industry all around the world. It is used just as often in relatively small transactions, as well as in transactions representing millions of dollars. Letters of credit are rather easy to obtain because most banks have personnel knowledgeable in the matter and are qualified to process these documents. Subject to international regulations, letters of credit have proved to be one of the most effective forms of collecting or making the payment.

Obtaining a letter of credit is almost like applying for a loan. In order for the bank to commit to make a payment to a seller on your behalf, it will require you to provide proof of your ability to pay the bank back the amount of the transaction. The bank will look for financial stability, enough liquidity (cash or assets that can be converted to cash) to cover the debt, and may even accept certificates of deposit and other assets as assurances for payment of the letter of credit. In addition, there are fees associated with securing, processing, and collecting letters of credit. When importing, there is a transaction fee, amendment fees, and payment fees, which are all based on a percentage of the transaction amount with a minimum amount to be met. When exporting, there are flat fees, such as for advising, confirmation (subject to country risk conditions), collections, and amendments. Fees based on percentages with a minimum amount are for assignment of proceeds/transfers and payment negotiations.

All letters of credit originate with a contract for sale or purchase of goods. This contractual obligation extends through the letter of credit, in that letters of credit are irrevocable and therefore cannot be altered or canceled without the consent of the party from whom you are purchasing the goods.

Therefore, upon receiving a copy of a letter of credit, it is critical to review all information for accuracy of the terms of the sale and completeness. If manufacturing of the product in question is involved, make sure you will be able to meet the deadline. Always take into account any unforeseen events that may delay the manufacturing process, such as a possible shortage in the supply of any of the components or any mechanical problems that might arise with the manufacturing equipment. Also, you must take into consideration shipping and delivery time frames to avoid missing the specified date on the letter of credit, which will result in the delay of the payment for the goods.

Using a hypothetical case for an example, it will be easier to visualize the sequence of events in the course of a letter of credit from inception through collection.

> IMPORTS, an importing company in Miami, purchases women's footwear from a manufacturer in Brazil for $25,000. The manufacturer requests that IMPORTS pay with a letter of credit, at which time IMPORTS applies at the bank and successfully receives a letter of credit in the amount of the transaction. The bank then commits to paying the seller in Brazil the $25,000 once the terms of the letter of credit are met. The terms are that the manufacturer in Brazil provides the bank with documentary evidence that the footwear purchased by IMPORTS has been shipped, at the specified shipping date and manner — which was by ocean freight to Miami, then by truck to IMPORTS' warehouse. These are the steps IMPORTS went through to obtain a letter of credit:

Step 1: IMPORTS successfully negotiates sales terms with the footwear manufacturer in Brazil and, as agreed, applies to the bank for a commercial documentary letter of credit reflecting the terms agreed upon for the sale.

Step 2: IMPORTS' bank accepts the application, drafts the irrevocable letter of credit, and sends it to the manufacturer's bank in Brazil, requesting confirmation.

Step 3: The manufacturer's bank receives the letter of credit and contacts the manufacturer for review and acceptance of the terms and conditions outlined in the letter of credit.

Step 4: The manufacturer agrees with the terms and conditions of the letter of credit and consequently contacts a freight-forwarder to make arrangements and take care of the shipment and final delivery of the goods to IMPORTS' warehouse in Miami.

Step 5: The manufacturer presents the documents received from the freight forwarder, such as ocean bills of lading (a receipt from the shipping company stating that the goods were received and placed onboard the vessel for shipment), to their bank in Brazil, verifying that all the terms of the letter of credit have been met.

Step 6: The manufacturer's bank reviews all the appropriate documents to ensure full compliance with the terms of the letter of credit, confirms that everything is in order, and releases payment to the manufacturer.

Step 7: The documents are then returned to IMPORTS through its bank, at which time IMPORTS makes arrangements to clear the goods through Customs.

Open accounts

An open account is just like its name: open, meaning you have no real legal recourse should the buyer default in payment of the goods shipped by the seller. In the international trade industry, under an open account arrangement, the seller would send the goods to the buyer with an invoice including shipping costs and other related costs. Once the goods are received, the buyer sends the seller the payment, which could be in the form of an international money order, cashier's check, bank transfer, or any other form of electronic fund transfer acceptable to both parties. Due to its nature, open accounts are often used by large import export companies who know each other's track record, and default is not a real issue.

As a start-up exporting business, you may be asked to accept open account terms; unfortunately, it is somewhat expected of the small exporter to accept these terms in order to build a business and reputation in the international trade industry. Although it involves taking risks that you may not want to take, more often than not, taking these types of risks pays off. Using common sense and doing a background check on the company requesting you to accept open account terms may be worth trying while you are still fairly new to the industry. If you decide to try a sale with open account terms, keep in mind that you have to make allowances in your budget to accommodate a possible large gap between the time you ship the goods and the time you get paid. Also, it is very important to take into consideration the country where the buyer is located when deciding whether to offer open account terms to a new customer. Sometimes local politics play a role in payments' being delayed. On the flip side, as a start-up importer, it is not very likely that you would be able to secure a shipment of goods under an open-account arrangement. Again, not many exporters are willing to take a chance on small start-up companies with little or no references as well as a limited credit record.

Documentary draft

Documentary drafts work pretty much like a check that you would write from your regular checking account, and unfortunately carry the same risk of not having the funds to back it up. Documentary drafts are also referred to as bills of exchange, probably because title of the goods does not transfer to the buyer until the draft is paid or makes some form of legal commitment to paying the draft when due. Documentary drafts are classified into three different types of drafts: sight drafts, time drafts, and date drafts.

Sight drafts are used when the vendor does not want to relinquish title to the merchandise until they reach the buyer's warehouse or other final destination and the goods are paid in full. When the goods have been transported by ocean freight, the buyer has to approve and sign the original ocean bill of lading and return it to the carrier who delivered the goods before the goods can be released. However, this rule does not apply when the goods are shipped by airfreight, and the buyer can claim the goods without the endorsement of the air waybill — a bill of lading for air transportation. Even though this is the formal way of handling sight drafts, it is common practice for the exporter to actually endorse the ocean bill of lading — along with the sight draft, invoices, and other documents required for the transaction — and forward it to the buyer's bank through the exporter's bank.

As soon as the ocean bill of lading has been endorsed by the seller, the seller's bank notifies the buyer. At that point, the buyer pays the draft, the seller's bank turns over the bill of lading, and the goods are then released to the buyer. The disadvantage of this form of payment is that there is no guarantee on behalf of the bank to back up the draft — the buyer could very well decide not to accept the goods after they have been shipped and arrived at the final destination, leaving the seller without payment and without the goods until they are returned. Although the buyer would not receive the goods because of non-payment, the seller would still have to cover the cost of getting the goods back.

Time drafts work the same as if the seller had sold the goods to the buyer on credit. Time drafts actually state the grace period the buyer has in which to pay the draft, such as, "payable within 60 days after acceptance." Once the time draft is signed, the word "accepted" is written on the document, the buyer takes possession of the goods, and the buyer is then formally committed to paying the draft.

Date drafts are similar to time drafts in that under both circumstances, the buyer can delay the payment of the goods after they have been received. However, date drafts do not have the flexibility of allowing payment to be done within a certain time frame; these documents actually have specific due dates for the full payment of the draft.

Cash in advance

Cash in advance is a simple form of payment, but it is not commonly used because it is too risky for the buyer to submit payment without having received the goods first. There are more negative ramifications to this form of payment than positive. For instance, there is always the possibility of a dishonest seller who either sends lesser-quality items than agreed upon or delays shipment of the goods. On the other hand, cash in advance is quite a favorable business deal for the seller, who has use of the money even before the goods are shipped.

Consignment

In the international trade industry, sale by consignment works pretty much the same way as in the domestic market, but at a much larger scale and at higher risk. When an exporter sells merchandise in consignment to a buyer overseas, the exporter still keeps title to the merchandise until such time that the goods are actually sold. However, once the merchandise is sent to the buyer to be sold in consignment, the exporter no longer has control as to how long it will take for the goods to sell and ultimately receive payment. It may not be the most cost-effective way for the exporter to do business, but at times, it may be the most feasible.

Foreign bank checks

Accepting checks from foreign banks for goods is not as commonly used anymore due to the availability of electronic bank transfers. However, should you ever be approached by a buyer who requests that you accept a check from a bank abroad, be aware that domestic banks still honor these checks. Foreign checks can be drawn on U.S. banks or foreign banks. Those drawn on U.S. banks are processed the same way as domestic checks. Foreign checks drawn on foreign banks represent somewhat of a risk to the seller in the United States in that most banks will exchange foreign checks according to the average daily currency exchange rate for that specific country's currency. Therefore, depending on the going rate at the time the checks are processed, the seller may end up losing money on the deal. In addition, as a general rule, banks will charge a processing fee for redeeming foreign checks.

Electronic bank transfers

Often used in the international trade industry, electronic bank transfers are a simple form of payment that is also time- and cost-effective for both parties involved. However, it depends on when the funds are actually transferred as to who is at risk should one of the parties default in the transaction. For instance, if the seller requires the buyer to transfer the funds prior to the buyer actually receiving the goods, the buyer is running the risk of the seller defaulting on the terms of the sale. On the other hand, should the buyer require the seller to ship the goods prior to transferring the funds, the seller is then at risk of not receiving the payment. Banks will charge a nominal fee to the buyer for processing the transfer and to the seller for accepting the transfer.

Factoring and forfaiting

Factoring and forfaiting are alternative ways to process payment for goods sold in the international market. Factoring is when export receivables are sold to a company that will assume responsibility for collecting those receivables. If the buyer ends up not paying for the goods received, then the factor (the company that purchased the export receivable) ends up losing the amount of the receivable. However, factors would not exist if there were not a source of revenue for them. Factors generate their revenue through fees that ensure a profit for them and cover their own costs, as well as the costs associated with the financial risks. Because this type of transaction represents such a risk to the factors, as a general rule, they prefer to be aware ahead of time as to whom the buyer is so that they can decide whether to accept the proposed transaction. Forfaiting is a similar form of collecting export receivables but is normally only used when the receivables are for sales over a quarter of a million dollars. Therefore, due to the large amount of money involved, forfeiting requires affording long-term credit to the buyer as well as bank guarantees.

Having a thorough understanding of the financial matters affecting the management of your business is essential for your success. Although you could contract with an accountant to take care of your finances, it is ultimately in your best interests that the company realize a profit. There is a lot to running a business; however, the tools and information provided here will help you set up and operate your business to be finance-conscious. Knowing the mechanics of running the fiscal portion of your business and being able to understand where your company stands financially at any given time will allow you to make sound business decisions.

Chapter 6

Product Classification — Understanding the Harmonized Tariff Schedule

The Harmonized Tariff Schedule of the United States (HTS) is at the heart of every import into the U.S. If you import, you will definitely be working with this tariff schedule as it will dictate how much you will be paying in duties on the products. The HTS is an internationally standardized system of products and numbers designed in the form of a hierarchical structure that describes all possible goods that can be traded. Published by the United States International Trade Commission, which is the federal agency responsible for determining the possible impacts certain imports may have on domestic companies, the HTS provides tariff rates and statistical categories for all products that enter into the United States. Based on the international Harmonized System, which is a classification system of goods traded worldwide, the HTS essentially provides duty rates, or tax rates, for all of these items. Changes and modifications to the international classification system within the HTS are made periodically through legal action by the World Customs Organizations (WCO), the intergovernmental agency whose focus is exclusively on Customs-related issues worldwide. However, duty rates are established by U.S. Customs and Border Protection. The first 97 chapters of the HTS reflect the international classification structure of the Harmonized Commodity Description and Coding System, as standardized by the WCO in 1989.

The HTS establishes the duty rate that must be paid for every item that you can possibly imagine importing. Duty rates are assigned to whole items, as well as components for whole items. Duty rates are quite specific, and great care must be taken when determining a particular product's duty rate to avoid incorrect duty payment, which can result in penalties assessed by Customs. For instance, the duty rate of a specific product may vary according to its condition or stage of completion at the time of importing. For instance, a tennis racket, not strung, has a 3.9 percent duty rate; however, a tennis racket, strung, has a duty rate of 5.3 percent. Duty rates are assessed on the value of the goods at the time of importation (transaction value), which includes the costs associated with the transaction — packing costs, commissions, royalties, and so on. If for some reason the duty cannot be assessed based on the transaction value, it can be assessed based on any of the following:

- Transaction value of identical goods

- The transaction value of similar products, as long as Customs has previously accepted this value

- The value of the resale price of the merchandise in the United States, which is called deductive value, with deductions for items such as commissions and transportation costs

- The computed value, which is determined by adding the cost of materials and labor, packing costs, profits, and other routine expenses

Duty rates are also based on the trading status of the country of origin. Most products are imported under Normal Trade Relations (NTR) status, which means these are products originating from countries that the U.S. does not have any trade restrictions with, and the standard duty rate applies. These products appear under Column 1 of the HTS. It is also possible for goods to be imported duty-free, or at a reduced duty rate lower than those assigned under NTR status. These would be goods originating from developing countries and goods under special programs such as the Generalized System of Preferences (GSP), the Israeli Free Trade Act, the North America Free Trade Act (NAFTA), the Caribbean Basin Initiative (CBI), and the Dominican Republic-Central America Free Trade Agreement (DR-CAFTA). *These are all discussed at length in Chapter 12.*

Duties assigned under these programs are reflected with a notation under the special column part of column 1. If the imported product originates from one of the trade-restricted countries — Cuba, North Korea, Iran, Syria, or Sudan — then the duty rate will be different and will appear under column 2. For example, shoes classified under 6402.19.50 in the HTS being imported from a Normal Trade Relations country have a duty rate of 76 cents a pair, plus 32 percent of the value. However, the same shoes being imported from a trade-restricted country will have a duty rate of $1.50 a pair, plus 66 percent of the value. Trade-restricted countries are those that the United States has designated as countries supporting terrorism.

The HTS is divided into two main parts: notes and classifications. The notes segment includes, among other things, rules of classification, discussion on trade programs such as NAFTA, and a list of recent changes to the document. The classifications portion is where the products are actually listed and classified, and is subsequently divided into 22 sections, which are further divided into chapters. At the beginning of each chapter, you will find notes regarding the products classified within that chapter. These notes will address key issues, such as lists of products that are not classified within that chapter, acceptable definitions, explanations of the chapter headings, and other relevant information.

This international categorizing system is identified by the first four- to six-digit level classification of the products. The initial classification is then extended to an eight-digit level classification to provide duty rates for products specific to the United States. Product classification begins with a two-digit code for the broadest category of the product, and it is then sub-divided by adding additional digits to make the classification more product-specific.

To give you an idea of the extent and complexity of the HTS classification system, an excerpt of the HTS's table of contents is included. This excerpt concentrates more specifically on Section XII, as well as its corresponding page in the tariff. The importation of shoes will be used as an example to follow that product from the HTS Table of Contents excerpt, to the actual HTS page that lists the shoes, to a breakdown of the item number, so that you can better understand what how the product classification system works. The excerpt from the tariff's table will also be used to discuss in more detail the significance of each column.

Recreated excerpt from The Harmonized Tariff Schedule of the United States (2009) (Rev. 1)
Table of Contents

SECTION XII: FOOTWEAR, HEADGEAR, UMBRELLAS, SUN UMBRELLAS, WALKING STICKS, SEATSTICKS, WHIPS, RIDING-CROPS AND PARTS THEREOF; PREPARED FEATHERS AND ARTICLES MADE THEREWITH; ARTIFICIAL FLOWERS; ARTICLES OF HUMAN HAIR

Chapter 64 Footwear, gaiters, and the like; parts of such articles

Chapter 65 Headgear and parts thereof

Chapter 66 Umbrellas, sun umbrellas, walking sticks, seatsticks, whips, riding crops, and parts thereof

Chapter 67 Prepared feathers and down and articles made of feathers or of down; artificial flowers; articles of human hair

---

Excerpt from the Harmonized Tariff Schedule of the United States

Harmonized Tariff Schedule of the United States (2009) (Rev. 1)
Annotated for Statistical Reporting Purposes

XII
64-5

Heading/ Subheading	Stat. Suf-fix	Article Description	Unit of Quantity	Rates of Duty		
				1		2
				General	Special	
6402		Other footwear with outer soles and uppers of rubber or plastics:				
		Sports footwear:				
6402.12.00	00	Ski-boots, cross-country ski footwear and snowboard boots	prs.	Free		35%
6402.19		Other:				
		Having uppers of which over 90 percent of the external surface area (including any accessories or reinforcements such as those mentioned in note 4(a) to this chapter) is rubber or plastics (except footwear having foxing or a foxing-like band applied or molded at the sole and overlapping the upper and except footwear designed to be worn over, or in lieu of, other footwear as a protection against water, oil, grease or chemicals or cold or inclement weather):				
6402.19.05		Golf shoes	. . . .	6%	Free (AU,BH,CA, CL,D,E,IL,J+,JO, MA,MX,OM, P,PE,R,SG)	35%
	30	For men	prs.			
	60	For women	prs.			
	90	Other	prs.			
6402.19.15		Other	. . . .	5.1%	Free (AU,BH,CA, CL,D,E,IL,J+,JO, MA,MX,OM, P,PE,R,SG)	35%
	20	For men	prs.			
	41	For women	prs.			
	61	Other	prs.			
		Other:				
6402.19.30		Valued not over $3/pair	. . . .	Free		84%
	31	For men	prs.			
	61	Other	prs.			
6402.19.50		Valued over $3 but not over $6.50/pair	. . . .	76¢/pr. + 32%	Free (AU,BH,CA, CL,D,E,IL,J+, MA,MX,OM, P,PE,R) 7.6¢/pr. + 3.2% (JO) 19¢/pr. + 8% (SG)	$1.58/pr. + 66%
	31	For men	prs.			
	61	Other	prs.			
6402.19.70		Valued over $6.50 but not over $12/pair . . .	. . . .	76¢/pr. + 17%	Free (AU,BH,CA, CL,D,E,IL,J+, MA,MX,OM, P,PE,R) 7.6¢/pr. + 1.7% (JO) 19¢/pr. + 4.2% (SG)	$1.58/pr. + 35%
	31	For men	prs.			
	61	Other	prs.			
6402.19.90		Valued over $12/pair	. . . .	9%	Free (AU,BH,CA, CL,D,E,IL,J+,JO, MA,MX,OM, P,PE,R,SG)	35%
	31	For men	prs.			
	61	Other	prs.			
6402.20.00	00	Footwear with upper straps or thongs assembled to the sole by means of plugs (zoris)	prs.	Free		35%

Breakdown of Harmonized Tariff Schedule by Column

Heading/subheading column

The product classification is made up of four digits, with the first two (64) being the chapter where the goods are located. With each set of digits that is added, the description of the product gets more specific.

For example, 6402.19.50 would be broken down as follows:

64　　　Chapter 64, Footwear, gaiters and the like; parts of such articles

　02　　　Other footwear with outer soles and uppers of rubber or plastics

　　.19　　Sports footwear

　　　.50　Valued over $3, but not over $6.50/pair

Stat. suffix column

The numbers that appear under this column are a direct reference to Customs rulings that have been done pertaining to that particular product, which is Customs' determination as to what duty rate applies to that particular product. While using the HTS online, you can click on that number. Using the same product as above for an example, clicking on the "31" will direct you to a site where Customs rulings on this particular product have been made.

Article description

This column describes in detail the product to clearly identify it and differentiate it from similar products that may fall under a different duty rate.

Unit of quantity

The unit of quantity must be identified, as it will clarify in what unit of quantity the duty rate was assessed, e.g. by individual item, by pairs, or any other unit.

Rates of duty

The rates of duty column is where the amount of duty you will have to pay on the imported products is determined. This column is further sub-divided into the three following columns:

General: Typically referred to as column 1, the general column states the typical duty rate from the majority of the countries that import this good. Duty rates are typically expressed in terms of quantity/cost rate, or as a percentage of the value of the good. However, in some instances, such as in the example we are using, duty is being assessed on both a quantity/cost rate and a percentage of the value of the goods.

$$76¢/pr. + 32\%$$

In other words, if you were to import a dozen pairs of shoes valued at $10 dollars a pair from a country falling in the category of Normal Trade Relations status, the total amount of duty owed would be $47.52.

12 pairs of shoes x $10.00/each =[value]	$120.00
12 pairs of shoes x 76 cents/pair = [cost]	$9.12
$120.00 (total [value] of importation) x 32 % duty rate =	$38.40
Total amount of duty owed= [cost] + [duty]	$47.52

Special: The special column indicates special duty rates assigned to specific countries or under certain trade programs. Going back to our sample imported goods, these goods would be imported duty-free if imported from Australia (AU) under the United States-Australia Free Trade, Canada (CA) under Goods of Canada, and Mexico (MX) under Goods of Mexico, just to explain a few of all the programs listed.

Column 2: Contains the duty rates specifically assigned to trade-restricted countries, such as North Korea, Cuba, and other countries.

The Harmonized Tariff Schedule may seem somewhat complex when you first look at it, but once you familiarize yourself with it, you will find it is not as complicated as it seems. In addition, all abbreviations and references made in the Harmonized Tariff Schedule are spelled out and explained within the document. If you would like to have a hard copy of the Harmonized Tariff Schedule, you can order a copy from the Government Printing Office. As updates and amendments are made throughout the year, you will receive copies of those changes so that your copy is always current. The Harmonized Tariff Schedule can also be accessed online through the U.S. Bureau of Customs and Border Protection's Web site at **www.cbp.gov**, as well as at the United States International Trade Commission's site at **www.usitc.gov**.

U.S. Customs and Border Protection Rulings on Product Classifications

Although the United States International Trade Commission publishes and updates the Harmonized Tariff Schedule on a regular basis, there may be times when you as the importer may not have a clear understanding of how to classify the product you are intending to import under the HTS, or you may have other schedule-related questions. If that is the case, you can contact Customs and request a ruling addressing issues, such as the proper classification or valuation of certain merchandise, proper country of origin marking, or even if the goods being imported qualify for duty-free or deferred-duty treatment. If you have the slightest doubt, do not hesitate in contacting Customs for an answer. There are times when there is such a fine line between one classification of one product and another with very distinct duty rates that it is best that you seek expert assistance rather than guessing. If you have any concerns regarding goods planned for importation, whether it is a duty rate or any other compliance issue, it is recommended to request a ruling as soon as possible in order to avoid any problems at the time of importing. Although requesting a ruling from Customs can result in extended waiting periods ranging anywhere from several months to a year, it is worth the wait, as using the improper classification and, therefore, duty rate can result in penalties being assessed by Customs. For example, say you are considering importing handmade wooden umbrellas from China and you are not sure if the duty rate for handmade wooden umbrellas is the same as the duty rate for handmade aluminum umbrellas. Requesting a ruling from Customs will provide you with the proper duty rate. A Customs ruling, which is always provided in writing, is the agency's official interpretation of that particular case.

Rulings can be requested by the importer, the exporter, an authorized agent, or anyone else who has a direct interest in the issue being addressed with the ruling request. The written petition for a ruling can be fairly simple; however, the more information you provide to Customs, the better off you will be, as Customs will have a better understanding of what you are asking for. Once Customs issues a ruling, that interpretation is legally binding for both Customs and the importer who made that particular request. All rulings issued are published, posted on Customs' Web site, and distributed to all ports of entry and other reporting agencies throughout the country. Ruling requests for tariff classification-related issues should be done in writing and addressed to the National Commodity Specialist Division of the U.S. Customs and Border Protection at One Penn Plaza, 10th Floor, New York, NY 10119, Attn: CIE/Ruling Request.

Chapter 7

Importing

You may be interested in importing, but what does it actually mean to be an importer? An importer is considered to be someone who brings merchandise into the United States from a foreign country. The business of importing can be challenging at times due to the number of regulations that have to be met; however, it is very rewarding. You will have the opportunity to meet people from places across the globe with whom you probably never imagined you would be working. Doing your homework in respect to procedures and researching your goods will make your experience in the exporting industry satisfying.

Identify the Goods that Will Get You in the International Trading Game

Conducting business with partners who are overseas is a rewarding experience, but it can be challenging. Conducting business transactions with individuals you have never met can be a bit scary, and it can be even worse if you are not familiar with the products. You should attempt to enter the industry working with products or services that are familiar to you. Maybe in your current or previous employment, or even in a business you may have owned earlier, you were directly involved with certain products and became knowledgeable about them. Starting up your import business with such products would make it easier for you to market them; you would be able to get a good idea as to its possible target market, its benefits, and uses, thus providing the knowledge necessary to conduct successful sales transactions.

If your line of work prior to starting your own business did not afford you the opportunity to actually work with any product in particular, then select a product that may interest you and go from there. There are numerous sites on the Internet that contain information regarding certain products or categories of merchandise as they relate to importing into the U.S. One of those sites is the Customs and Border Protection Web site, which contains a list of restricted and prohibited items that cannot be imported in the U.S., such as drug paraphernalia, dog and cat fur, and ceramic tableware, to name a few. The Web site address is **www.cbp.gov/xp/cgov/travel/vacation/kbyg/prohibited_restricted.html**. Another good Web site to visit is the World Trade Organization's site, **www.wto.org**, which contains international trade statistics and a detailed analysis of international trade by sector and product that will be helpful when determining what to import or export and from where. This site in particular will give you a good idea as to what products are trading well and where. Just because you are a beginner does not mean you have to limit yourself to just one product to trade. You may start by importing or exporting goods that are related, such as bed linens and bath towels. However, you must be realistic and limit your options so that you may thoroughly educate yourself about the particular goods or services. Once you become familiar with those products, then you may cautiously consider expanding your line of products.

Importing goods that you are not familiar with can be risky. Unlike the U.S., not all countries have export regulations established for quality control purposes of goods leaving the country. As a result, numerous products, unsafe for consumption, have been imported to the U.S. from such countries. One of the biggest safety concerns has been children's toys that were imported into the U.S. with high lead content in the paint. Choosing the right product or products to begin with is critical to your success. You will want to carve out a niche of the market by specializing in a particular line of product.

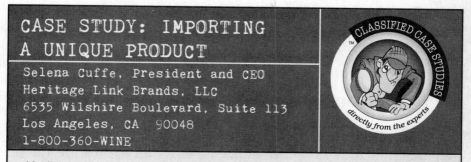

CASE STUDY: IMPORTING A UNIQUE PRODUCT

Selena Cuffe, President and CEO
Heritage Link Brands, LLC
6535 Wilshire Boulevard, Suite 113
Los Angeles, CA 90048
1-800-360-WINE

Heritage Link Brands is the largest importer and distributor of indigenous-produced wines from Africa and its Diaspora. They received the prestigious Black Enterprise Small Business of the Year Award for 2009.

The story of Heritage Link Brands is that of a business that was built based on filling an existing gap in the market — that of importing into the United States and distributing wines produced by black South Africans. President and CEO Selena Cuffe attributes her company's success to having enough passion to withstand not only cultural challenges, but also the multiple regulations that must be met. She started the company in 2005 after a visit to South Africa, where she attended a wine festival in Soweto. It was during that trip that she became aware of the $3 billion wine industry in Africa and decided to start a business as part of that industry. That industry has since grown into a $5 million industry, with her company alone generating more than $1 million in revenues in 2008.

Heritage Link Brands is truly a success story of an import company starting from the ground up. Cuffe and her husband started the company with $70,000 they had in savings and credit cards. A strong belief in what they were doing combined with excellent marketing of the product propels the success; the company's imported wines sell at more than 1,000 restaurants, retailers, and grocery stores. The company experienced tremendous growth in a relatively short period of time. "We started in Massachusetts but grew rapidly," Cuffe said. "Within three months after launch, we were in 26 states, and by the second year, we were in 41 states."

As the company has continued to grow, so has its importing and distributing strategies. Heritage Link Brands has recently expanded its imported product line to include wines from countries other than Africa but made by African-descent individuals. In addition, the company has partnered with Sam's Club, Disney and, most recently, sealed a deal with American Airlines, which serves the Seven Sisters and One World wines onboard its flights, both domestic and international.

Do Your Homework

Once you have identified the goods that are of interest to you, and you are comfortable enough to be able to discuss them intelligently, then begin market research. Determine if there is a market for this product, and figure out how extensive that market may be. Some products may have a large market in certain regions and may not be marketable at all in others. For instance, you decide to import snow skis and snow boards. There will obviously be a market for such products in states where it snows. However, the demand for such products may be higher in some of those states than others; find out which. Initially, you might want to try to narrow down your selection to commonly used products, such as apparel and footwear, that are not as complicated and are not highly regulated, as opposed to products that are more complex, such as electronics and cosmetics.

If you are considering importing a particular product, conduct an assessment of your product's potential for success in the domestic (U.S.) market. A reasonable way to judge how your product will perform is to evaluate how that particular product is doing in other countries that are somewhat comparable to the United States. This information can be accessed in the World Trade Organization's Web site (**www.wto.org**), which contains a vast amount of statistical information broken down by product and country, making it easy to understand. The same holds true if you are considering exporting a certain product to a particular country — take into consideration how that product is doing in the domestic market. Also take into account cultural, economic, political, and environmental differences, which may affect the outcome of your evaluation. For example, when evaluating the possibility of exporting specialty Christmas decorations, economically they would not do as well in the poorer countries because the number of people who would actually have the money to spend on things like that is a lot lower. Remember that even though the country you select to use for comparison may be similar to the U.S. in certain ways, no two countries are completely alike, and the overall attitude of the general population will not be the same in two countries. Differences like that will not make your evaluation accurate. For instance, the movement in the U.S. for environmental protection consciousness is on the rise; however, this attitude does not hold true in other countries. Most importantly, avoid getting into the importation and distribution of items that are of substandard quality or run the risk of having safety issues. The ramifications of importing defective or substandard goods are more complicated than what you will be ready to deal with as a start-up business. For instance, importing defective or substandard products can result in your entire shipment being rejected by your customer, or even your getting involved in a lawsuit.

Research and Select Suppliers for These Goods

When you are ready to import, one of the first areas you need to take care of is identifying the countries that produce the goods you want. You may find that the products are available in a number of different countries, allowing you plenty of flexibility when it comes time for selecting suppliers, who are individuals or companies from whom you acquire the goods you intend to import or export. On the other hand, you may also find that few countries have the products you want, which means fewer suppliers from which to choose. Selecting a supplier is a critical decision, especially as you are starting a business and do not have much of a financial cushion to accommodate unforeseen disasters.

You are probably asking yourself, how and where do I even start looking for suppliers overseas? You can certainly look on the Internet for sources by simply searching for "foreign suppliers;" however, the list will be endless and, aside from being time-consuming, all you would end up with would be names of suppliers, with no practical way of knowing if they are a legitimate company or a fraudulent operation. As Internet fraud is on the rise, this is one major drawback of looking for this information online.

A better way to find suppliers overseas is through trade publications, magazines, and other periodicals published to target the import export industry. Most of the trade publications are also available online by subscription or through memberships to the various international trade organizations. Suppliers and manufacturers advertise in these publications, sometimes including references to current and past clients, therefore giving you the opportunity to contact these references even before you call the supplier. Contacting a prospective supplier's past clients is always a good idea, especially if the information is readily available, so that you can get references on matters such as the quality of the product they received from that supplier and whether the product was delivered on time and as promised.

Local economic development councils (or corporations) may also be good sources of information regarding contacts overseas. Their work with local industry is conductive to obtaining and making available public information such as this. Even if they did not have the information readily available, then due to the nature of their business, they would know where to secure sources of possible suppliers. Another option is to check with agencies within your state, such as Enterprise Florida in the state of Florida. Enterprise Florida has many services available to small businesses, one of these being international trade assistance, providing the Florida business owner with information such as lists of suppliers and manufacturers overseas. You can also contact trade-regulating governmental agencies, such as consulates from the countries where you want to locate a supplier. Consulates are where representatives of a foreign government represents the legal interests of their people. Professional trade organizations for importing and exporting, such as the American Association of Exporters and Importers, the American Importers Association, and others are also reliable sources of information that can provide you with lists of potential suppliers as well as provide great sources of networking opportunities in the industry. *See Chapter 15 for more on these organizations.* Look into associations such as the American Importers Association (**www.americanimporters.org**) and the Professional Association of Exporters and Importers (**www.paei.org**). These, and a number of other international trade-related organizations, can be found online, as well as in advertisements in trade publications.

After you have narrowed down the list to just the right supplier that is carrying exactly what you want, you must take into consideration the country where the supplier is located. Even though the import export business operates in a global market, sometimes there are factors relating to that specific country that affect your ability to effectively conduct business with the newfound supplier. Some of these factors, such as being a trade-restricted country, may not be deal-breakers, but they certainly should influence your final decision, as the duty rate on goods imported from such countries will be higher.

Find out from your Customs broker, a person empowered by U.S. Customs and Border Protection to assist importers and exporters, if the U.S. places any restrictions on imports originating from that country and whether those restrictions are temporary in nature, or if they have been in place for a while. Your Customs broker can also advise you if that particular country has a preferential trade agreement with the U.S., such as the North American Free Trade Agreement (NAFTA). Preferential trade agreements are covenants made between countries for reducing tariffs for certain products to the agreeing countries. There are several trade agreements in place, and those involved in international trade should take advantage of them. *Chapter 11 of this book is dedicated to the discussion of the multiple trade agreements in which the U.S. participates.*

Evaluate the level of actual trading activity with this particular country: How much is this country importing or exporting? Does it have a large manufacturing base and, therefore, exports a large volume of products? It does not necessarily have to be related to your particular product, but just the overall trade activity will be a strong indicator of the viability of successful trading with this country. The level of development of the particular country also needs to be taken into consideration because trading with developed countries is generally easier and comes with fewer obstacles than dealing with developing countries. Developed countries, being more advanced, have procedures and regulations in place, similar to those of the United States, which make trading safer and less complicated. You may find that the prices of goods from suppliers located in developing countries could be lower than those of suppliers located in developed countries, but the cost of having to resolve legal issues, should they arise, may turn out to be more than the original savings you experienced.

In addition, take into consideration the location of the supplier or manufacturer. Depending on their location, transportation costs may add up so that it is not financially feasible for you to purchase the desired goods from this particular supplier. Besides the shipping cost associated with moving the goods from the supplier's nearest port to your port of entry, there are also transportation costs for moving the goods from the supplier's manufacturing plant to the shipyard. The farther away the supplier's manufacturing plan is located from its nearest port, the higher the cost of transportation will be. What about labor costs? Labor is one of the largest factors in determining the price of the final product. Wages in developing countries are lower, which reduces the final cost of the product to you; however, ethical questions arise in regard to some of the poor working conditions in some of these countries.

A different area of concern is your familiarity with a country, and your ability/inability to speak and understand the language. Understanding the language may not seem important, as U.S. business partners abroad tend to speak English, too. However, that is not always the case, and unless you find a trustworthy translator to speak for you while negotiating business deals, not knowing the language can be a serious hindrance. Not only is it difficult to work through a translator during meetings that are in person, but it is even worse when trying to conduct business over the phone because you do not have the benefit of seeing the other person's body language to gauge the situation. Finally, being familiar with the country and its culture can provide you with some guidance as to what may be expected of you. For instance, some countries still harbor issues with women in the business world and may refuse to deal with you if you are a woman, or with any of your female employees. You have to be prepared to deal with this situation in the best way possible to complete your business transaction. There are also countries where the only way to conduct business is by "paying off" corrupt companies and, at times, government officials. If you are aware that this situation is taking place in the region or the country where your supplier is located, you may reconsider how important it is to you to purchase from that particular supplier.

Bureau of Customs and Border Protection

As with any type of business, when you enter the international trade industry, it is in your best interests to get to know early on who the key players are, such as the regulatory agencies and your contacts for particular issues. In the import export business, there are a number of regulatory agencies involved, and it will depend on the merchandise being imported as to which agency will regulate that product. For example, if you are exporting firearms, ammunition, or other similar products, the Bureau of Alcohol, Tobacco, Firearms, and Explosives (ATF) is involved. When it comes to agricultural-related products and merchandise, the U.S. Department of Agriculture is involved, and the primary agency overseeing all exports is the Bureau of Customs and Border Protection (CBP). Customs provides management oversight and assistance to the 327 official ports of entry into the U.S. — there are 20 field operations offices that oversee this. Customs' offices at these ports of entry carry out transactions related to the importation of goods, such as clearing cargo, performing agricultural inspections, and collecting duties.

As with many other governmental agencies, the events that took place on September 11 also affected and changed the way that CBP operated. The CBP, known as U.S. Customs prior to September 11, was originally part of the U.S. Department of Commerce. Its main function was to regulate the Tariff Act of 1930; however, after September 11, the agency was reorganized, renamed, and moved out from under the Department of Commerce. At that time, Customs was renamed as U.S. Customs and Border Protection (CBP) and was teamed with other border enforcement agencies to become what is now the U.S. Department of Homeland Security. Therefore, in its new role, Customs' main mission became that of homeland security — not only through the inspection and clearance of goods coming in the country, but also by taking a more active role in securing our borders.

As part of the Homeland Security team, CBP is also responsible for detecting and preventing terrorists and weapons intended for terrorist activity from entering the United States, as well as regulating international trade. Customs' new mission integrated well with its prior duty of protecting and facilitating international trade, as well as assessing and collecting duties, taxes, and other fees associated with the import and export of goods. In order to properly collect duties due and better manage what is actually being imported into the U.S., processing imports with Customs is quite document-intensive. For that reason, so many importers secure the services of Customs brokers to process their importation paper work. These individuals, being licensed through Customs, are very knowledgeable of all the processes and requirements to successfully import your products.

In addition, Customs also regulates the movement of goods, people, and carriers between the U.S. and other countries, as well as protects borders from bringing in illegal drugs and other hazardous products. Customs law enforcement activities also include detecting and investigating any illegal international trade activity, such as unlawful importation of arms and other fraudulent transactions intended to avoid paying appropriate fees.

Although Customs is responsible for enforcing laws pertaining to the protection of U.S. borders, it is also responsible for educating importers about the rules and regulations affecting importation. This effort was put into effect with the implementation of informed compliance and shared responsibility, as mandated by the Customs Modernization Act of 1993.

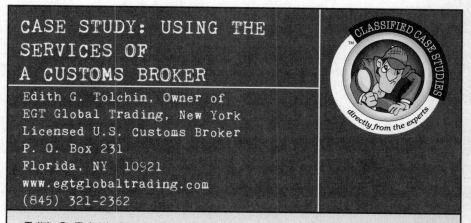

CASE STUDY: USING THE
SERVICES OF
A CUSTOMS BROKER

Edith G. Tolchin, Owner of
EGT Global Trading, New York
Licensed U.S. Customs Broker
P. O. Box 231
Florida, NY 10921
www.egtglobaltrading.com
(845) 321-2362

Edith G. Tolchin has been a licensed Customs broker and sourcing consultant for many years. During her years in the industry, she has been witness to many success stories of small import export companies that have grown and become successful. Companies that have been wise in their decision-making process have known when to secure the services of experts, such as Customs brokers, as they "learn the ropes" of importing and exporting. "Novice importers [and] exporters should always use the services of licensed Customs brokers for at least their first international trade transaction," Tolchin said.

In the 35 years that she has been involved in the import export business, Tolchin has seen many changes in procedures and regulations; the knowledge and expertise of a Customs broker can be priceless in effectively clearing imported shipments through Customs. Customs brokers will prepay duties, prepare necessary documentation, and deliver the shipment to your inland delivery destination, Tolchin said. "They are also qualified to consult on Customs issues and can prepare a binding ruling request to determine classification (and import duties) for your products."

Informed compliance

In December 1993, the Customs Modernization, or "Mod," Act was signed into law, amending several sections of the Tariff Act of 1930 that, when passed, had a major impact on more than 20,000 commonly imported goods into the U.S. Two of the provisions that emerged from the Mod Act were informed compliance and shared responsibility. These provisions were based on the principle that if importers, exporters, and all other "players" involved in international trade were thoroughly informed as to all of Customs' rules and regulations relating to international trade, then there would be no reason for these individuals to not adhere to these rules. Thus, all those involved in international trade would be expected to adhere to those rules by exercising reasonable care when importing into the U.S. In this context, by "reasonable care," Customs refers to how you as the importer would make every reasonable effort to abide by all rules and meet all regulations established.

The concept of informed compliance was designed to benefit both Customs and the importer under the principle that when voluntary compliance is reached, Customs will be able to cut back on the use of its resources. This would be accomplished by not having to spend time and funds conducting unnecessary examinations or extended entry reviews for shipments by importers that are found to be compliant on regular basis.

Therefore, both the CBP and the importing community share the responsibility for implementing these requirements. For instance, Section 484 of the Tariff Act states that it is your responsibility (the importer) to use reasonable care when classifying and determining the value of the goods that will be imported. You must also provide Customs with any other pertinent information that will help them assess the appropriate duties and determine if that particular shipment meets all the legal requirements. Customs' responsibility, on the other hand, is to assess or change the final classification and value of goods being imported.

In an effort to meet its informed compliance responsibilities, Customs' Office of International Trade has issued numerous informed compliance publications regarding revised requirements, regulations, or procedures, and a number of classification and valuation issues. In addition, to assist in exercising reasonable care, Customs has issued a checklist intended to provide importers with guidance in exercising such reasonable care. The checklist can be found in one of the many Customs publications on informed compliance, titled "What Every Member of the Trade Community Should Know About: Reasonable Care (A Checklist for Compliance)." The checklist can be accessed online i at **www.cbp.gov** by searching within the site for "informed compliance checklist."

Required documentation

There are numerous documents that an importer needs to be familiar with during the process of importing merchandise into the United States. Not all documents discussed in this book are developed by the importer or the importer's representative, but it is important that the importer be familiar enough with these documents to be able to identify any errors or discrepancies in them. It is the responsibility of the importer, however, to ensure accuracy in all documentation related to the import being processed, as it will have a direct impact on the successful processing of the cargo. Starting with the requirement to file a request for an importer's number and continuing with the purchase agreement — where your importation transaction begins — all documents related to the importation process will be discussed as follows:

Customs Form 5106: Application for Importer's Number

Before you import your first shipment, you must first apply to U.S. Customs and Border Protection for an importer's number. The process is relatively simple because you can fill out the form, Form 5106, online and obtain a reply within days. The form is found on the CBP's Web site (**www.cbp.gov**), under "Forms." This is the first step you need to take when you are going to import. As an individual importer, once you receive a number, which normally is the same as your federal employer identification number or social security number, you are ready to begin with the process of importing your goods. Proceed by preparing the appropriate paperwork discussed in this chapter.

Importer Identification Number Application Form — 5106

DEPARTMENT OF HOMELAND SECURITY U.S. Customs and Border Protection **IMPORTER ID INPUT RECORD** 19 CFR 24.5	Approved OMB NO. 1651-0064 Exp. 09-30-2012 See back of form for Paperwork Reduction Act Notice. 1. TYPE OF ACTION *(Mark all applicable)* ☐ Notification of importer's number ☐ Change of address* ☐ Change of name* ☐ Check here if you also want your address updated in the Fines, Penalties, and Forfeitures Office *NOTE--If a continuous bond is on file, a rider must accompany this change document.

2. IMPORTER NUMBER *(Fill in one format):--*

2A. I.R.S. Number   2B. Social Security Number

2C. ☐ Check here if requesting a CBP-assigned number and indicate reason(s). *(Check all that apply.)*   ☐ I have no IRS No.   ☐ I have no Social Security No.   ☐ I have not applied for either number.   ☐ I am not a U.S. resident

2D. CBP-Assigned Number

3. Importer Name

4. DIV/AKA/DBA   ☐ DIV ☐ AKA ☐ DBA   5. DIV/AKA/DBA Name

6. Type
☐ Corporation ☐ Partnership ☐ Sole Proprietorship ☐ Individual ☐ U.S. Government ☐ State/Local Governments ☐ Foreign Governments

7. Importer Mailing Address *(2 32-character lines maximum)*

8. City   9. State Code   10. ZIP

11. Country ISO Code *(Non-U.S. Only)*

12. Importer Physical Location Address *(2 32-character lines maximum, see instructions)*

13. City   14. State Code   15. ZIP

16. Country ISO Code *(Non-U.S. Only)*

17a. Has importer ever been assigned a CBP Importer Number using the same name as in Block 3?   ☐ No ☐ Yes *(List number(s) and/or name(s) in Block 17c.)* | 17b. Has importer ever been assigned a CBP Importer Number using a name different from that in Block 3?   ☐ No ☐ Yes *(List number(s) and/or name(s) in Block 17c.)*

17c. If "Yes" to 17a and/or 17b, list number(s) and/or name(s)

I CERTIFY: That the information presented herein is correct; that if my Social Security Number is used it is because I have no IRS Employer Number, that if my CBP assigned number is used it is because I have neither a Social Security Number nor an IRS Employer Number, that if none of these numbers is used, it is because I have none, and my signature constitutes a request for assignment of a number by CBP. | 18. Printed or Typed Name and Title | 19. Telephone No. Including Area Code

20. Signature X   21. Date

22. Broker Use Only

Previous Editions are Obsolete   **CBP Form 5106 (03/99)**

Purchase agreement

A purchase agreement developed for use in international trade — most commonly referred to as an international purchase agreement — differs in many ways from agreements used for domestic transactions. The international purchase agreement contains terms and conditions of significant importance, which are in place to avoid any misunderstandings that could arise as a result of conducting business with international entities. There is not an international purchase agreement form that is used as a standard. However, keep in mind that the more specific the agreement is, the less opportunity there will be for later dispute regarding any of the terms. One of the key elements is appropriately identifying the buyer and the seller. Not only is it important for legal reasons, but it also can actually make a difference when it comes to Customs. For instance, in the case of a parent company selling to its subsidiaries, Customs valuation of the merchandise and assessment of dumping duties, which is the sale of goods at less than the normal price, may be different than if there was not some type of connection between the exporter and the importer.

Pricing is another element that needs to be explained in detail in the purchase agreement. You must carefully examine the price calculation sheet, which is prepared by the supplier and breaks down all the costs associated with your purchase, then is normally attached to purchase agreements. This information will be valuable for considering all the costs associated with the importation of those goods when developing a price for the sale of those goods in the domestic market. Furthermore, to be sure that you are getting the best price form the seller, you can request that the seller agree to concede you the best price for those goods as it grants to any other buyer during the terms of the purchase agreement. Also, the purchase agreement must disclose if the buyer is benefiting from any rebates, discounts, allowances, or price escalation clauses.

When negotiating a purchase of goods in bulk to import, it is important to clearly state the quantity of goods you intend to purchase for two main reasons. The first reason is that the quantity of goods being purchased will have a direct impact on the price of the goods. For instance, if you, as the buyer/importer, commit to purchasing the seller's entire stock of goods, even if it is over a determined period of time, the seller will likely offer you a better price than if you only commit to buying a limited amount. The same holds true if you specifically state in the purchase agreement that you commit to buying all of a certain product that the seller will manufacture within a specified amount of time. In this instance, the seller more than likely will also discount the price of the goods because of the commitment to purchase such large quantities. The second reason is that under U.S. law, the purchase agreement is legally enforceable if the parties have agreed upon the quantity of goods to be sold and imported, even if the price has not been established.

Another critical aspect to disclose in the agreement is the method of payment you will be using and whether you have sought financing for the purchase of the goods. If you are applying for financing, then you must state the type of financing for which you applied. This will give the seller an indication of what documentation you will require so that he or she can provide it to the financial institution you are using for you to obtain such financing. Moreover, the financing clause in the purchase agreement must also clearly state whether you will be released from the agreement should the requested financing not go through.

Not a consideration in domestic purchase agreements, but of paramount importance in international purchase agreements, is that of fluctuations of currency. This is mostly a concern when the purchase agreement is long-term, as there exists the possibility of fluctuation in currency, therefore inevitably affecting one of the parties involved. The best way to approach this issue is by both parties coming to an agreement, such as splitting the difference 50/50 in price or cost due to a fluctuation in currency, and clearly stating it in the purchase agreement.

In respect to implementing some safeguards into the international purchasing agreement regarding the quality of the goods being imported, the importer can request in the agreement that a pre-shipment inspection be conducted. Because importers normally do not have representatives abroad who can physically conduct an inspection, importers can hire private companies that actually perform inspections on behalf of the buyers. The downside to hiring an inspection company is that it can be costly, and it can delay the shipment of the goods by almost a month. There are many variables associated with determining the cost of the inspection, as it will depend on the goods, their location, packaging, and other such elements, thus you will not really know the cost until you actually get an estimate. Getting an estimate and actually conducting the inspection is what causes the time delay. Nevertheless, the cost of receiving damaged or poor quality products can turn out to be more costly to the importer than just paying for inspection. However, whether you go through an inspection or not, addressing the warranty terms in the purchase agreement is crucial. From the seller's point of view, it is most advantageous to limit or eliminate all warranty provisions from the purchase agreement. This is because under U.S. law, unless the seller expressly limits its warranty, the seller will be liable for all damages the importer may incur from the defective products.

The international purchase agreement must also clearly state at what point (the date) the importer actually takes title to the goods purchased. Normally — and unless otherwise stated in the purchase agreement — title of the goods and risk of loss transfers to the importer once the goods are delivered from the seller to the carrier, and payment is received for the goods. However, in any dispute, United Sates law recognizes and enforces the transfer of title, which was specified under the international purchase agreement. Transfer of title can take effect upon arrival in the United States and clearing Customs, or even upon arrival at the port of export.

Lastly, but of great importance, is addressing whether the laws of the seller's country will govern the terms of the agreement, or if the laws of the importer's country will govern the terms. Even though it is a negotiated issue, the laws of the seller's country usually end up governing the agreement because the seller has more leverage during negotiations The reason is that, contrary to common belief, studies have shown that normally the sellers are the ones with the most leverage. This has been attributed to various reasons, but the most significant is the skill level of the seller, who likely has received some form of formal training in sales. Therefore, it is critical that you, as the importer, be aware of how the prevailing laws will impact the outcome of the purchase agreement.

Customs Form 7501: Entry Summary

The entry summary is the most important document when importing goods into the United States. Customs Form 7501 contains detailed information on the importer and the products being imported. Thus, Customs uses this form as a "receipt" of the importation and is able to determine the appropriate amount of duty that will be owed to them as a result of the importation. The entry must be filed with Customs within five working days from the arrival of the shipment and must specify whether the goods are for domestic consumption, or for storage in a warehouse that will be removed for domestic consumption at a specified later date. A sample entry summary is as follows:

Form Approved OMB No. 1651-0022

DEPARTMENT OF HOMELAND SECURITY
U.S. Customs and Border Protection
ENTRY SUMMARY

1. Filer Code/Entry No.	2. Entry Type	3. Summary Date
4. Surety No.	5. Bond Type	6. Port Code	7. Entry Date

8. Importing Carrier	9. Mode of Transport
12. B/L or AWB No.	13. Manufacturer ID
16. I.T. No.	17. I.T. Date	18. Missing Docs
21. Location of Goods/G.O. No.	22. Consignee No.

10. Country of Origin	11. Import Date
14. Exporting Country	15. Export Date
19. Foreign Port of Lading	20. U.S. Port of Unlading
23. Importer No.	24. Reference No.

25. Ultimate Consignee Name and Address	26. Importer of Record Name and Address
City State Zip	City State Zip

27. Line No.	28. Description of Merchandise			32.	33.	34.
	29. A. HTSUS No. B. ADA/CVD No.	30. A. Grossweight B. Manifest Qty.	31. Net Quantity in HTSUS Units	A. Entered Value B. CHGS C. Relationship	A. HTSUS Rate B. ADA/CVD Rate C. IRC Rate D. Visa No.	Duty and I.R. Tax Dollars Cents

Other Fee Summary for Block 39	35. Total Entered Value $	**CBP USE ONLY**		TOTALS
	Total Other Fees $	A. LIQ CODE	B. Ascertained Duty	37. Duty
		REASON CODE	C. Ascertained Tax	38. Tax
			D. Ascertained Other	39. Other
			E. Ascertained Total	40. Total

36. DECLARATION OF IMPORTER OF RECORD (OWNER OR PURCHASER) OR AUTHORIZED AGENT

I declare that I am the ☐ Importer of record and that the actual owner, purchaser, or consignee for CBP purposes is as shown above, **OR** ☐ owner or purchaser or agent thereof. I further declare that the merchandise ☐ was obtained pursuant to a purchase or agreement to purchase and that the prices set forth in the invoices are true, **OR** ☐ was not obtained pursuant to a purchase or agreement to purchase and the statements in the invoices as to value or price are true to the best of my knowledge and belief. I also declare that the statements in the documents herein filed fully disclose to the best of my knowledge and belief the true prices, values, quantities, rebates, drawbacks, fees, commissions, and royalties and are true and correct, and that all goods or services provided to the seller of the merchandise either free or at reduced cost are fully disclosed. I will immediately furnish to the appropriate CBP officer any information showing a different statement of facts.

41. DECLARANT NAME	TITLE	SIGNATURE	DATE
42. Broker/Filer Information (Name, address, phone number)		43. Broker/Importer File No.	

CBP Form 7501 (04/05)

Bill of Lading

Although a bill of lading is a contractual document between the supplier and the carrier company that will transport the goods, it is wise to become familiar with the document to understand the terms and information it contains. There are two kinds of bills of lading: a negotiable bill of lading and a non-negotiable, or straight, bill of lading. The negotiable bill of lading is a document prepared by the freight forwarder that is handling the transportation of the goods, which is then issued by the ocean freighter-steamship company — which is actually transporting the goods. This document is used as evidence of ownership of the merchandise being imported to obtain possession of the goods. In addition, when collection and payment is done through banks, such as under a letter of credit, the exporter must endorse the bill of lading and deliver it to the bank in order to collect payment for the shipment.

The non-negotiable bill of lading is issued by the supplier covering the goods from the point of origin, such as the manufacturing plant to the port from which the goods will be shipped. The purpose of the non-negotiable bill of lading is to state that the carrier who will transport the cargo has taken possession of the goods and will transport them to the final destination indicated in the document. *Bills of lading are further discussed in the Chapter 8 in greater detail.*

Customs Form 3461

Customs Form 3461 is a form the importer can file with Customs prior to the delivery of goods, requesting a special permit that will allow immediate entry and delivery of goods upon arrival in the United States. If the application is approved by Customs, the goods are immediately released to the importer upon port arrival. Customs Form 3461 is most commonly used when importing the following products: tariff rate quota merchandise, articles that will be used in any type of trade show, and fresh fruits and vegetables arriving from Canada or Mexico. The benefits of using this form are most evident when importing fruits and vegetables, as these goods have a limited shelf life, thereby allowing the importer to take these goods to the market immediately.

North American Free Trade Agreement (NAFTA) Certificate of Origin

As part of the agreement under NAFTA, goods from Canada and Mexico may be imported into the U.S. at a reduced duty or duty-free rate if they meet the established criteria. Eligibility for this kind of concession is product-specific and can be determined by looking into the headnotes section of the Harmonized Tariff Schedule. Further, in order to benefit from the reduced-duty rate or duty-free status of the goods, the importer must provide Customs with a certificate of origin obtained from the supplier, certifying the goods' country of origin. A copy of the NAFTA Certificate of Origin follows:

DEPARTMENT OF HOMELAND SECURITY
U.S. Customs and Border Protection

OMB No. 1651-0098
Exp. 03-31-2012
See back of form for Paperwork Reduction Act Notice.

NORTH AMERICAN FREE TRADE AGREEMENT
CERTIFICATE OF ORIGIN
19 CFR 181.11, 181.22

Please print or type

1. EXPORTER NAME AND ADDRESS	2. BLANKET PERIOD
	FROM
	TO
TAX IDENTIFICATION NUMBER:	
3. PRODUCER NAME AND ADDRESS	4. IMPORTER NAME AND ADDRESS
TAX IDENTIFICATION NUMBER:	TAX IDENTIFICATION NUMBER:

5. DESCRIPTION OF GOOD(S)	6. HS TARIFF CLASSIFICATION NUMBER	7. PREFERENCE CRITERION	8. PRODUCER	9. NET COST	10. COUNTRY OF ORIGIN

I CERTIFY THAT:

- THE INFORMATION ON THIS DOCUMENT IS TRUE AND ACCURATE AND I ASSUME THE RESPONSIBILITY FOR PROVING SUCH REPRESENTATIONS. I UNDERSTAND THAT I AM LIABLE FOR ANY FALSE STATEMENTS OR MATERIAL OMISSIONS MADE ON OR IN CONNECTION WITH THIS DOCUMENT;
- I AGREE TO MAINTAIN AND PRESENT UPON REQUEST, DOCUMENTATION NECESSARY TO SUPPORT THIS CERTIFICATE, AND TO INFORM, IN WRITING, ALL PERSONS TO WHOM THE CERTIFICATE WAS GIVEN OF ANY CHANGES THAT COULD AFFECT THE ACCURACY OR VALIDITY OF THIS CERTIFICATE;
- THE GOODS ORIGINATED IN THE TERRITORY OF ONE OR MORE OF THE PARTIES, AND COMPLY WITH THE ORIGIN REQUIREMENTS SPECIFIED FOR THOSE GOODS IN THE NORTH AMERICAN FREE TRADE AGREEMENT AND UNLESS SPECIFICALLY EXEMPTED IN ARTICLE 411 OR ANNEX 401, THERE HAS BEEN NO FURTHER PRODUCTION OR ANY OTHER OPERATION OUTSIDE THE TERRITORIES OF THE PARTIES; AND
- THIS CERTIFICATE CONSISTS OF [ ] PAGES, INCLUDING ALL ATTACHMENTS.

11a. AUTHORIZED SIGNATURE	11b. COMPANY
11c. NAME *(Print or Type)*	11d. TITLE
11e. DATE *(MM/DD/YYYY)*	11f. TELEPHONE NUMBER ▶ (Voice) (Facsimile)

CBP Form 434 (04/97)

Arrival notice

Once the imported goods arrive at the port, the transportation carrier will notify you, as the importer, or the Customs broker, if one was used for this transaction, that the goods have arrived. The importer or Customs broker is then responsible for filing with Customs the required documentation within five days of receipt to make entry and obtain a release for the goods.

Commercial invoices

A commercial invoice is a document, normally forwarded with the Bill of Lading, that specifies the products sold and amount due. Commercial invoices must be written in English and include specific information such as purchase prices, quantity, description of the goods, transportation charges, installation service, country of origin, and any finance charges that may apply. As the importer, it is your responsibility to inform the exporter of all the information required by Customs on the commercial invoice documents. Customs can decline to release a shipment of goods if the commercial invoice does not contain all the information required. *Commercial invoices are further discussed in the next chapter.*

Pro forma invoice

When a shipment of goods you have imported arrives without a commercial invoice, you can prepare your own, called a pro forma invoice, and submit it to Customs to process the entry of the goods. The pro forma invoice is used by the importer to report the price paid for the goods imported and can only be submitted to Customs with a bond. However, the original commercial invoice still needs to be produced by the supplier within 50 days of entry, or the importer's bond will be forfeited.

Marine and air casualty insurance

Verify that marine and air casualty insurance has been secured before the goods you have purchased are exported, especially when the supplier has sold you the goods free on board (FOB) or port of entry. This means that the goods are considered to have been delivered to the buyer the moment the goods are placed on the ship or airplane for transportation. Therefore, the buyer bears the risk of loss or damage, as well as all costs related to the shipment from that point on.

Failure to acquire marine and air casualty insurance can result in only recovering $500 per package on ocean shipments and $20 per kilogram on air shipments, even when it can be proved that the carrier was at fault. The issue of insurance should be discussed with the exporter prior to the exportation of the goods, as sometimes the exporter secures insurance that will pass the cost on to the importer, and if you secure insurance as well, you will be paying twice for insurance on the same shipment.

Importation bond

In order to import into the United States, you, the importer, must obtain an importation bond from a surety company, which is a company that only issues surety bonds, or from an insurance company that issues surety bonds. Importation bonds, or surety bonds, are used to guarantee all payments due to Customs, including duties and any other charges that may be due. Importation bonds are available in two types: single transaction bonds and continuous bonds. Single transaction bonds are used for individual importations and are mostly suitable for those importers who have few imports a year. The amount of a single transaction bond would be for an amount equal to the total value of the imported merchandise (including taxes, duties, and any other applicable fees). In cases where the imported goods are subject to quota requirements, the bond would have to be for an amount three times the total value of the import.

Continuous bonds cover all importations of a sole importer for a one-year term. These have to be for a minimum amount of $50,000 or for an amount equal to 10 percent of the total importation fees, taxes, and duties paid the previous 12-month period of operations. The bond amount would be for whichever amount is greatest. Because the surety company is guaranteeing payment of all fees due on your behalf, then should you default payment, the importer must go through a credit check and demonstrate the ability to financially back up the amount of the bond.

Temporary importation under bonds

Temporary import bonds, or temporary importation under bonds, (TIB), are used by importers when goods are going to be imported into the United States for a limited time — normally up to a year — and subsequently exported to their point of origin. The TIB is made in an amount that will cover the cost of the imported products and guarantees that the products will be exported within a year. Products imported under a TIB are normally samples to be tested, products and equipment to be used for trade shows, or goods to be inspected before deciding whether to purchase the products Should the goods not be exported before the TIB expires, the bond is forfeited, and the duties due to Customs could be up to twice as much the amount they would have been if paid upon entry into the U.S. Once the importer is ready to return the goods entered under a TIB (this must be before it expires), the importer must file an "Application for Exportation of Articles under Special Bond," Customs Form 3495, in order to avoid penalties.

Importing Goods Using Mail Service

Under certain circumstances, you are allowed to enter goods into the U.S. domestic market using the regular mail system. The process is straightforward and lends itself for importers who are importing a limited amount of merchandise, valued at $2,000 or less. When importing by mail, your overseas supplier simply packs the goods, enclosing the invoice for the goods in the parcel and attaching a Customs declaration form on the outside of the parcel, which describes the goods enclosed and the value. Once the package arrives in the United States, a Customs officer prepares an entry for the parcel charging a $5 fee per entry prepared. The package is then delivered by U.S. mail service, at which time duties owed plus the $5 service fee is collected by the postal service to be forwarded to Customs.

However, any merchandise valued over $2,000 imported by mail will require filing a formal entry form, as discussed earlier in this chapter. Also, all textile importations (all countries included) will require filing a formal entry, regardless of the value. There are several other exceptions to the rules related to importing by mail of certain articles with a value of $250 or more, such as footwear, handbags, and billfolds. However, because the exceptions are so many and so product-specific, your best bet before you try to import any product by mail would be to contact Customs via their Web site at **www.cbp.gov** to determine if your product would fall into any of the exception categories.

Chapter 8

Exporting

Being an exporter can be as exciting and challenging as being an importer, only that the challenges are just a little different — you are considered to be an exporter when you ship merchandise. There are countless benefits to exporting from the United States. First and foremost, as an exporter, if you manufacture the products you export, you will be contributing toward the overall reduction of unemployment rates in America by creating manufacturing jobs. At a more personal level, exporting will help your business thrive and become more competitive in the marketplace. Just think of the potential for market expansion: 67 percent of the world's purchasing power is outside the U.S. That means that the potential for succeeding in exporting is larger than if you were to restrict your business to the domestic market, as the majority of the buying power is outside the continental U.S. Because of these benefits, and the numerous other benefits small businesses experience as a result, the government has programs in place to assist with exporting activities. Exporting is extremely beneficial to the nation's economic welfare. The U.S. is one of the largest exporters in the world, 4th to the European Union, China, and Germany, according to the CIA World Factbook, and enjoys the acceptance of most countries throughout the world to import U.S.-made products.

As a result, the U.S. government has put forth a great deal of effort to promote exportation, while also realizing the need to enact certain export controls; therefore, the Export Administration Act of 1979 (EAA) was established to regulate exports and minimize circumstances that would prevent or limit the ability of American businesses to take part in world-wide commerce. In addition, the EAA establishes regulations designed to prevent the exportation of technology and other goods that could be used by other countries in the development of technology and weaponry that may ultimately have an adverse effect on the national security of the U.S. Export controls are also necessary to regulate the exportation of products and substances that may be hazardous to the public health and the environment. However, the EAA has also taken care in minimizing the restrictions imposed on the exportation of other products such as agricultural products and commodities, recognizing the significance of preserving a healthy agricultural industry in the United States. Hence, choosing the products you are considering for export will affect the ease with which you will be able to export them, and if you choose wisely, you will have a positive impact on your financial bottom line.

Find Your Market Niche — The Right Products for You

What exactly are you interested in exporting? Are suppliers or manufacturers for that particular product readily available? As a new exporter, there are several details you must take into consideration before selecting products to export. Eventually, you may be able to manage exporting various products, but until you are familiar and comfortable with the exportation process, it will be better to start with a single line of products, rather than diversifying too much. If you try to take on too many products at once, you are really not giving yourself the opportunity to learn the ins and outs of any of the products. Therefore, all you will know will be generalities and no specifics, which will be a hindrance when you are trying to make a sale and you are not really prepared to fully discuss the product with a prospective buyer abroad.

Knowledge and experience with the product

It will be a lot easier for you to find suppliers for the products you wish to export if you are knowledgeable and familiar with that particular product. To start, begin by looking into your background for possibilities. Think about your previous jobs or hobbies you enjoy. Being familiar with the product or product line will enable you to communicate more efficiently with the suppliers in the U.S., especially when it comes to specifying what you want. You will be able to clearly express what it is you are looking for in this product in terms of quality and price range, as well as what exactly it is that you do not want this product to be. In addition, you will be better poised to realize when a supplier is trying to sell you a low-grade product that you know will not sell in the U.S. or abroad. At the same time, you will be able to better promote your product to prospective buyers across the borders, as you will be able to relate to its uses and benefits. Better yet, you may even have a manufacturing company and have your own product line to export; all you have to do is find buyers overseas.

Need of the product in the foreign market

Thoroughly evaluate your product's potential for success in the foreign marketplace. One way to determine the product's potential abroad is to take a look at how that particular product is doing in its domestic market. If it is doing well, then you might want to evaluate potential markets that have comparable needs and market conditions as you find in the U.S. You may also consider exporting products whose sales are declining in the U.S. due to modern technology, but may be the perfect product for developing countries that are not as technologically advanced as the United States is.

The potential for exporting is endless. There will always be items that people want that are not accessible in their countries. Hence, doing some targeted market research — looking into how the product will do in certain markets — will point you in the right direction. *See Chapter 11 for more on marketing research.*

Advantages and disadvantages of the product

What are the benefits and drawbacks of the product you are considering exporting over already existing similar products? Research the product you are considering exporting and evaluate how it measures up to existing products. There is no such thing as a perfect product, although you might have come across a much better or more appropriate product for a foreign country than the one already on the market. Regardless of what the advantages or disadvantages may be, you need to be aware of it, because you do not want to come as a surprise while you are in the marketing process.

Quality of the product

In the international trade business, there are always opportunities to buy low-cost goods, which can then be exported for sale abroad at low prices, making it attractive to the end buyer. Although it may seem like a good proposition at first, you run the risk of buying not only low-cost goods, but also low-quality, and compromising quality for low prices is not the way to go. Sometimes paying a little more will get you further in the global marketplace than purchasing cheap, substandard products that you will not be able to get rid of later. In addition, the last thing you want is to develop a bad reputation among buyers in other countries. Always assure yourself of the quality of the product you are considering sourcing for exportation. If the product does not meet your standards as a consumer, then the product does not meet the standards for exportation. *For more information about product safety as it relates to product quality, see Chapter 13.*

Identifying and Selecting Suppliers

Finding the supplier that will best suit your needs is just as important as finding the right product to export. There are numerous avenues available to locate suppliers, such as trade magazines, Small Business Development Centers, and the most common way — the Internet. Looking for suppliers online can get a little overwhelming if you do not know how to narrow your search. Once you have an idea of what type of product you are looking at exporting, joining international trade chat groups is a great way to go about your supplier search. For instance, Yahoo!, a Web portal and search engine, has an extensive international trade chat group, which has subdivided itself by product category, country, and so forth. In addition, there are several well-known, long-established sites on the Internet that are reliable sources for suppliers. The Web site for the Thomas Register provides a comprehensive directory of American manufacturers and distributors, along with addresses, phone numbers, fax numbers, e-mail addresses, and Web sites. The Web address for the Thomas Register is **www.thomasnet. com.** Another commonly used Web site for identifying suppliers is **www. WAND.com**, which is an international business-to-business directory. This particular business directory is broken down by product type, which makes it easier to bring together buyers and sellers.

Industry-specific trade directories are also great sources for identifying possible suppliers. Trade associations always publish membership lists with the name of the industry, a contact person, telephone numbers, a Web site, and a brief description of the member's specialty. If you are looking at initially sourcing goods locally, your local Economic Development Council (Corporation) and chamber of commerce also publish local business directories.

Once you have identified suppliers you might be interested in working with, conduct a thorough background check. Research the supplier's reliability for being able to produce the quality and quantity of goods in which you are interested. You can do this by contacting previous or current customers. Also, take into consideration the company's longevity. Often, a company's reliability can be credited as one of the key elements that have kept the company running for an extended period of time. Ask for references and follow up on those references; it will prove to be worth the time you spend on it.

While looking for suppliers, you might also run into merchants who sell closeout, surplus, or liquidation merchandise, which could be merchandise from the previous season that did not sell or merchandise that will no longer be manufactured by the company. Depending on the type of product being liquidated or closed out, this merchandise has the potential of moving quickly — you can purchase it at reasonably low prices. By keeping the prices low, the products will be that much more attractive to overseas buyers. As you are breaking into the exporting business, exporting closeouts, surplus, and liquidation merchandise can be good test material, as you will not be committing to any long-term deals with the merchant. These sales are normally one-time deals.

Most important, however, is building and maintaining a good working relationship with your suppliers. As you start your business by placing one order at a time, paying it in full and on time, and building your relationship with good communication and honoring sale/purchase terms, you may end up with exclusive deals on certain products, which gives you an advantage over competitors. Maintaining a solid relationship with suppliers is one of the keys in operating a financially successful exporting business.

Identifying Countries You Want to do Business With

When you have determined what you would like to export, you must also research to learn what products are being exported and to which countries.

These databases will give you a good idea as to what countries you need to be looking at to find prospective buyers for your goods. Some excellent sources of statistical information include:

- **The U.S. International Trade in Goods and Services Report,** published by the U.S. Department of Commerce at **www.census.gov/foreign-trade/index.html**. This site contains a wealth of export and import statistics, information on regulations affecting export, and an assortment of reports on trade-related issues.

- **U.S.A. Trade Online Web site** at **www.usatradeonline.gov.** This contains statistics on imports and exports for thousands of commodities traded worldwide. Trade statistics are provided using the Harmonized Tariff Schedule product classification system, and you can get product-specific statistics at the port of entry level as well as district level.

- **The International Trade Administration** at **www.ita.doc.gov**. This organization promotes international fair trade, and various services related to export assistance are available through their Web site, including possible trade leads. More specifically, you will find information on the top 30 U.S. trading partners throughout the world, industry-specific export data, and statistical information on the exportation of products from the major metro areas in the U.S.

After you have gathered enough information on what is being traded where, select the countries that seem to have had a growing market (in previous years) for the product you are considering exporting. That will be an indicator that the growth is recent and likely will continue to move in that direction, at least for a while, unless unforeseen drastic changes occur in the industry. You can also analyze the information to determine if there seems to be a trend, even a slight one, that may indicate some growth in the market you are interested in. That will be the time to consider moving that product, possibly allowing you to get ahead of the competition.

Although you may be concentrating your efforts on finding the countries that will meet your market expectations, you must also take into consideration the financial and political stability of those countries, as well as their relationship with the United States. Doing business with politically or economically unstable countries can result in a disastrous situation. Lastly, before making a final decision, seek the counsel of agencies that are involved in exporting assistance. These agencies will be better prepared to advise you and guide you in the right direction. *Such agencies and their particular expertise are discussed later in this chapter.*

Finding trading partners across international borders

Finding customers across international borders is just as important as finding the right supplier in the United States. There are several ways you can establish trading relationships in foreign countries. You can conduct business directly with a foreign retailer, work with an overseas distributor, or work with an overseas agent. Whichever avenue you choose, you must feel comfortable with the situation if you want to be successful. That is not to say that if one way of establishing trading partners ends up not working for you, then you cannot change methods. However, consistency and long-term relationships go a long way when you are trying to conduct business, especially one that reaches across the globe.

Foreign retailer

Foreign retailers can be governmental agencies, hospitals, schools, or private concerns, such as businesses who import (into their country) products for their consumption or use. Working with individual foreign retailers means that the selection of products you will be able to sell and export will be limited because the selection of products will be based on the foreign retailer's particular needs. Consequently, you would need to establish relationships with a number of independent retailers in order to maintain a fair amount of merchandise moving at all times, which in turn will keep the stream of revenues flowing. Individual foreign retailers can be identified through international trade publications, trade shows and, of course, the Internet.

Overseas distributors

Overseas distributors are independent business people who import (into their country) merchandise for resale. Their profit comes from the markup they charge to the end customer. These distributors have contractual agreements with both the exporter and the end customers, but there is no relationship between the exporter and the end customer. Because these overseas distributors offer services to multiple U.S. exporters, it is often advantageous to offer them some sort of incentive, such as exclusive representation of certain territories, in exchange for agreeing not to market merchandise from competing exporters. Part of their responsibilities, as your overseas distributor, is to advertise and promote your products for sale. On the down side, when using an overseas distributor you actually lose control of the pricing of your goods because they actually set the price of the goods for sale to the end consumer — which may be detrimental to your sales, as the distributors may be pricing your goods too high or too low.

Overseas agents

Overseas agents are independent sales representatives for multiple U.S. exporters who are not in competing markets. Exporters normally use these agents when they are selling products to a small market or when the products are big-ticket items, such as heavy equipment that are normally not kept in stock abroad for sale at a later date. Although they may not be very knowledgeable about the products they are representing, overseas agents are of considerable value for their personal contacts in the country they live in, as well as for the inside information to which they have access. These contacts often are helpful in opening up doors to markets that otherwise would have been difficult, or even impossible, to reach. These individuals do not have any contractual arrangement with the end buyer, nor do they have any control over pricing or marketing of the products; their compensation is based entirely on commission.

Trade leads through government agencies

Regardless of how you want to do business abroad — whether it is directly with a foreign retailer, through an overseas agent, or overseas distributor — there are multiple government agencies that can help you locate these leads. Use the following list of sources for assistance in securing trade leads which you may refer to when you are ready to start exporting:

U.S. Small Business Administration (SBA) — International Trade Division

U.S. Export Assistance Centers at **www.sba.gov/aboutsba/sbaprograms/ internationaltrade/useac/index.html:** As part of their international trade program, the Small Business Administration has created and established U.S. Export Assistance Centers throughout the United States, in major metropolitan areas. The centers provide small- and medium-sized businesses with export assistance through an array of services available such as the Agent/Distributor Service (ADS). This service is used to find overseas-based agents and distributors in foreign countries. Based on the requirements and expectations provided by the exporter, the agency conducts an overseas search to identify foreign prospects that have already reviewed the exporter's prerequisites and product's information.

Likewise, these agents and distributors have expressed interest in representing the exporter. The agency then provides the U.S. exporter with the list of potential contacts for the exporter to evaluate and make a final decision.

For a list of U.S. Export Assistance Centers, refer to the above-mentioned U.S. Small Business Administration's Web site. This site also includes links to a number of other Web sites, such as the Federation of International Trade Associations and Trade Port, which contain a wealth of export-related information.

U.S. Department of Commerce

International Trade Administration at **www.trade.gov:** The U.S. Department of Commerce's International Trade Administration works with 20 other federal agencies to provide information to the U.S. exporter, which assists them in selecting markets and products to export. Their Web site is a portal to U.S. government agencies and other organizations whose purpose is to assist U.S.-based businesses with their international trade needs. The Web site makes it easier for the newest business owners in the international trade arena to find the path to success. There are direct links to the Export-Import Bank, United States Department of Agriculture, and the SBA Web sites that have information on trade leads and useful market research data.

International Trade Administration

Customized Market Research at **www.trade.gov/cs:** The Customized Market Research program is administered by the U.S. Commercial Service — a division of the International Trade Administration. The Customized Market Research document is a personalized report that addresses questions and matters related to your particular commodity or service. Trade specialists working for the U.S. Commercial Service will work with your company to help you get started in exporting. If you are already exporting, they will provide assistance to help you expand sales to new foreign markets. U.S. Commercial Service trade specialists, located throughout the United States and in more than 80 countries, conduct interviews and surveys in order to generate your company's report. The completed report contains information such as the overall marketability of the products, distribution and promotion practices, potential business partners, main competitors, trade restrictions, and competitive pricing for your products.

U.S. Department of Commerce

Business Contact Program at **www.commerce.gov/TradeOpportunities/index.htm:** The Business Contact Program of the U.S. Department of Commerce (DOC) is a service provided by its foreign commercial service officers that helps exporters identify and qualify leads for possible distributors, agents, and customers abroad. DOC's foreign commercial service officers are located around the world are experts in programs and products in the countries that represent more than 95 percent of the markets for U.S. products.

U.S. Department of Commerce

Commercial News USA at **www.thinkglobal.us:** Commercial News USA (CNUSA) uses a combination of electronic bulletin boards and paper media to provide worldwide exposure for U.S. products and services. The printed format of this source is the official export promotion magazine of the Department of Commerce, and it is distributed at industry-related trade shows worldwide. The magazine is printed bimonthly, with special editions printed in Spanish and Chinese, and distributed through U.S. embassies and consulates in 176 countries. The electronic distribution of CNUSA reaches the private sector, as well as governmental agencies, with over 2 million subscribers in strategic foreign markets. The lists include information such as the exporter's name, contact information, and his or her products and services available for trade. CNUSA has nearly 20 different industry categories, such as information technology, agriculture, and electronics.

U.S. Department of Commerce, U.S. Commercial Service Agency

Gold Key Matching Service at **www.buyusa.gov/home/export.html:** The Gold Key Matching Service is one of the many country-specific programs sponsored by the U.S. Commercial Service. The U.S. Commercial service is an agency operating under the U.S. Department of Commerce. The program provides assistance to U.S. businesses in securing one-on-one appointments with potential business partners in China. The service also includes market research and interpreter services — when needed — for meetings and on-site briefings that may be necessary. However, the service is relatively expensive, lending itself mostly to the larger exporting companies.

National Trade Data Bank

Commercial Service International Contacts (CSIC) and County Directories of International Contacts (CDIC) at **www.stat-usa.gov/tradtest. nsf:** Commercial Service International Contacts contains information about companies around the world that are interested in importing U.S. products into their countries. In addition, the directory contains product-specific and contact information for these companies. The Country Directories of International Contacts (CDIC) has a list of country-by-country directories of private and public agencies that are helpful to the U.S. exporter. Both of these lists can be accessed through the National Trade Data Bank Web site, listed above.

National Trade Data Bank

Global Trade Directory at **www.stat-usa.gov:** The National Trade Data Bank Global Trade Directory includes trade-related information, such as legal issues relating to exporting, reports based on market research, foreign contacts, country-specific commercial guides, policy and trade practices, and trade statistics. Updated monthly, the STAT-USA/Internet Web site contains a collection of reports regarding U.S. finance and economic data, market research, and international trade statistics.

International Company Profiles

www.buyusa.gov/home/export.html: The International Company Profile is a background report prepared by the Department of Commerce's commercial officers overseas regarding a specific foreign company. The report is quite comprehensive, including information about the type of organization, its size, number of employees, year it was established, region covered, product lines, financial and trade references, principal owners, the company's language preference to conduct business, and even a statement as to the company's overall reputation.

Trade leads through private-public agencies

In addition to governmental agencies, there are also private sector agencies and private-public partnerships that provide international trade assistance to businesses based in the U.S. These are private agencies that receive government funding and sometimes are even partnered with government agencies for the day-to-day operations In most states you will find some of these private-public partnership agencies that offer assistance to the small- to medium-sized businesses and normally have an international trade department.

For instance, Enterprise Florida is a private-public partnership in the state of Florida whose primary mission is to promote economic development in the state through the various programs available to business owners. One of those programs is offered through the International Trade & Business Development Field Offices. Among the many other trade assistance services offered to Florida companies, these offices offer export-counseling services such as helping you select the target market for your particular product or service, assistance with export marketing missions, and an electronic trade leads network. Field offices located throughout the State have international marketing professionals available to assist the Florida exporter to successfully participate in the global marketplace.

Another example is the International Trade Center at The University of Texas at San Antonio's Institute for Economic Development. The International Trade Center was established in 1992 and is one of the leading trade assistance agencies in Texas, providing local companies with trade consulting services and market research assistance. The center also provides new businesses, as well as already established organizations, with a variety of training programs to facilitate their entering the international market or expanding their already existing market. The advantages of working with this type of agency is that you benefit from expertise in the industry from both the private and the public sector, and the fees for the services are normally nominal.

Pricing Goods for the International Market

Proper pricing of your product is one of the most crucial elements in selling your products on the international market. In the domestic market, there are certain basic elements such as costs, market demand, and competition that are taken into consideration when determining the price for goods. However, when pricing goods for the international market, you must also take into consideration the additional costs that will be absorbed by the importer, which will be taken into account when determining the final sale price of your exported goods. Before the importer of your products can establish a final price for those goods to sell them in his or her country, extra costs will be added, such as Customs fees, value-added taxes, and tariffs. Taking all this into consideration, if your initial price is too high, the products may end up being priced out of the market, which in turn may result in the importer not buying goods form you again due to the inability to sell them.

Establishing pricing policies

The first step in establishing the price of merchandise for sale in the international market is to establish the overall pricing policy objectives. The price should be low enough to generate interest on the consumers' end, but yet high enough to make the sale profitable. Exporters will also need to consider the extent to which currency fluctuations will adversely influence the affordability of a product overseas. Therefore, the final price should depend on:

- The competition of a target market

- Level of demand in the foreign market for the product

- The total costs necessary to bring the product to the market

There are three pricing strategies to consider: low-price, moderate-price, and high-price. Keep in mind, however, that pricing strategy decisions should be made on a case-by-case and country-by-country basis.

Low-price strategy: A low-price strategy is usually considered a short-term approach most suitable for when the exporter is trying to move excess inventory fast. Using this strategy may discourage new competition, and might even reduce the market share of existing competitors. Exporters using this strategy should be aware of, and abide by, all anti-dumping regulations.

Moderate-price strategy: The moderate-price strategy may enable U.S. exporters to penetrate the market easier, retain adequate profit margins, and develop a market share. Using a moderate-price strategy will enable you, as the exporter, to achieve long-term participation in the market.

High-price strategy: A high-price strategy is more suitable for an exporter who is selling a new or unique product or is trying to sell a product with a "top of the line" image. Even though you will be able to generate a higher profit margin with this strategy, you may also end up limiting the product's marketability.

Factors to consider when setting your product's price

Conversely, regardless of which pricing strategy you choose, there are several factors you must take into consideration when setting a price for the products you will be exporting.

Cost

First, you must think about all of the costs for which you, the exporter, will be responsible. Some of these costs may not apply if you are exporting goods purchased from a domestic supplier, but the steps below can help you determine your costs.

1. Figure out materials and labor costs related to the production of the goods to be exported.

2. Calculate the factory overhead costs directly related to the production of such goods.

3. Deduct any charges that are not related to the goods that are to be exported, such as domestic marketing expenses.

4. Include in your calculation other costs associated with the sale, such as expenses related to travel, any market research, promotional items, translation costs — if any — freight forwarder fees, and packing materials.

5. Allow for a realistic profit or mark-up.

6. Give yourself a realistic price margin to allow for unexpected expenses directly related to the exportation of the merchandise.

Competition

Looking at what your competition is doing is just as important in the global market as it is in the domestic market. Before setting your prices, carefully evaluate your competition's pricing policies in each of the foreign markets you intend to enter yourself. If you are looking at entering a market where there is a lot of competition, you might want to reevaluate the costs associated with the exportation of your goods, especially if you are a first-time exporter. This may require minor adjustments where possible so that you can enter the market either at a reduced rate than your competition, or so you can just match the going price and establish your market share. If you, however, are entering a foreign market where you will be introducing a new product, then you might be able to get away with charging higher prices than you would for the same product on the domestic market.

Market demand

Just as in the domestic market, product demand plays a crucial role in setting the price of your product in a global market. You can only charge for a product as much or as little as the market will bear, if you want to remain in business. Market demand will also be determined by how your product relates to the nature of the market in which you are trying to sell your products. Take into consideration the demographics of the market area where you want to export your product. Factors such as age, level of education, income, and the socioeconomic class of the area will determine the demand for your particular product or lack thereof.

The following export costing worksheet is a good tool to use that will help you determine the price for goods to be exported. This worksheet is just a guide, and not all the information will be applicable in every instance. However, whatever numbers you are able to plug in will be helpful in guiding you in the right direction as to setting a price:

**Costing Worksheet
for Product Export**

Customer Information
Name _____   Telephone No. _____
Address _____   Fax No. _____
_____   E-mail address _____

Product Information
Product _____   Number of units _____
Net weight (units) _____   Dimensions _____
Gross weight _____

Product Charges
Price (or cost) per unit _____   Total _____
Profit (or markup)   _____
Sales commissions   _____
FOB, factory price   _____

Fees — Packing, Marking, Inland Freight
Freight forwarder (if applicable)   _____
Financing costs   _____
Packing costs for exportation   _____
Marking and labeling expenses   _____
Inland freight to: _____   _____
FOB, city and port   _____
Other charges   _____

Port Charges/Document
Unloading
Heavy lift unloading (extra charge)   _____
Loading aboard ship   _____
Consular document (if required)   _____
Certificate of origin (if required)   _____
Export license (if required)   _____
Other charges   _____

Freight
Ocean or air _____
Based on _____ Weight _____ Measure
On deck _____ Under deck _____
Rate _____

Insurance
Coverage required _____ (rate & amount)
CIF, port of destination price _____

See the accompanying CD-ROM for a template of this form.

Preparing Goods for Shipping

Preparing goods for shipping overseas is a serious matter. It is your responsibility that the goods you sold to a foreign merchant arrive undamaged to the predetermined point of delivery. Packaging merchandise to be shipped abroad is not the same as packaging merchandise to be transported across several state lines by truck or even by air. Goods shipped overseas are handled multiple times, from the time they are packaged at the supplier's plant until the time they arrive at their final destination. During the shipping process, these goods are exposed to an array of circumstances such as moisture, pilferage, and excess weight, all of which may damage the goods if they are not packaged properly.

Packaging

Air shipments normally do not require as heavy packing as ocean shipments. They should, however, still be adequately packaged and protected against damage during transportation, as well as from theft. When shipping by air, standard domestic type packing is oftentimes acceptable if the goods are not fragile in nature. Otherwise, using high-test cardboard of tri-wall construction boxes (at least 250 pounds per square inch) will suffice. Depending on the air carrier and the product you are shipping, you may also ship you merchandise by air in pallets. You will have to contact the air freight company to request their specifications for shipping by air with them.

When shipping by ocean freight, details are a little different because there are more options as to how you can ship.

Less than container load (LCL)

Although cargo to be shipped by ocean freight is typically carried in containers, sometimes it is shipped as break bulk cargo, also referred to as less than container load (LCL). Merchandise shipped LCL is generally stacked on pallets and shrink-wrapped so it can be held together and is easier to handle. Forklifts can easily lift and move these pallets for loading and unloading, and moving around the warehouse. However, shipping LCL gives you a higher cost per unit than larger volume shippers who can ship by a full container load (FCL), so your shipping expenses result in higher transportation costs. Thus, when packaging your goods to be shipped as break bulk cargo, there are several issues of concern that must be taken into consideration to ensure the merchandise will arrive at its final destination without damage. Whether you package your merchandise yourself or have a third party do it for you, you must make sure that the packaging has been done correctly so that in case of damage or loss, the cargo issuance will cover the damages. It is not uncommon for cargo insurance companies to refuse to cover damages to shipped merchandise if it was not packaged properly.

Further, palletized merchandise shipped by ocean freight is exposed to tremendous strain during the shipping process, at times being exposed to the weather as well as being handled and moved around multiple times, in addition to the normal handling of transportation prior to arrival at the port. The palletized merchandise is typically loaded aboard the ship using nets, slings, conveyors, or chutes, all of which is geared to handle the merchandise at the greatest speed possible — not so much handling with the greatest care. In addition, steamships make stops at various ports, and whenever they load, they do not rearrange pallets or containers on the ship to have the lighter shipments at the top. Pallets are stacked without reservations, and the same holds true for containers, therefore increasing the possibility of damage to the merchandise at the bottom of the stack. The cargo is stacked with the sole purpose of maximizing capacity in the ship. However, the stress to the crates and pallets does not end there. Handling facilities overseas are not always as sophisticated as they are in the U.S., and the crates could be damaged during unloading or while being transported, if they are dragged, rolled, pushed, or even dropped. That is why it is so important to take all available measures to make sure your merchandise is packaged safely.

Full container load (FCL)

If you are shipping large quantities of merchandise to the same buyer abroad, the safest and most cost-effective way of shipping the goods is by FCL. Containers are large metal boxes that can be obtained from carriers, steamship companies, or independent leasing companies. Containers are available in various sizes, from 20 feet long to 53 feet long, with the 40-foot container being the most commonly used for exporting. The 40-foot container can accommodate approximately 2,347 cubic feet or 42,000 pounds of merchandise. The best way to determine what size container you need is by the weight and size of your cargo. Also playing a part in determining the correct container size is the availability of containers and equipment that can handle the container, any weight limitations on the road at both your product's point of origin and point of destination, and the ship's configuration. Using containers to ship your goods can drastically reduce and eliminate damage and pilferage to your goods. Once a container is packed, it is then locked and sealed, and sent to the port either by road or by rail. After it arrives at the port, it is placed on the ship and not opened until it reaches the buyer at its final destination or at the port of entry for inspection by Customs. When the container is sealed by the exporter, the cargo is said to be transported under "shipper's load and count," which means the exporter, not the carrier company, is responsible for declaring the actual merchandise included in the container, the weight, and the price counts. Basically, under a shipper's load and count, a note states that your product was loaded and counted by you, the shipper, without being checked by the company that is exporting it for you. It is important to report this information accurately because any misrepresentation of this type of information is considered fraud.

If the buyer does not specify any packaging requirements, follow these guidelines to ensure the safe arrival of your product at its port of destination.

- Make sure that the packages and packing filler is made of moisture-resistant material.

- When appropriate, make sure to follow the required product-specific guidelines, such as hazardous materials packing requirements as specified in the Code of Federal Regulations, 49 CFR, Part 172 available through the Electronic Code of Federal Regulations at **www.ecfr.gpo.access.gov**.

- To avoid theft and pilferage, do not write what the contents of the packages are on the outside of the packages; use straps, seals, and shrink-wrap boxes.

- Goods should always be placed on pallets containerized when at all possible.

- To provide proper bracing in the container, make sure the weight is evenly distributed, regardless of size.

- Pack your merchandise in strong containers, fill them to capacity, — or as close to it as possible — and adequately seal the container for added safety.

Whether you are shipping LCL or using containers, a common element that must be taken into consideration when packaging goods is moisture. This is a prime concern because not only can it develop in the hold of a ship as a result of condensation, but it is also not uncommon for cargo to be loaded or unloaded in the rain. There is also the possibility that the port of destination may not have covered storage facilities, which — in addition to the moisture issue — creates another concern of theft.

As you explore all the options available to you for shipping merchandise overseas, keep in mind that transportation costs are determined by weight and volume. Using specially reinforced and lightweight packing materials developed for exporting is recommended, thereby minimizing volume and weight, as well as ensuring the goods are securely packaged.

Labeling

Properly labeling and marking export shipping cartons will make a big difference in successfully completing an export transaction. There are specific marking and labeling requirements that must be met when exporting products from the U.S. These regulations have been established to ensure proper handling of the merchandise, conceal the identity of the contents, assist your customers in identifying shipments, and to verify compliance with environmental and safety standards. Also, your customer overseas will normally let you know which export marks should be placed on the cargo coming in. In addition to the export marks requested by your customer, there are a number of markings that are required to appear on cartons to be shipped. The markings should be placed on three sides of the container with waterproof ink or pre-printed labels and stickers for some of the common markings, such as "Made in the U.S.A.," which are available through suppliers of shipping and packaging materials. These marks include:

Shipper's mark: The shipper's mark is used to identify the exporter and normally used by the buyer to identify the cargo.

Country of origin: In this case, shipping from the United States, you would simply state "Made in the U.S.A."

Weight marking: Weight marking is done in both pounds and kilograms.

Precaution markings: These are the typical markings normally seen in boxes. These markings include "Do not freeze," "Fragile," "Keep dry," and others. They must be stated both in English and in the language of the country where the goods are being shipped.

Number of packages and size of cases: If you are shipping more than one box or pallet, you must number each one and specify how many there are in total. For example, if you shipped a total of 10 pallets, you must then number each pallet and state "3 of 10" on one of the sides of the pallet. That way, it is easier to account for the total number of pallets or boxes in the shipment. The number of packages, as well as the size of the cases, must be specified in both inches and centimeters.

Handling marks: These are the international pictorial symbols that are standard on shipments, such as arrows pointing up on the side of the boxes indicating which side of the box must be up.

Port of entry: State the name of the city and the port abroad where your goods will arrive.

Hazardous materials labels: If you are shipping hazardous materials, you must use the universal symbols adopted by the International Air Transportation Association and the International Maritime Organization. Required hazardous materials labels include:

- Radioactive material
- Corrosive
- Flammable liquid
- Biohazard

Labeling and marking your packages as they are ready for shipment is one of the most critical steps in the exportation process. Customs and Border Protection strictly enforce freight labeling regulations, thus correctly marking your cargo will save you from running into unpleasant situations during the final leg of your export process. It is strongly encouraged to use the services of freight forwarders, who facilitate the movement of cargo to and from foreign destinations, to help ensure full compliance with applicable regulations. *The full scope of freight forwarders role in the import and export business is discussed later in Chapter 14.*

Required Documentation

For the first—time exporter, the concept of understanding and managing all the documentation required to export merchandise from the United States may seem somewhat intimidating. The truth is, however, that the key in overcoming such an overwhelming feeling is in knowing that not all of the forms are needed with every transaction. The documents needed in any particular transaction will depend on the merchandise being shipped, as well as the requirements of the U.S. government and the government of the buyer's country. Once you get to know what forms are needed for what and you learn how to process them, things will seem less intimidating. The paper trail — or document trail — is to keep track of the goods as they move from one place to another, and to make sure they are ultimately delivered to the appropriate party. Keep in mind that accuracy in processing these forms is crucial in successfully getting your products intact across international borders, as well as ultimately getting paid.

Bills of lading

The bill of lading is a contractual document issued by the transportation carriers. It is a contract between them and you stating that they have received the shipment and have agreed to take it to its final destination for a determined dollar amount. A thorough bill of lading can be used to cover the entire transportation of the cargo from its point of origin to its final destination abroad. Individual bills of lading, however, may be issued for the domestic portion of the transportation, as well as for the marine or air transportation portion of the shipment. For example, you might want to use an individual bill of lading to move your products from your warehouse or distribution center to the port from where the goods will be shipped.

Inland bills of lading are used for the domestic portion of the route and are normally taken care of by the trucking or railroad companies transporting the merchandise to the port of export. Transportation by ocean freight is covered by a marine bill of lading, issued by the steamship company and prepared by the exporter or freight forwarder. These are issued in three originals, one of which is used by the buyer to obtain possession of the goods upon arrival at the port. When transporting goods by air, an Air Waybill will be issued by the airline carrier, which is a non-negotiable bill of lading. Bills of lading can be issued as negotiable bills of lading or as straight, also known as non-negotiable bills of lading, previously discussed in Chapter 7.

Shipper's Export Declaration

The Shipper's Export Declaration (SED) is a form required by the U.S. Census Bureau to control all U.S. exports and gather trade statistics, although you do not always need one to export goods to Canada. It is the only form of all export documents that is actually filed with a United States governmental agency. The form is required for any export made by an individual or a business holding a valid export license and is necessary for individual shipments that are more than $2,500 in value. If your product is being shipped by mail and is valued more than $500, you will also need to fill out an SED form. The SED is prepared by the exporter or designated agent, such as a freight forwarder or Customs broker. It is then given to the steamship or air carrier company transporting the goods, who in turn files the form with U.S. Customs and Border Protection prior to clearing the port. It is critical that the SED is filled out correctly, as there are legal repercussions should the information prove to be false, either by accident or intentional. Civil and criminal penalties include a $10,000 fine and up to five years in prison. Further, the exporter or agent filling out the SED must certify to having read the instructions set forth in the U.S. Census Bureau's booklet "Correct Way to Fill Out the Shipper's Export Declaration." The SED is available online at no charge from the U.S. government Printing Office (**www.gpo.gov**), and it is submitted to a U.S. Customs and Border Protection agent by the exporter or freight forwarder.

Inspection certificate

The inspection certification may be required by some countries and buyers; therefore, before the merchandise is shipped, the inspection is conducted, and a certificate for such inspection is produced. The purpose of this certificate is to attest to the specifications of the merchandise being shipped. If the buyer is going to require that an inspection be conducted, then it must be specified in the contract and quotation for the goods. Inspection certificates are usually requested for certain commodities, such as equipment and machinery, because it would be very costly — not only in shipping costs but also in possible loss of sales — to return this type of merchandise should it be defective. Inspections of this type are customarily performed by an independent testing organization that is responsible for producing the inspection certificate. Depending on the circumstances, the inspection certificate is delivered by the inspection company directly to the buyer or the buyer's government, if they are the ones requiring the inspection. However, when the sale transaction involves documents such as a letter of credit, and it specifies that an inspection certificate is required in order to collect payment, the exporter must then provide the financial institution with the inspection certificate to collect payment for the shipment.

Commercial invoice

The commercial invoice (discussed in Chapter 7) is the invoice prepared by the exporter for the buyer abroad that confirms all aspects of the sale agreement for the merchandise sold. Sometimes the commercial invoice varies from the terms of the original pro forma invoice, which is the invoice used by the importer to report the price paid for the goods imported, as a result of further negotiations between the exporter and the buyer after the initial sales agreement was reached. The original commercial invoice is forwarded through financial institution channels for payment or sent directly to the buyer when the purchase was made on an open account. Multiple copies of the commercial invoice are typically made because copies have to be sent with the bill of lading and other transportation documents. The commercial invoice should itemize the merchandise by price per unit and specify the terms of payment because often, foreign governments use these invoices as a basis to determine the true value of the goods, especially when it comes to assessing Customs duties. It must also include any other information that may be required by the countries involved, depending on the goods being shipped. Some foreign governments also use commercial invoices as a means to control imports, therefore requiring such elements as its form, content, language to be used, and number of copies to be made available.

Consular invoice

The consular invoice is only required in some countries, and it is used to allow clearance of your merchandise into the country requiring it. For example, some Latin American countries require consular invoices to determine the origin of the merchandise or to approve the price of the goods as being reasonable. It contains information such as the name of the consignor, name of the consignee, value of the shipment, and a description of the goods in the shipment. When such document is required, it used in addition to the bill of lading, the commercial invoice, and any insurance documents accompanying the shipment. The consular invoice form can be obtained from the end country's embassy or consulate in the U.S.

Certificate of origin

Several countries require that the merchandise entering the country include a certificate of origin indicating the location where the goods were manufactured. The document certifies that, to the best of your knowledge as the exporter, the products originated from the country specified in the document. Although you would prepare and sign the certificate of origin, the document must be certified by a third party as to the legitimacy of the origin of the products addressed. This certification is normally performed by your local chamber of commerce. Certificates of origin must not be confused with country of origin markings. Some countries require that the products themselves specify the country of origin, and that labels be placed on the packages specifying the country of origin of the goods.

A significant certificate of origin to be familiar with is the NAFTA Certificate of Origin (sample included in Chapter 7), which contains product-specific and country of origin criteria. The criteria is met when the products are qualified products originating from one of the NAFTA countries as discussed earlier in the previous chapter. The following is a sample of a certificate of origin for product origination from countries other than NAFTA countries:

Certificate of Origin – CPB Form 3229

OMB No. 1651-0016
Exp. 10-31-2011

DEPARTMENT OF HOMELAND SECURITY
U.S. Customs and Border Protection

CERTIFICATE OF ORIGIN

(ARTICLES SHIPPED FROM INSULAR POSSESSIONS, EXCEPT PUERTO RICO, TO THE UNITED STATES 1)

19 CFR 7.3

1. PORT

2. DATE

3. CERTIFICATE NO.

4. NAME OF PERSON COMPLETING CERTIFICATE

5. NAME OF FIRM

6. SHIPPERS EXPORT DEC. NO.

7. DATE FILED

8. CARRIER (Vessel or Airline)

9. DESTINATION (Port of)

10. CONSIGNED TO

11. LOCATION OF CONSIGNEE (City and State)

12. MARKS AND NUMBERS	13. QUANTITY	14. DESCRIPTION OF ARTICLES	FOREIGN MATERIALS 2		MATERIALS DESCRIBED IN GENERAL NOTE 3 (a)(iv)(B)(2) 3		
			15. Description	16. Value	17. Description	18. Date Imported into Insular Possession	19. Date Incorporated into Imported Goods

20. INSULAR POSSESSION WHERE MERCHANDISE WAS PRODUCED OR MANUFACTURED

21. INSULAR POSSESSION OF WHICH MATERIALS ARE THE GROWTH, PRODUCT, OR MANUFACTURE

22. ADDRESS OF SHIPPER

I declare that I am the person named above, acting in the capacity indicated; that the description and other particulars of the merchandise specified above are correct as set forth in this certificate; that the said merchandise was produced or manufactured in the insular possession named above, and from the materials grown, produced, or manufactured in the insular possession also named above, or of the United States, or of both; that if foreign materials were used therein, their description and value are shown above.

23. SIGNATURE OF SHIPPER

VERIFICATION OF CBP OFFICER   I hereby certify that I have investigated the foregoing statements and am satisfied that they are correct to the best of my knowledge and belief.

24. DATE

25. SIGNATURE OF CBP OFFICER

SEE BACK OF FORM FOR FOOTNOTES AND PAPERWORK REDUCTION ACT NOTICE.

CBP Form 3229 (06/09)

Export packing list

The export packing list goes along with the merchandise and describes the shipment in detail. It includes information such as the name of the shipper, name of the consignee, measurements of the packages, any serial numbers, the weighs of the individual packages, and any other important information specific to that shipment. Packing lists itemize the contents of each individual package. They also state the type of package being used to ship the goods, such as box, drum, crate, or carton. Once completed, packing lists are inserted in waterproof envelopes labeled as "Packing list enclosed," and attached to the outside of the container or package.

Insurance certificates

Insurance certificates provide proof of coverage secured for the exported goods. Sometimes contracts, purchase orders, or commercial invoices may contain stipulations requiring insurance certificates in order for the exporter to be able to collect payment for the goods. Insurance certificates generally indicate the type and amount of coverage, as well as identify the merchandise in terms of packages and marks. It is important that you — as the exporter — make sure that the information contained in the insurance certificate is exactly the same as the information included in the invoices and bills of lading.

Dock receipt and warehouse receipt

These documents are used to transfer accountability of the products when moved by a domestic carrier to the shipping port and are then left with the steam ship company or the air freight company for exportation of the goods. These are the receipts issued by the shipping company that will be transporting the merchandise abroad, after the ground carrier has delivered the merchandise for export to the port. Therefore, both of these documents are necessary, along with the other required paperwork for exporting.

Export controls

The United States differs greatly from other countries in its export controls perspective: The philosophy of the U.S. government is that all exported goods and technical documentation are subject to the government's regulations. Most countries operate under a philosophy of freedom of exportation, unless there is a specific need to control the exports. Export controls vary from drastic in the form of embargoes, as is the case with North Korea and Cuba, to very minimal, as is the case with Canada.

In addition, export controls are enforced by different governmental agencies, depending on the products being exported. For instance, some of the goods enforced by individual governmental agencies include narcotics and dangerous drugs (licensed by the Department of Justice); nuclear material (licensed by the Nuclear Regulatory Commission); and the exportation of arms, ammunition, and related defense articles (licensed by the Department of State). However, as a general rule, the export and re-export of most commercial items that are obviously not for military use are regulated by the Export Administration Regulations (EAR). The Bureau of Industry and Security (BIS), which falls under the Department of Commerce, enforces the Export Administration Regulations. Thus, as you commence transactions to export a particular product, it is a good idea to look into the EAR, Part 730 at **www.access.gpo.gov/bis/ear/ear_data.html**. It contains a complete list of agencies involved in export controls and the products they license so that you involve the appropriate agency in your transaction.

It would be impossible under the context of this book to discuss all the regulations. However, you need to be aware that they are in place and are important to adhere to when exporting from the U.S. The EAR database is available online and will be helpful in determining if a certain export is subject to the regulations, how to request a commodity classification, and how to apply for an export license.

Export licensing requirement

Anything that is sent out of the United States to a foreign country is considered an export, regardless of how the transfer took place. Exported items could be commodities, technology, information transmitted via e-mail, fax, or even information downloaded from a Web site, some of which may be subject to export licensing regulations.

The requirement for an export license, as mandated by the Export Administration Act of 1979, is dependent upon various elements, such as the product's technical characteristics, the end user, the intended use, and the destination of the exported product. As the exporter, ask yourself the following questions in determining whether you need a license:

- What are you exporting?
- Where are you exporting the product to?
- Who are you shipping the product to?
- What will the product be used for?

The crucial element that will determine whether you need a license is the nature of the product you are planning to export. A large percentage of products that are exported do not need a license. However, the products that require a license have an export control classification number (ECCN) assigned to them by the Export Administration Regulations. The ECCN is a five-digit number that identifies the technology level and the capabilities of a particular product. This number — combined with the customer, the country of destination, and its intended use — is what will determine if an export license will be required. All ECCNs are listed under the Commerce Control List (CCL), which is included in the EAR as Part 774 (**www.gpo. gov/bis/ear/pdf/774.pdf**). You can try to determine if the product you are considering exporting has an ECCN and is listed in the CCL. However, it can get a bit confusing, and you want to be 100 percent sure as to whether you need a license because the penalties for exporting without a license when one is required are severe. Exporting without a license constitutes a violation of the Export Administrative Act of 1979 and the Export Administration Regulation, which could result in being subject to criminal penalties of up to 20 years in prison and up to $1 million dollars per violation. Other administrative penalties may also apply for up to $11 million dollars per violation.

If you are not sure that you have made the correct determination as to the ECCN or simply cannot figure it out on your own, you can contact the product's manufacturer. If the particular product has been exported before, they should have the ECCN available. If going that route does not turn out any results, you may want to request an official ECCN classification from the Commerce Department's Bureau of Industry and Security (BIS) using the Simplified Network Application Process Redesign (SNAP-R) at **www.bis.doc.gov/snap/index.htm**.

The products you are shipping to the final destination and end user are also important determinants of the need for an ECCN because exports are not allowed to countries embargoed by the U.S., such as Cuba, North Korea, and Sudan. Therefore, the U.S. requires that a destination control statement, which is basically a notification to the carrier stating that the shipment is prohibited from being diverted to a destination contrary to U.S. laws, be placed on all commercial invoices and bills of lading. Shipments to Canada that are intended for consumption in Canada are the only ones exempt from this requirement. The U.S. Department of State maintains a list, called the Directorate of Defense Trade Controls, that includes all the embargoed countries and the extent of the embargo and is updated regularly. The list is available in the U.S. Department of State Web site at **www.pmddtc.state.gov/embargoed_countries/index.html**. In addition, the U.S. prohibits exportations to particular groups or individuals who are engaged in the development of weapons of mass destruction, and those involved in drug trafficking or terrorism.

Lastly, the purpose for which the products exported will be used is of equal concern in determining its viability for export. This is because the goods regulated by the BIS are classified as dual-use items, meaning that they have both commercial and military applications, such as navigational and telecommunications equipment. In addition, export restrictions have been established for products that are in short supply in the U.S. in an effort to protect the economy by avoiding the exhaustion of such goods, as is the case with petroleum and petroleum products.

Export license application

Should it be determined that you need a license, you should then proceed to acquire and file the export license application, Form BIS-748P — "Multipurpose Application Form" — with the Bureau of Industry and Security. You can request the form by calling the Export Counseling Division at (202) 482-4811 and mailing it to: Bureau of Export Administration, U.S. Department of Commerce, 14th Street and Pennsylvania Avenue NW, Room 2007, Washington, DC 20044.

You may also file your application electronically through the Simplified Network Application Process Redesign (SNAP-R) at **www.bis.doc.gov/ snap/index.html**. The application form can be used to request approval to export and re-export. The requirements to fill out and submit the application for the export license are specified in the form itself.

The export license is considered to be a grant of authority to conduct a particular type of export from the appropriate licensing agency. It is issued to individual exporters to export a particular product to specific destinations. Licenses are granted on a case-by-case basis and can be issued for single or multiple transactions within a specified time frame, although export licenses are normally issued for two-year periods. It is critical that the application be filled out in its entirety and with utmost accuracy. Any omissions or errors will result in your application not being processed and returned to you, thus delaying your ability to export your product. Once approved, the license is sent to the exporter containing the authorization number and the expiration date. This information must be included in your shipper's export declaration document that accompanies the shipment.

Exporting under "No license required" (NLR) designation

Having said all that, it is important to note that most exports from the U.S. do not require an export license; thus, most exports are done under the "NLR" designation. You do not need an export license when the product being exported is not listed on the Commerce Control List (CCL), or the product is listed on the CCL but the country of destination is not marked under the "reason for control" column in the Commerce Country Chart. Based on the country where the goods are being exported to, the Commerce Country Chart outlines all the appropriate licensing requirements. The CCL is used together with the Commerce Country Chart to determine if a license will be required for the exportation of the products listed under the CCL. Both of these charts can be found online and in the Code of Federal Regulations Part 738, Supplement No. 1. The following excerpts of the CCL (the Table of Contents and the Commerce Country Chart) will give you a good idea of the complexity of trying to figure out whether the products you plan to export have an ECCN and if you need a license to export such products:

Excerpt — Commerce Control List, Table of Contents

Commerce Control List - Table of Contents   Supplement No. 1 to Part 774 - ToC 54

ECCN	Description
2B117	Equipment and process controls, other than those controlled by 2B004, 2B005.a, 2B104 or 2B105, designed or modified for the densification and pyrolysis of structural composite rocket nozzles and reentry vehicle nose tips
2B119	Balancing machines and related equipment, as follows (see List of Items Controlled)
2B120	Motion simulators or rate tables (equipment capable of simulating motion), having all of the following characteristics (see List of Items Controlled)
2B121	Positioning tables (equipment capable of precise rotary position in any axis), other than those controlled in 2B120, having all the following characteristics (See List of Items Controlled)
2B122	Centrifuges capable of imparting accelerations above 100 g and having slip rings capable of transmitting electrical power and signal information
2B201	Machine tools, other than those controlled by 2B001 for removing or cutting metals, ceramics or "composites", which, according to manufacturer s technical specification, can be equipped with electronic devices for simultaneous "contouring control" in two or more axes
2B204	"Isostatic presses," not controlled by 2B004 or 2B104, capable of achieving a maximum working pressure of 69 Mpa (10,000 psi) or greater and having a chamber cavity with an inside diameter in excess of 152 mm (6 inches) and specially designed dies, molds, and controls therefor
2B206	Dimensional inspection machines, devices or systems, other than those controlled by 2B006
2B207	"Robots" or "end-effectors", other than those controlled by 2B007, specially designed to comply with national safety standards applicable to handling high explosives (for example, meeting electrical code ratings for high explosives) and specially designed controllers therefor
2B209	Flow forming machines, or spin forming machines capable of flow forming functions, other than those controlled by 2B009 or 2B109, and mandrels
2B225	Remote manipulators that can be used to provide remote actions in radiochemical separation operations or hot cells
2B226	Controlled atmosphere (vacuum or inert gas) induction furnaces capable of operation above 1,123 K (850 °C) and having induction coils 600 mm or less in diameter, and designed for power inputs of 5 kW or more, and power supplies specially designed therefor with a specified power output of 5 kW or more
2B227	Vacuum or other controlled atmosphere metallurgical melting and casting furnaces and specially configured computer control and monitoring systems therefor
2B228	Rotor fabrication and assembly equipment, rotor straightening equipment, and bellows-forming mandrels and dies
2B229	Centrifugal multiplane balancing machines, fixed or portable, horizontal or vertical
2B230	"Pressure transducers" capable of measuring absolute pressure at any point in the range 0 to 13 kPa, with pressure sensing elements made of or protected by nickel, nickel alloy with more than 60% nickel by weight, aluminum or aluminum alloy
2B231	Vacuum pumps with an input throat size of 380 mm or greater with a pumping speed of 15 m³/s or greater and capable of producing an ultimate vacuum better than 13.3 mPa
2B232	Multistage light gas guns or other high-velocity gun systems (coil, electromagnetic, electrothermal, and other advanced systems) capable of accelerating projectiles to 2 km/s or greater
2B290	"Numerically controlled" machine tools not controlled by 2B001 or 2B201
2B350	Chemical manufacturing facilities and equipment, except valves controlled by 2A226 or 2A292
2B351	Toxic gas monitoring systems and their dedicated detecting components (i.e., detectors, sensor devices, and replaceable sensor cartridges), as follows, except those systems and detectors controlled by ECCN 1A004.c (see List of Items Controlled)
2B352	Equipment capable of use in handling biological materials
2B991	Numerical control units for machine tools and numerically controlled machine tools, n.e.s.
2B992	Non-"numerically controlled" machine tools for generating optical quality surfaces, and specially designed components therefor
2B993	Gearmaking and/or finishing machinery not controlled by 2B003 capable of producing gears to a quality level of better than AGMA 11
2B996	Dimensional inspection or measuring systems or equipment not controlled by 2B006
2B997	"Robots" not controlled by 2B007 or 2B207 that are capable of employing feedback information in real-time processing from one or more sensors to generate or modify "programs" or to generate or modify numerical program data
2B998	Assemblies, units or inserts specially designed for machine tools controlled by 2B991, or for equipment controlled by 2B993, 2B996 or 2B997
2B999	Specific processing equipment
2D001	"Software", other than that controlled by 2D002, specially designed or modified for the "development", "production" or "use" of equipment controlled by 2A001 or 2B001 to 2B009
2D002	"Software" for electronic devices, even when residing in an electronic device or system, enabling such devices or systems to function as a "numerical control" unit, capable of coordinating simultaneously more than 4 axes for "contouring control"
2D018	"Software" for the "development", "production" or "use" of equipment controlled by 2B018
2D101	"Software" specially designed or modified for the "use" of equipment controlled by 2B104, 2B105, 2B109, 2B116, 2B117, or 2B119 to 2B122

Export Administration Regulations   December 11, 2009

Excerpt — Commerce Country Chart

Commerce Control List Overview and the Country Chart

Supplement No. 1 to Part 738–page 1

Commerce Country Chart

Reason for Control

Countries	Chemical & Biological Weapons CB 1	CB 2	CB 3	Nuclear Nonproliferation NP 1	NP 2	National Security NS 1	NS 2	Missile Tech MT 1	Regional Stability RS 1	RS 2	Firearms Convention FC 1	Crime Control CC 1	CC 2	CC 3	Anti-Terrorism AT 1	AT 2
Afghanistan	X	X	X	X		X	X	X	X	X		X		X		
Albania[2,3]	X	X		X		X	X	X	X	X		X				
Algeria	X	X		X		X	X	X	X	X		X				
Andorra	X	X		X		X	X	X	X	X		X				
Angola	X	X		X		X	X	X	X	X		X				
Antigua & Barbuda	X	X				X	X	X	X	X		X		X		
Argentina	X		X	X		X	X	X	X	X	X	X		X		
Armenia	X	X		X		X		X	X	X	X	X		X		
Aruba	X	X				x		X	x			X	X	X		
Australia[3]	x					x		x	x	X		X		X		
Austria[3,4]	X	X				X	X	X	X	X						
Azerbaijan	X	X	X	X		X	X	X	X	X		X		X		
Bahamas, The	X	X		X		X	X	X	X	X	X	X	X	X		
Bahrain	X	X	X	X		X	X	X	X	X		X		X		

Export Administration Regulations

December 23, 2009

Automated Export System (AES)

The international trade industry is a paper-intensive industry with little room for error. In addition, as you have learned so far, there are always multiple agencies or entities involved with any one transaction — all of which, combined, allows plenty of room for mistakes to be made. However, with advances in technology, improvements are constantly being made to streamline the document filing process and make it as error-free as possible. The implementation of the Automated Export System (AES) aims to do just that. The AES is a fairly new way for exporters to declare, electronically, international exports to Customs and Border Protection. The AES has been in place for a relatively short time, when you take into consideration how long exports were processed completely paper-bound using the shipper's export declaration (SED). The AES was implemented in stages, starting with a few trial ports filing entries using both SED and AES electronically in 1995 until it was fully implemented by all seaports of entry in July 1997. The AES is a nationwide system in operation for all forms of transportation and at all ports.

The AES is a system by which all the export information required by all the agencies involved in the export of your product can be filed and submitted to Customs electronically. This system provides an alternative to filing the required documents, such as the ED, on paper, therefore expediting the review process and cutting back on the number of possible mistakes. The AES was designed to ensure that exporters abide by all the laws regulating exporting and improve the collection and processing of trade statistics.

Once you decide you are ready to export certain goods, shipping arrangements are made by your agent, if you are using an agent or a freight forwarder. If you are not using an agent, then the shipping arrangements are made by you. At that point, the shipment's information that would be included in the SED is transmitted using the AES. As the information is received, the AES authenticates the information against editing tables and files containing the requirements established by the various U.S. government agencies involved. At that point, it generates a confirmation message back to the exporter with either approval to export or an error message outlining missing or erroneous information in the submittal. If there were any errors or information missing, you would then file the corrections using the AES for approval to proceed. Lastly, within ten calendar days after the shipment departed from the port, the carrier transmits the entire export manifest electronically, also using AES. The export manifest contains the lists of the merchandise that will be loaded onboard of the carrier. Once the process is completed, the system electronically sends you confirmation that all the necessary documents have been filed successfully and provides you with an international transaction number (ITN).

There are many benefits to using the AES, but the most important benefit is that because of its high-tech editing system, you are sure to comply with all the current export reporting requirements in the U.S. In addition, using the AES decreases the cost and reduces the time associated with filing your export documentation by providing you feedback right away if there are any errors or omissions, thus eliminating costly delays of additional paperwork. In addition, AES uses technology that is available to the small business as well as large companies.

As a newcomer to the industry, it is important that you stay abreast of all the changes in the industry that affect the way you do business, such as the implementation of the AES. Even though it is common to be resistant to change, in the long run, changes in the system such as this are for the benefit of everyone involved.

Exporting Incentives

Although the government has established certain export controls, above all it has recognized the significantly positive impact exporting has on the U.S. economy. As a result, the government has established incentives in different forms to encourage exporting. There are tax incentives and industry-specific incentives, which normally are in effect for a specific length of time. There are also incentives provided by local trade assistance agencies established in an effort to help promote exports in the area, and although not of a financial nature, they are provided by facilitating trade missions, trade leads, and trading partnerships across the globe at little or no cost to the local companies.

An example of an industry-specific incentive is the Dairy Export Incentive Program (DEIP). This program was designed to help U.S. dairy product exporters be able to compete in the global market. This is accomplished by the U.S. Department of Agriculture's paying cash bonuses to exporters, which allows them to sell their products in the global marketplace at prices lower than it actually costs them to acquire that particular product. Taking advantage of this program ultimately allows the U.S. dairy exporter to compete for a segment of the market with competitors whose products are subsidized by other countries.

Another incentive for exporting goods has to do with taxes, through the establishment of the Interest-Charge Domestic International Sales Corporation (IC-DISC). The IC-DISC is a tax-deferral method that can result in tax savings up to 20 percent and can be taken advantage of by small- to medium-sized domestic corporations. One of the requirements is that the company be established for the sole purpose of exporting. The mechanics of setting up an IC-DICS are significantly complex, however, not beyond the capabilities of most accountants. Another form of tax incentive for exporters is in the form of duty drawback, which is when the exporter is refunded duties or taxes by the government when importing manufacturing components, or when products are imported and then re-exported.

Chapter 9

Importing and Exporting

In previous chapters, the process of importing and exporting were discussed individually. Necessary documentation, regulating agencies, and the mechanics of each process were also discussed at length. This chapter, however, will discuss how you can run a successful business of importing products, or components thereof, then re-exporting those goods. There are incentives for such operations and ways of conducting a financially successful operation by paying lower prices on your manufacturing components, as well as saving significantly in the payment of Customs duties and other fees.

Normally, when talking about importing goods into the U.S., the initial assumption is that the merchandise imported will be distributed throughout the United States for domestic consumption. However, imported goods do not always end up in the domestic market. Quite often, these goods are used as components or raw materials in the manufacturing process of products that end up being exported. For example, in the automobile industry, some of the electronics and other components are actually manufactured overseas and imported to be used in the final assembly of the vehicle. Therefore, the product imported is then re-exported as part of the vehicle that was manufactured for sale abroad.

Another situation where goods are imported for re-exportation is when merchandise is imported in bulk, brought into a warehouse or distribution center, and prepared for sale and distribution abroad. For example, as an importer with a distribution business, you may purchase bed sheets and other linens from a manufacturer overseas at a discounted price. The linens are brought into your distribution facility, where they are labeled with your name brand, repackaged, and prepared for sale. Meeting all the labeling and country of origin markings discussed in previous chapters, these goods are then sold to overseas importers who consequently sell the goods in their country.

There are, however, a couple of commonly used U.S. Customs programs and procedures for avoiding payment of Customs duties when goods are imported and re-exported, or receiving a refund for duties already paid on goods that were imported but re-exported. This can be done through the duty drawback program and TIB procedure — Temporary Importation under Bond.

CASE STUDY: SUCCESS IN BOTH IMPORTING AND EXPORTING

Gerard L. Gigon, President/CEO
Tecnicor International, Inc.
Gigon & Associates
105 Lazell Street
Hingham, MA 02043
(617) 686-0094

Tecnicor International, Inc. was incorporated in Massachusetts as a C corporation in 1992, importing cork composition rolls and sheets and natural cork products from Portugal, as well as decorative materials from Spain. The company would then export converted material that had been imported from Portugal along with materials that had been sourced from U.S. manufacturers. The company started relatively small but grew to a business netting more than $7 million in sales.

Gigon attributes this success to a number of factors combined. "Tecnicor used the import/distribution business to establish a customer base and company reputation," Gigon said. In addition, customer service was the key. Tecnicor worked hard to get to a 95 percent on time delivery performance against stated service goals on an average of 2,700 shipments a year. They also worked to use inventory investments to reduce lead times — that way, U.S. customers did not have to wait four to six weeks for delivery.

One of the methods employed by Tecnicor to reduce the distribution time to the customer was using public warehouses in various states such as Florida, Texas, Illinois, and California, in addition to their primary location in Massachusetts. The company used $150,000 in sales in a certain region as the threshold to determine the need for a public warehouse in that region. In addition, according to Gigon, public warehouses can help you grow the business without the risk of adding employees or managing people from a distance.

Gigon has a few words of advice to the new import export business owner:

- Communicate in simple "business" English, and do not use colloquial expressions.

- Make sure you have fax as well as e-mail capability for written communications, and always confirm key points or arrangements in writing.

- Find a bank that offers secure and reasonable cost wire transfer systems to pay for imports and to collect receivables for exports.

- Review the U.S. Customs Harmonized Tariff Schedule to determine the duty rates for the products being imported because products often can fall into more than one classification, affecting the duty rate.

- Lastly, study and try to understand the cultural and business differences between the countries: supplier country to U.S. or U.S. to customer country.

Duty Drawback Program

The duty drawback program is considered to be the most complex program administered by Customs because it involves every facet of Customs transactions, including imports and exports. It is a program that has been around since 1789 when the first tariff act was enacted in the U.S. However, as is the case with many of the laws affecting trade, it changes from time to time, affecting the conditions under which the duty drawback is payable. Duty drawback is a way in which, as an importer, you can get refunded 99 percent of duties and other fees that you paid to Customs at the time of importation of goods when they are re-exported. The duty drawback program was established to enable domestic manufacturers to compete in the global market. The benefit of using duty drawback is that you can apply to Customs for a refund after those imported goods, for which you paid duties, have been exported or have been destroyed. However, on the down side, the process to take advantage from duty drawback is quite complex, and you run the risk of being assessed substantial penalties due to poor record management or improper filings. To be able to claim your refund, Customs must be able to track the specific commodities that were imported and then exported.

Types of drawbacks

The following are various applications for drawbacks, established under Title 19, Section 1313, of the United States Code of Federal Regulations:

Manufacturing drawback

There are two types of manufacturing drawbacks: direct identification manufacturing drawback and substitution manufacturing drawback.

Direct Identification Manufacturing Drawback — This program can be used when the goods for which you will be requesting a drawback were imported as raw material or as components to be used in the manufacturing of a finished product, which is ultimately exported. Once the finished product is exported, you can apply for drawback of the duties paid on the imported components of the product.

Substitution Manufacturing Drawback — In order to promote using U.S. manufactured raw materials in the manufacturing process rather than importing them, Congress enacted legislation establishing the Substitution Manufacturing Drawback process. Under this program, when a manufacturer has imported raw materials or components to be used in the manufacturing process, but is then able to use U.S. made components instead, the importer is allowed to apply for drawback on duties paid on the imported components that were not used and were ultimately returned.

Under both types of manufacturing drawback programs, the manufacturer must maintain accurate records as to the amount of waste of imported products during the manufacturing process. The manufacturer must also maintain detailed records that can be referenced by Customs to verify the utilization of the imported components in the manufacturing process of the finished product. Records must be maintained for a period of three years from the date the drawback payment claim was filed, or five years from the date the raw materials or components were imported — whichever is longer. In addition, the manufacturer must have an importer's identification number as well as applying for a manufacturing drawback ruling. Drawback rulings specify Customs' terms and conditions under which manufacturing must take place in order to qualify for a drawback.

Drawback rulings can be general or specific. A general manufacturing drawback ruling is designed to simplify the drawback process for certain common manufacturing operations. These operations could be piece goods operations, manufacturing of petroleum, or petroleum derivative products, and operations involving orange juice or its derivatives. A complete list of manufacturing operations that qualify for general manufacturing drawback rulings can be found in Customs regulations Section 191.7 of the Code of Federal Regulation (19 CFR, section 191.7). If your operation falls under one of the general manufacturing drawback rulings and you anticipate operating without any variation thereof, all you need to do is send a letter of notification to conduct operations under that specific general ruling (stating the ruling number). The letter of notification to operate under a general manufacturing drawback ruling is submitted to any of the drawback offices where the drawback entries will be filed. The following five drawback offices — or centers — located throughout the United States are the locations where you would submit the letter of notification to conduct operations under these rulings and receive additional assistance on drawbacks procedures.

U.S. Customs and Border Protection
9915 Bryn Mawr Avenue
3rd Floor
Rosemont, IL 60018
(847) 928-6077

U.S. Customs and Border Protection
2350 N. Sam Houston Parkway East
Suite 100
Houston, TX 77032
(281) 985-6890

U.S. Customs and Border Protection
Port of Los Angeles – Seaport
301 E. Ocean Boulevard
Long Beach, CA 90802
(562) 366-5706

U.S. Customs and Border Protection
1100 Raymond Boulevard

Room 310
Newark, NY 07102
(973) 368-6950

U.S. Customs and Border Protection
555 Battery Street
Room 109
San Francisco, CA 94111
(415) 782-9245

However, if your operation does not fall within one of the general manufacturing drawback rulings, under Section 191.7 of the Code of Federal Regulations, you would need to apply for a specific manufacturing drawback ruling under Section 191.8. To apply for a specific manufacturing drawback ruling, three copies of the application are required to be sent to the following places: U.S. Customs Service Headquarters, Duty and Refund Determination Branch, Office of Regulations and Rulings, Washington, D.C. 20229. Appendix B to Part 191 of Title 19 (19 CFR, Part 191) has samples of the formats to follow when applying for either one of the specific manufacturing drawback rulings. Although samples are provided in the Code of Federal Regulations for your use, the format is lengthy and of a technical nature, often resulting in the need to seek the assistance of experts such as international law attorneys.

Jet aircraft engines drawback

In situations when a jet aircraft engine was manufactured abroad but imported to be overhauled, repaired, rebuilt, or reconditioned in the Untied Sates, it would qualify for duty drawback at the time of exportation. That is if the work was done with imported merchandise, including parts, and the importer can provide evidence of having paid duties on such goods.

Imported salt used for curing drawback

Salt imported in bond that is used to cure fish taken by licensed vessels for commercial purposes and salt used to cure fish on the shores of U.S. navigable waters qualifies for drawback of 99 percent of duties paid. In addition, salt used to cure meats in the United States for exportation purposes qualifies for a drawback refund as long as it is in amounts greater than $100.

Products manufactured with domestic alcohol

Taxes paid on domestic alcohol that has been used in the manufacturing process of specific products that are consequently exported or shipped to any of the U.S. island territories may qualify for drawback of those taxes paid.

Unused merchandise drawback

This type of drawback applies when goods are imported into the U.S. and are then exported or destroyed without being used. Goods are considered "not used" when they are exported without having been processed into new products with a new name, character, or use. When this is the case, the importer can then apply for a drawback on these products as long as exportation or destruction of the merchandise takes place within three years after importation.

Rejected merchandise drawback

An importer/manufacturer can apply for rejected merchandise drawback when the merchandise received from the supplier abroad is either defective or does not meet the specifications of the goods sold. When an importer intends to file duty drawback under these circumstances, the manufacturer must return the goods to Customs within three years of the import date for inspection and processing. At that time, the importer may be able to recover 99 percent of the duties paid as drawback.

Packaging materials drawback

As an importer, you can also receive 99 percent of duties paid on the material used for packaging goods that were destroyed or exported that qualify for drawback.

Finished petroleum derivatives drawback

The ruling establishing qualifications and procedures under this application is probably the most complex one of all drawback applications and requires the interpretation of an expert to address each specific petroleum-related drawback issue. Unless you intend to be involved in the importing and exporting of petroleum and petroleum products, this type of drawback will not be applicable to you. Nevertheless, as in all other drawback applications, it has its limitations as to what qualifies for drawback, time frame allowed in which to request your drawback, and procedures for requesting a drawback.

Exportation Procedure and Drawback Claim Process

In order to process a duty drawback claim, the drawback claimant who will be exporting or destroying the goods must first complete and file a Drawback Entry, along with other supporting documentation. The Drawback Entry — Customs Form 7551 — is a document that contains a detailed description, along with other information, regarding the exported, or destroyed products, on which drawback is being claimed. Supporting documentation also includes verification that the products on which the manufacturing drawback is being claimed were exported within five years after importation. For surplus or rejected merchandise, the drawback period is three years. In addition, you must include supporting documentation that establishes the date, nature of the exportation, and the identity of the exporter.

According to U.S. Customs and Border Protection's regulations, the procedure to establish exportation for drawback purposes must include:

- Actual documented evidence of exportation such as originally signed — or certified copy thereof issued by the carrier — freight waybill, cargo manifest, air waybill, or bill of lading.

- Export summary.

- For mail shipments, a certified export invoice.

- Notice of transfer for articles manufactured to a foreign-trade zone — foreign trade zones are discussed later in this section.

U.S. Customs and Border Protection Draw Back Entry Form — CBP Form 7551

Section III - Manufactured Articles

35. Quantity & Description of Merchandise Used	36. Date(s) of Manufacture or Production	37. Description of Articles Manufactured or Produced	38. Quantity and Unit of Measure	39. Factory Location

Section IV - Information on Exported or Destroyed Merchandise

PERIOD COVERED _____ TO _____

40. Exhibits to be attached for the following:

☐ Relative Value ☐ Petroleum ☐ Domestic Tax Paid Alcohol ☐ Piece Goods ☐ Waste Calculation ☐ Recycled
☐ Harbor Maintenance Fee ☐ Merchandise Processing Fee ☐ Other Taxes/Fees

41. Date (MM/DD/YYYY)	42. Action Code	43. Unique Indentifier No.	44. Name of Exporter/Destroyer	45. Description of Articles (Include Part/Style/Serial Numbers)	46. Quantity and Unit of Measure	47. Export Destination	48. HTSUS No.

Section V - Declarations

☐ Same condition to NAFTA countries - The undersigned herein certifies that the merchandise herein described is in the same condition as when it was imported under above import entry(ies) and further certifies that this merchandise was not subjected to any process of manufacturer or other operation except the following allowable operations:

☐ The undersigned hereby certifies that the merchandise herein described is unused in the United States and further certifies that this merchandise was not subjected to any process of manufacture or other operation except the following allowable operations:

☐ The undersigned hereby certifies that the merchandise herein described is commercially interchangeable with the designated imported merchandise and further certifies that the substituted merchandise is unused in the United States and that the substituted merchandise was in our possession prior to exportation or destruction.

☐ Merchandise does not conform to sample or specifications.   ☐ Merchandise was defective at time of importation.   ☐ Merchandise was shipped without consent of the consignee.

☐ The undersigned hereby certifies that the merchandise herein described is the same kind and quality as defined in 19 U.S.C. 1313(p)(3)(B), with the designated imported merchandise or the article manufactured or produced under 1313(a) or (b), as appropriate.

☐ The article(s) described above were manufactured or produced and disposed of as stated herein in accordance with the drawback ruling on file with CBP and in compliance with applicable laws and regulations.

> The undersigned acknowledges statutory requirements that all records supporting the information on this document are to be retained by the issuing party for a period of three years from the date of payment of the drawback claim. The undersigned is fully aware of the sanctions provided in 18 U.S.C. 1001 and 18 U.S.C. 550 and 19 U.S.C. 1593a.
>
> I declare that according to the best of my knowledge and belief, all of the statements in this document are correct and that the exported article is not to be relanded in the United States or any of its possessions without paying duty.

☐ Member of Firm with Power of Attorney   ☐ Officer of Corporation   ☐ Broker with Power of Attorney

Printed Name and Title	Signature and Date

CBP Form 7551 (07/08)

TIB — Temporary Importation under Bond

Temporary Importation under Bond is a procedure whereby certain items may be entered into U.S. Custom's territory — for a limited time and under certain conditions — duty-free. Products such as items used as models or samples and merchandise imported for repair are entered under a TIB because they are not intended to be entered into the domestic market. To enter imported goods under a TIB, you have to post a bond for twice the amount of the Customs duty that would have otherwise been due upon importation instead of paying the duty, taxes and other applicable fees. You would use a TIB when you intend to export or destroy the imported merchandise within a specified time; otherwise, you would be responsible for paying Customs for liquidated damages, which would be twice the normal amount of duty that would have been owed.

Items eligible for TIB

Only the following items, as listed under subheadings 9813.00.05 through 9813.00.75 of the Harmonized Tariff Schedule of the U.S., qualify for a TIB entry:

- *Subheading 9813.00.05* — Articles to be repaired, altered, or processed.

- *Subheading 9813.00.10* — Models of women's wearing apparel imported by manufacturers for use solely as models in their own establishments.

- *Subheading 9813.00.15* — Articles imported by illustrators and photographers for use solely as models in their own establishments, in the illustrating of catalogues, pamphlets, or advertising matters.

- *Subheading 9813.00.20* — Samples solely for use in taking orders for merchandise.

- *Subheading 9813.00.25* — Articles solely for examination with a view to reproduction, or for such examination and reproduction (except photo-engraved printing plates for examination and reproduction); and motion picture advertising films.

- *Subheading 9813.00.30* — Articles intended solely for testing, experimental, or review purposes, including specification, photographs, and similar articles for use in connection with experiments or for study.

- *Subheading 9813.00.35* — Automobiles, motorcycles, bicycles, airplanes, airships, balloons, boats, racing shells, and similar vehicles and craft, and the usual equipment of the foregoing; all the foregoing that are brought temporarily into the United States by nonresidents for the purpose of taking part in races or other specific contests.

- *Subheading 9813.00.40* — Locomotives and other railroad equipment brought temporarily into the United States for use in clearing obstructions, fighting fires, or making emergency repairs or railroads within the United States, or for use in transportation otherwise than in international traffic when the Secretary of the Treasury finds that the temporary use of foreign railroad equipment is necessary to meet the emergency.

- *Subheading 9813.00.45* — Containers for compressed gasses, filled or empty, and containers or other articles in use for covering or holding merchandise (including personal or household effects) during transportation and suitable for reuse for that purpose.

- *Subheading 9813.00.50* — Professional equipment, tools of trade, repair components for equipment or tools admitted under this heading and camping equipment; all the foregoing imported by or for nonresidents sojourning temporarily in the United States and for the use of such nonresidents.

- *Subheading 9813.00.55* — Articles of special design for temporary use exclusively in connection with the manufacture or production of articles for export.

- *Subheading 9813.00.60* — Animals and poultry brought into the United States for the purpose of breeding, exhibition, or competition for prizes, and the usual equipment thereof.

- *Subheading 9813.00.70* — Works of the free fine arts, engravings, photographic pictures, and philosophical and scientific apparatus brought into the United States by professional artists, lecturers, or scientists arriving from abroad for use by them for exhibition and illustration, promotion, and encouragement of art, science, or industry in the United States.

- *Subheading 9813.00.75* — Automobiles, automobile chassis, automobile bodies, cutaway portion of any of the foregoing and parts for any of the foregoing, finished, unfinished, or cutaway, when intended solely for sow purposes.

Obtaining a TIB

How you obtain a TIB depends on how the merchandise is being imported. For instance, if the merchandise is being imported as cargo, you can either hire a broker to clear the merchandise through Customs, or you may go directly to the port of entry to clear the shipment. You must also make arrangements in advance to secure a Customs bond for the importation, which would be in an amount twice the amount of what would be owed for duties or taxes on that importation. Because it is so critical that the bond is secured for the correct amount owed, you should contact an import specialist for assistance at the port of entry where your merchandise will be entering U.S. territory.

However, if you are importing goods as accompanying baggage as you enter the United States, which is common for business travelers, there are two ways to acquire the TIB. The most effective way is to make arrangements ahead of time, by contacting a Customs broker who would make the appropriate arrangements and conduct the necessary transactions ahead of time. If it is not possible to make arrangements before traveling, then the process of securing a TIB can be a bit cumbersome. The importer, in this case the traveler, would have to go to the Customs office at the port of entry, which often is in a separate building from the main airport, and fill out a Customs Entry Summary CF 7501. At that time, the importer would have to post the bond to cover the temporary importation, which would require a trip to a surety office for that purpose.

Exportation requirements under a TIB

Before any merchandise is exported, the TIB must be canceled with U.S. Customs and Border Protection at the port of exportation using Customs Form CF 3495, "Application for Exportation of Articles Under Special Bond." To verify that the merchandise previously imported was then exported under a TIB, Customs requires that the following items be included:

1. A copy of the bill of lading, which proves that the goods were actually loaded onto a ship.

2. A reference to the original entry number, which is line 1 of the Customs Form 7501.

3. A merchandise description on the bill of lading that matches the description for that product as it appears on Customs Form 7501. The description must be concise and include information such as serial numbers and any other identifying information.

When the merchandise is being exported as accompanying baggage, the traveler must take the merchandise to the entry office where the TIB was issued so that Customs can physically verify that the merchandise is leaving the country. If the merchandise is being exported from a port other than the original port of entry, then the person exporting the goods must take the merchandise to the international arrival area of the airport. There, a Customs inspector will fill out a Customs Form 3495, "Application for Exportation of Articles Under Special Bond," so that the traveler may complete the exportation. A copy of this form must then be submitted to the original port of entry, where the merchandise was brought in the country.

U.S. Customs and Border Protection Form 3495

	Form Approved OMB No. 1651-0004
DEPARTMENT OF HOMELAND SECURITY **U.S. Customs and Border Protection**	Exp. 12-31-2010

APPLICATION FOR EXPORTATION OF ARTICLES UNDER SPECIAL BOND

19 CFR 10.38

TO CBP PORT DIRECTOR

1. TO: CBP Port Director *(Address)*	2. FROM: *(Name and Address of Importer or Agent)*

ATTACH COPY OF EXPORT INVOICE DESCRIBING ARTICLES TO BE EXPORTED

3. Name of Exporting Carrier	4. Date of Departure	5. Country of Origin	6. No. of Export Packages
7. Port of Entry	8. Entry Number Date		9. Date Bonded Period Expires
10. Date Articles Available for CBP Examination	11. Signature of Importer or Agent		12. Date

(FOR CBP USE ONLY)
NOTICE TO IMPORTER TO DELIVER ARTICLES TO BE EXAMINED AND IDENTIFIED FOR EXPORTATION

13. Place of CBP Examination	Date
14. Date	15. CBP PORT DIRECTOR BY:

REPORT OF EXAMINATION

☐ 16. The articles covered by this application have been examined and agree with the invoice in content and No. of export pkgs. and are approved for export.

17. No. of Export Packages	18. Date of Delivery for Exportation	19. Marks and Numbers on Export Packages

☐ 20. The articles covered by this application do not agree with the invoice in content or in number of packages as follows

21. SIGNATURE OF EXAMINING CBP OFFICER	22. DATE

REPORT OF EXPORTATION

23. Home of Exporting Conveyance *(Vessel, Railroad, Airline and Flight Number)*

24. Date of Departure	Paperwork Reduction Act Statement: An agency may not conduct or sponsor an information collection and a person is not required to respond to this information unless it displays a current valid OMB control number and an expiration date. The control number for this collection is 1651-0004. The estimated average time to complete this application is 8 minutes. If you have any comments regarding the burden estimate you can write to U.S. Customs and Border Protection, Office of Regulations and Rulings, 799 9th Street, NW., Washington DC 20229.
25. Manifest No.	
26. SIGNATURE OF CBP OFFICER	

(CBP officer must return one copy of this form to port of origin upon exportation.)	*(Previous Editions are Obsolete)*	CBP Form 3495 (06/09)

To avoid having to pay liquidated damages, it is paramount that the original port of entry receives confirmation of exportation of the merchandise brought in under a TIB. If the merchandise imported under a TIB is to be destroyed within the original bond period, rather than exported, the importer needs to contact the Customs office at the original port of entry to determine what the exact requirements are to do so. To satisfy Customs destruction requirements, therefore satisfying the bond requirements, the merchandise would have to be destroyed to the point where it would no longer have any commercial value.

Chapter 10

Foreign-trade Zones and Customs Bonded Warehouses

Part of operating a profitable business is to always look for cost-effective ways of doing business. Notice that this is not the same as looking for "ways to save money," because in saving money, sometimes you will not necessarily end up ahead of the game, and instead it may end up costing more in the long run. Thus, finding better ways to do business, although it may take some investment of both time and money, more often than not will result in profitable business deals, as is the case with foreign-trade zones and bonded warehouses. Foreign-trade zones and bonded warehouses are not for everyone involved in importing and exporting. However, they are worth looking into to see if they would be applicable to your operation because the cost-savings opportunities associated with these types of programs are quite significant and worth the investment.

Using Foreign-trade Zones to Your Advantage

The foreign-trade zones (FTZ) program was established through the enactment of the Foreign-Trade Zones Act of 1934. The act was designed to "expedite and encourage foreign commerce" in the United States by designating certain geographical areas within or adjacent to Customs ports of entry, where Customs would treat merchandise as if it were outside the U.S.

domestic market. The tariff and tax relief afforded to the U.S. importer and exporter through the implementation of this act was designed to reduce their costs of operations, thereby retaining employment opportunities in the U.S, as well as creating new employment opportunities, rather than sending them abroad.

The Foreign-Trade Zones Act is administered through two sets of regulations: the Code of Federal Regulations (Title 15) and the Customs and Border Protection Regulations (Title 19 of the Code of Federal Regulations, Part 146).

Through the FTZ regulations, the FTZ Board is authorized to grant authority to private and public organizations to establish, maintain, and operate foreign-trade zones. The board, located in the Department of Commerce, comprises the secretary of commerce (chair of the board) and the secretary of the treasury. The commissioner of U.S. Customs and Border Protection also plays a key role, more specifically in issues relating to Customs security, control, and other matters. The board also regulates the administration of foreign-trade zones, has the authority to inspect and examine the operations and location of zones, and ultimately has the authority to revoke any grant of authority previously issued to any zone for repeated violations of the FTZ Act.

U.S. Customs and Border Protection FTZ coordinators (CBP officers, import specialists, entry specialists, or agricultural specialists) supervise foreign-trade zones through compliance reviews and visits. Customs is responsible for the movement of merchandise in and out of the zones and for the protection of Customs' revenues by ensuring the proper collection of duties. In addition, the Customs' port director, of ports where foreign-trade zones are located, is responsible for overseeing foreign-trade zone activity as the representative of the FTZ Board. The port director controls the admission, handling, and disposition of merchandise in the foreign-trade zone, as well as the removal of such merchandise from the zone.

What are Foreign-trade Zones?

Foreign-trade zones are isolated, enclosed areas located in or near a Customs port of entry. Foreign-trade zones are directly supervised by U.S. Customs through an audit-inspection system. Customs does not verify compliance by having constant, on-site supervision of the zones; rather, it verifies compliance through audits and spot checks. Although FTZs are considered to be outside U.S. Customs territory, they are still subject to the laws and regulations of the United States, as well state and local laws of the FTZ's location. Merchandise brought into a foreign-trade zone can be assembled, manufactured, processed, mixed, manipulated, destroyed, re-exported, salvaged, repaired, exhibited, repackaged, relabeled, cleaned, tested, stored, and sampled. Merchandise, except that which is illegal or not allowed by any existing regulations, may be brought into a foreign-trade zone without being subject to the Customs laws of the United States. Goods entered into a foreign-trade zone are only subject to Customs duties if they are removed from the zone and entered into U.S. Customs territory. In this context, U.S. Customs territory means all of the United States where the tariff laws apply, which includes all 50 states, the District of Columbia, and Puerto Rico.

There are two types of foreign-trade zones: general purpose zones and subzones.

General purpose zones are established for a variety of uses by individual businesses. This type of zone can be operated by a private enterprise or by the public sector. Normally, a general purpose zone storage or distribution space is leased to users in warehouse-type facilities, which have easy access to various modes of transportation. Some of the most common uses for general purpose zones are storage, distribution, testing, repackaging, and rearing of goods. Manufacturing and processing of goods can be allowed in these general-purpose zones, however, approval for such operations must be acquired first from the FTZ Board.

Subzones are special-purpose zones that are approved by the FTZ Board to conduct certain manufacturing activities at a specific geographic location. Subzones can also be established for distribution facilities. Companies operating under subzone status enjoy the same benefits as general-purpose zones, with the only difference being that subzones are located outside general-purpose zone areas. Subzones are sponsored by general-purpose zones, which is why they are able to operate outside the geographic confines of the general-purpose zones. However, they must be located within 60 miles from the nearest port of entry. This type of authority is normally granted when a company's operations cannot be accommodated or relocated to an existing general-purpose zone area.

For example, FTZ No. 153's grantee is the City of San Diego. The zone is made up of multiple sites throughout the city, which are all part of the general purpose zone. However, FTZ No. 153 also has several subzones, such as Subzone 153C DNP Electronics, and 153D Callaway Golf Company.

Applying to establish a foreign-trade zone

The application to establish a foreign-trade zone is typically done by public entities such as state or local government, ports or port authorities, nonprofit corporations, and economic development agencies, who would ultimately become the grantee of the zone once the grant of authority has been granted, as one of the purposes of establishing a foreign-trade zone in a community is to stimulate the local economy. The grantee is the entity that is awarded the authority to establish and operate a foreign-trade zone pursuant to the grant, and is ultimately held accountable for the entity's activities and the activities of its operators, users, and other participants in that foreign-trade zone. The specific guidelines for a general purpose zone application, as prescribed by the FTZ Board, are available on their Web site, **www.ia.ita.doc. gov/ftzpage**. As an individual importer or exporter, you would likely not be in a position to submit an application for a general purpose zone yourself.

Rather, your role would be as a user of the zone — a user is the entity that establishes its operations within a foreign-trade zone.

Nevertheless, it is important that you have an idea of the application guidelines and process because it is the basis for operating within a general purpose zone and for establishing subzones. Basically, an application for a general purpose zone is submitted to the executive secretary of the FTZ Board by sending an electronic copy along with the original (hard copy) and three additional copies. The application should be submitted with a letter of transmittal, dated and signed by the authorized officer of the organization. The application package must include the following elements:

- **Executive summary:** The executive summary must describe the type of organization making the application as well as its legal authority to make such application. It must also state the type of zone being requested, proposed site and facilities, and general background on the project. The applicant also needs to state the relationship of the proposed zone project with the area's economic development plans and how the zone project will be financed.

- **Exhibit 1 — Legal authority to apply:** The applicant must provide evidence of its legal authority to apply for the zone project by providing a certified copy of the state's enabling legislation regarding foreign-trade zones, sections of the applicant's organization papers — or charter — that are relevant to foreign-trade zones, and a certified copy of a resolution authorizing the organization's officer to sign the application.

- **Exhibit 2 — Site description:** This section must include a description of the proposed site, including the legal description, and state the legal jurisdiction of the location of the site. It should also include a description of the facilities and services, current activities, transportation services available to the site, and any plans for expansion.

In addition, the applicant must discuss the zone's ability to meet Custom's adjacency requirement to a port of entry — a driving distance not to exceed 60 miles or 90 minutes' driving time.

- **Exhibit 3 — Operation and financing:** This exhibit should include information as to the proposed zone's operational plan, a statement of the applicant's right to use the facilities, plans for the implementation of security measures, plans for financial operating and capital costs, and a timetable for construction of a facility — if applicable.

- **Exhibit 4 — Economic justification:** The economic justification section of the application is the most critical and normally the longest part of the application. The required elements of this exhibit are numerous and the requirements very detailed; however, generally stated, the goal of this exhibit is to demonstrate to the Foreign-trade zones Board the need for establishing the zone and the valuable economic impact it will have in the community.

- **Exhibit 5 — Maps:** Several maps must be included in this exhibit such as a state map indicating the location of the zone, a street map with the zone site highlighted, and a blue print of the proposed facility with the boundaries outlined in red.

The application and approval process takes a long time. Normally, an application package, as described above, can take anywhere from six months to a year to put together — and even longer, depending on the complexity of the project. In addition, the estimated review and approval process can take six to eight months from submittal, if there are no corrections to the application.

As a private entity importing and exporting — and possibly manufacturing — you would either be establishing your operations within an already existing general-purpose foreign-trade zone, or applying to become a subzone. Establishing operations within an already existing general purpose zone is not as complicated as establishing a subzone. To be a zone user, a request is submitted to the FTZ Board stating the nature of your operation, exact location within the general purpose zone where you will be operating from, information about your company and its officers, and a description of what activities you plan to carry out in the zone. There are set guidelines as to how the application must be prepared and submitted to the board for approval, which are normally provided to the user by the grantee or zone operator. In addition, an operations manual, which describes the nature of your company and its operations, must be developed and approved by Customs prior to activation of the zone. Activation is when approval is received by Customs to commence operations under foreign-trade zone status. In addition, a security manual that describes in intricate detail the security measures you propose on implementing to protect Customs interests — prevent the removal of merchandise from the zone without proper duty being paid — must also be developed and approved by Customs prior to activation. As a user of the zone, you also have to conduct your operations in accordance with the established guidelines and regulations prescribed by the zone grantee.

If you own a manufacturing facility or run a distribution operation as part of your import export business, and there is a general purpose zone in your area, you might want to investigate the possibilities of activating your operations as a subzone. Subzone applications are submitted to and reviewed by the FTZ Board. The applications are detailed documents providing extensive information regarding the proposed zone project. Authority is granted by the board to conduct activity within the zone that is consistent with trade policy and yields net positive economic effects, taking into account the potential impact on other domestic operations. The application process for a subzone, whether it is a distribution operation subzone or a subzone with manufacturing authority, is almost as intricate and time-consuming as that of a general purpose zone, taking several months to accomplish.

Additionally, the review and approval process is almost as extensive as that of a general-purpose zone, taking several months to receive approval. The applicant should have a basic understanding of how foreign-trade zones operate and a good understanding of the procedures of the FTZ Board and Customs. The specific guidelines for the application of a subzone, as established by the Foreign-trade Zones Board, are available on their Web site, at **www.ia.ita.doc.gov/ftzpage/sz-application.html**. However, to give you a general idea of the scope of the application process, the basic guidelines, along with a brief description of each section, is provided herewith:

- **Application letter:** The application letter for a subzone is written by the zone grantee transmitting the application package. The letter will include an executive summary of your proposed operations, and how approval of this proposal will be beneficial for your community.

- **Economic justification:** This is the most extensive portion of the application. One of the key elements to cover in this section is an explanation as to why your proposed operation cannot be accommodated within the already existing general-purpose zone. Another very important element of this section, which is critical in the favorable outcome of the application, is providing detailed justification as to the project's nationwide economic benefits. Additional information that must be included in this section includes company-specific information such as management, employment practices, sourcing practices, and market and industry information related to your company.

- **FTZ-related savings:** In this part of the application, the applicant must discuss estimated annual savings directly related with the proposed subzone activities. The applicant must also include estimates as to the economic impact your company will experience operating as a foreign-trade zone. This includes costs directly associated with the operation of the subzone such as: recordkeeping fees, fees paid to the general-purpose zone, and inventory control costs.

- **Site description:** The site description requires a detailed description of the proposed site, including physical address, legal description, acreage, buildings (including square footage), and an explanation of the planned activities within that site.

- **Environmental impact:** In this section, you must address any potential environmental impacts, such as land use issues and zoning requirements.

- **Maps:** The application must include local and state maps indicating the proposed subzone's location. Street maps and location maps showing the proposed site's boundaries — outlined in red — must also be included.

- **Operation and financing:** The applicant, in this section, needs to address the ownership status of the proposed site, security measures that will be implemented in the site, and your commitment to working with Customs and Border Protection to meet current and future requirements for its automated reporting systems.

- **Products and components:** A detailed description of the manufacturing activity planned for the site must be included along with a description of the main products and components to be used in the manufacturing process — if applicable.

This is only a generalized description of the application guidelines, as the contents of the application are much more specific and detailed. If the concept of operating under foreign-trade zone status appeals to you, you may wish to seek professional assistance in the evaluation of its feasibility as well as in the application and submittal process. There are numerous consulting firms that specialize in foreign-trade zone and subzone applications. An excellent source for finding them is through the National Association of Foreign-trade Zones Web site at **www.naftz.org**.

Operating Under Foreign-trade Zones Status

Although authority to establish a foreign-trade zone is granted to the grantee by the FTZ Board, it is common for the grantee to contract with an operator to operate the zone. An operator can be a corporation, partnership, or an individual. However, in a subzone setting, the owner of the company will more than likely be the operator of the subzone. General operating procedures will be discussed herewith; however, details regarding recordkeeping requirements, security requirements, and specific foreign-trade zone operating requirements can be found in the *Foreign-trade Zones Manual* developed by the Department of Homeland Security, Customs, and Border Protection. As changes on rules and regulations are implemented by the corresponding governing bodies, this manual is updated to stay current. A copy of the manual can be obtained through the U.S. Government Bookstore at **http://bookstore.gpo.gov**.

Foreign-trade zones work to the importer and exporter's advantage, mostly when you are importing with intentions of re-exporting those goods, or exporting manufactured products using imported raw materials. Foreign-trade zones are also a good way to go when you are importing with an indefinite time table as to when you will be able to sell those goods in the domestic market, or even when you import merchandise subject to quotas. For instance, in cases where you are importing merchandise subject to quotas and the quota is filled, you may bring those goods into the foreign-trade zone until the quota is removed, or it opens again. An import quota is the total amount of a particular product that may be imported during the quota period, which is normally one year. Quotas are established to protect the domestic market, and although Customs has the authority to control the importation of quota merchandise, quotas are established by legislation. In the U.S., tobacco, wheat, sugar, cotton, apparel, and textiles are governed by quotas.

When you operate under foreign-trade zone status, you are able to compete at a more level playing field with your foreign competitors. You will be more competitive because not only will you be retaining quality labor locally, but your manufacturing costs also will be less due to reduced or eliminated duty payments. In addition, if you own multiple manufacturing, warehousing, or distribution facilities, you can transfer merchandise from one foreign-trade zone facility to another within the U.S. without having to pay duty on those goods.

The actual operation of your business as a foreign-trade zone will not differ that much from traditional importing and exporting operations. The difference will be more evident in the strict security requirements and extensive paper trail — or automated document trail. Operating under foreign-trade zone status requires strict compliance with Customs by maintaining accurate and up-to-date records of the movement of merchandise in and out of the zone. There will also be more forms involved in the operation of a foreign-trade zone than what is customary in a regular import export operation.

For example, to admit merchandise into a foreign-trade zone, you would use Customs Form 214 "Application for Foreign-trade zone Admission and/or Status Designation," which is submitted to Customs by the zone operator or Customs broker to request their approval to admit merchandise into the foreign-trade zone. The form is then presented at the port of entry, where Customs will review the application and conduct an inspection of the goods, or approve the application without an inspection if it falls within the low-risk shipment category. Customs will then issue a permit for admission of the merchandise into the zone. To transfer merchandise from one zone to another zone, managed by the same operator and within the same port of entry, Customs Form 6043 "Delivery Ticket" needs to be used. Ultimately, to remove goods from a foreign-trade zone for domestic consumption, you would use both Customs Form 3461 "Entry/Immediate Delivery" and Customs Form 7501 "Entry Summary." A copy of Customs Form 214 and 7501 are included for your reference.

U.S. Customs and Border Protection Form 214

CENSUS USE ONLY	DEPARTMENT OF HOMELAND SECURITY U.S. Customs and Border Protection **APPLICATION FOR** **FOREIGN-TRADE ZONE ADMISSION** **AND/OR STATUS DESIGNATION** 19 CFR 146.22, 146.32, 146.35-146.37, 146.39-146.41, 146.44, 146.53, 146.66		OMB No. 1651-0029 Exp. 01-31-2010
		1. ZONE NO. AND LOCATION *(Address)*	
		2. PORT CODE	

3. IMPORTING VESSEL (& FLAG)/OTHER CARRIER		4. EXPORT DATE	5. IMPORT DATE	6. ZONE ADMISSION NO.
7. U.S. PORT OF UNLADING	8. FOREIGN PORT OF LADING		9. BILL OF LADING/AWB NO.	10. INWARD M'FEST NO.
11. INBOND CARRIER	12. I.T. NO. AND DATE		13. I.T. FROM *(Port)*	

14. STATISTICAL INFORMATION FURNISHED DIRECTLY TO BUREAU OF CENSUS BY APPLICANT? ☐ YES   ☐ NO

15. NO. OF PACKAGES AND COUNTRY OF ORIGIN CODE	16. DESCRIPTION OF MERCHANDISE	17. HTSUS NO.	18. QUANTITY (HTSUS)	19. GROSS WEIGHT	20. SEPARATE VALUE & AGGR CHGS.
		21. HARBOR MAINTENANCE FEE (19 CFR 24.24) ▶			

22. I hereby apply for admission of the above merchandise into the Foreign-Trade Zone. I declare to the best of my knowledge and belief that the above merchandise is not prohibited entry in the Foreign-Trade Zone within the meaning of section 3 of the Foreign-Trade Zones Act of 1934, as amended, and section 146.31, Customs Regulations.

23. I hereby apply for the status designation indicated:
☐ NONPRIVILEGED FOREIGN (19 CFR 146.42)   ☐ PRIVILEGED FOREIGN (19 CFR 146.41)   ☐ ZONE RESTRICTED (19 CFR 146.44)   ☐ DOMESTIC (19 CFR 146.43)

24. APPLICANT FIRM NAME	25. BY *(Signature)*	26. TITLE	27. DATE
F.T.Z. AGREES TO RECEIVE MERCHANDISE INTO THE ZONE ▶	28. FOR THE F.T.Z. OPERATOR *(Signature)*	29. TITLE	30. DATE

PERMIT	Permission is hereby granted to transfer the above merchandise into the Zone.	31. PORT DIRECTOR OF CBP: BY *(Signature)*	32. TITLE	33. DATE
PERMIT	The above merchandise has been granted the requested status.	34. PORT DIRECTOR OF CBP: BY *(Signature)*	35. TITLE	36. DATE

37. The goods described herein are authorized to be transferred: ☐ without exception   ☐ except as noted below

PERMIT TO TRANSFER	38. CBP OFFICER AT STATION *(Signature)*	39. TITLE	40. STATION	41. DATE
	42. RECEIVED FOR TRANSFER TO ZONE *(Driver's Signature)*	43. CARTMAN	44. CHL NO.	45. DATE

FTZ OPERATOR'S REPORT OF MERCHANDISE RECEIVED AT ZONE	46. To the Port Director of CBP: The above merchandise was received at the Zone on the date shown except as noted below:		
	47. FOR THE FTZ OPERATOR *(Signature)*	48. TITLE	49. DATE

(See page 2 for Paperwork Reduction Act Notice.)   *Previous Editions are Obsolete*   CBP Form 214 (11/09)

U.S. Customs and Border Protection Form 7501

Form Approved OMB No. 1651-0022
EXP. 03-31-2012

DEPARTMENT OF HOMELAND SECURITY
U.S. Customs and Border Protection

ENTRY SUMMARY

1. Filer Code/Entry No.		2. Entry Type	3. Summary Date
4. Surety No.	5. Bond Type	6. Port Code	7. Entry Date

8. Importing Carrier	9. Mode of Transport	10. Country of Origin	11. Import Date
12. B/L or AWB No.	13. Manufacturer ID	14. Exporting Country	15. Export Date
16. I.T. No.	17. I.T. Date	18. Missing Docs	19. Foreign Port of Lading	20. U.S. Port of Unlading
21. Location of Goods/G.O. No.	22. Consignee No.	23. Importer No.	24. Reference No.

25. Ultimate Consignee Name and Address

26. Importer of Record Name and Address

City   State   Zip

City   State   Zip

27. Line No.	28. Description of Merchandise			32.	33.	34.
	29. A. HTSUS No. B. ADA/CVD No.	30. A. Grossweight B. Manifest Qty.	31. Net Quantity in HTSUS Units	A. Entered Value B. CHGS C. Relationship	A. HTSUS Rate B. ADA/CVD Rate C. IRC Rate D. Visa No.	Duty and I.R. Tax Dollars Cents

Other Fee Summary for Block 39	35. Total Entered Value	CBP USE ONLY		TOTALS
	$	A. LIQ CODE	B. Ascertained Duty	37. Duty
	Total Other Fees	REASON CODE	C. Ascertained Tax	38. Tax
	$		D. Ascertained Other	39. Other

36. DECLARATION OF IMPORTER OF RECORD (OWNER OR PURCHASER) OR AUTHORIZED AGENT

| | E. Ascertained Total | 40. Total |

I declare that I am the ☐ Importer of record and that the actual owner, purchaser, or consignee for CBP purposes is as shown above, **OR** ☐ owner or purchaser or agent thereof. I further declare that the merchandise ☐ was obtained pursuant to a purchase or agreement to purchase and that the prices set forth in the invoices are true, **OR** ☐ was not obtained pursuant to a purchase or agreement to purchase and the statements in the invoices as to value or price are true to the best of my knowledge and belief. I also declare that the statements in the documents herein filed fully disclose to the best of my knowledge and belief the true prices, values, quantities, rebates, drawbacks, fees, commissions, and royalties and are true and correct, and that all goods or services provided to the seller of the merchandise either free or at reduced cost are fully disclosed.
I will immediately furnish to the appropriate CBP officer any information showing a different statement of facts.

41. DECLARANT NAME	TITLE	SIGNATURE	DATE

42. Broker/Filer Information (Name, address, phone number)	43. Broker/Importer File No.

CBP Form 7501 (06/09)

While operating under foreign-trade zone status, the usual entry procedures and duty payments normally required by Customs on the entry of foreign merchandise are not applicable. Customary entry procedures and duty payment only apply at the time the merchandise enters the domestic market for consumption. At that time, the importer makes the determination of which duty rate would apply to the merchandise because you could pay duty on the original foreign materials —components for manufacturing of the final product — or on the final product. This is because at times, the duty rate on the final product is significantly less than the duty rate that would be paid on the individual components — it is called inverted duty.

For example, a halter (for horses or dogs) manufacturing company imports most of the raw materials — nylon webbing, rings, and clasps — from foreign countries to manufacture the halters in the United States. By the time all the costs of the raw materials and its respective duties paid are added up, along with the cost of labor, the finished product may have cost the manufacturer $5.00. However, if that same manufacturer imports the raw materials under foreign-trade zone status, not paying duty on those products, the final cost of manufacturing will be less. Taking it a step further, if the manufacturer sells the finished halter in the domestic market, he or she will only be paying duty on the halter itself, which may have a much lower duty rate than the individual duty rate of each of the components. In addition, the duty will be paid at the time the merchandise leaves the zone rather than when it was originally imported, thus delaying the payment of the duty.

Advantages of a foreign-trade zone

Foreign-trade zones offer many advantages to the business community. Even though the foreign-trade zones program has certain limitations and restrictions, the significant financial advantages often justifies operating under foreign-trade zone status. One of the biggest mistakes that a large number of international trade business owners make is that they do not plan adequately for its Customs duty payments, and operating under foreign-trade zone status allows the importer or exporter to avoid normal duties, quotas, federal excise taxes, and inventory taxes. It saves you time and money, but most of all it allows you to remain competitive in the global market. The following are the most common benefits that can be experienced while operating as a foreign-trade zone:

- Unlike TIBs, which are used when it is anticipated that the goods will be destroyed or re-exported within one to three years as permitted by these bonds, foreign-trade zones do not have such restrictions and have much more flexibility with the manipulation of the merchandise within the zone than when imported under a TIB.

- With foreign-trade zones, the avoidance of paying Customs duties is a significant advantage over Customs drawback. With drawback, the importer must pay the duties immediately and rely upon the Customs procedures to obtain the rebate of its duties. Although drawback allows free movement of merchandise within the U.S. Customs territory, the disadvantages of extensive documentation and the uncertainty of the outcome of the claim for drawback make using a foreign-trade zone more appealing.

- You can import and test new manufacturing equipment and send it back if you choose not to purchase it, without paying duty.

- Imported merchandise intended for re-export can be brought into a foreign-trade zone, manipulated as needed, and exported without paying duties.

- Duty is only paid on the imported value of the item less the scrap value. Imported value is the value of the product before adding the value of labor, overhead, and profit.

- You can import foreign merchandise and store it without time limitations, until such time that market conditions are more favorable, therefore increasing your profit margin on those goods.

- Imported goods that are not considered market worthy can be returned to the foreign supplier without having to pay any duty.

The number of companies that take advantage of operating under foreign-trade zone status are many, and the number continues to grow as more companies are realizing the significant savings available to them through this program. Automobile manufacturing companies and pharmaceutical companies are some of the biggest users of the foreign-trade zone program. Some of the other companies operating under foreign-trade zone status, to name a few, include Dell Computer (FTZ 183A), Conair Corporation (FTZ 75A), and Fuji Photo Film (FTZ 38C).

Disadvantages of foreign-trade zones

Although there are numerous advantages to operating under foreign-trade zone status, there are some drawbacks. For instance, foreign-trade zones are highly regulated, and there are strict recordkeeping and reporting requirements. The grantee of the foreign-trade zone is responsible for reporting its activities to the FTZ Board on an annual basis. Reports are intricate, requiring detailed information on operations such as the specific number of goods or components used in manufacturing that were imported, how many were scrapped, and how many were exported or entered into the domestic market.

In addition, a Security Manual and Operations Manual must be developed to meet Customs requirements and must ultimately be approved by Customs before you can begin operations under foreign-trade zone status. Failure to adhere to requirements outlined in the manuals or failure to comply with the foreign-trade zones regulations may result in the assessment of significant penalties by the FTZ Board.

Also, the initial set-up and start-up costs to operate as a foreign-trade zone can be quite expensive, especially if you need to upgrade your facility's security system. There are also application fees to the FTZ Board and consulting fees if you hire consultants to help you with the process.

Determining if foreign-trade zones are right for you

The advantages of operating under foreign-trade zone status are many, and the idea may seem quite appealing for the type of business you are engaged in or are considering starting. However, all factors — operational and financial — must be taken into consideration before taking such a leap. The following foreign-trade zones savings worksheet is a powerful tool that can be used to provide you with a general idea of the potential savings that can be achieved by operating under foreign-trade zone status, as well as providing you with a possible scenario as to where you can cut costs using this program. This worksheet has been used for many years by the National Association of Foreign-trade Zones for training purposes, as well as by countless prospective foreign-trade zone users to help them determine the financial feasibility of the program for their particular business.

In addition, the International Trade Administration's Web site contains a wealth of information on the foreign-trade zones program, including a simplified duty savings estimator for foreign-trade zone manufacturing. The form is an automated worksheet that can be used by small- to medium-sized U.S. manufacturers to complete a basic assessment of possible duty-saving opportunities if they were to operate under foreign-trade zone status. The worksheet can be found at **www.ia.ita.doc.gov/ftzpage/info/savingscalc.pdf**.

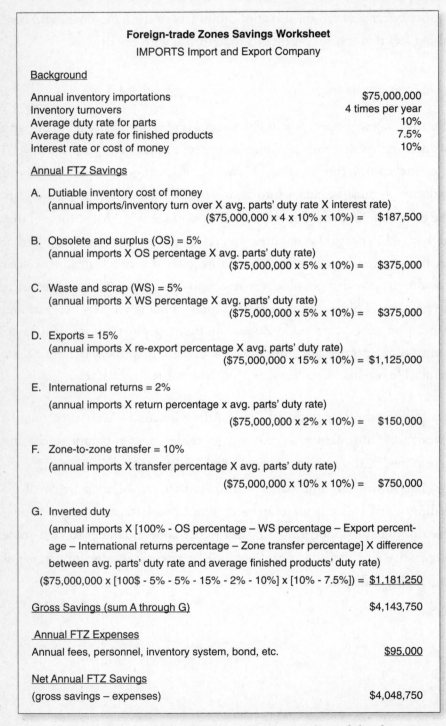

Foreign-trade Zones Savings Worksheet

IMPORTS Import and Export Company

Background

Annual inventory importations	$75,000,000
Inventory turnovers	4 times per year
Average duty rate for parts	10%
Average duty rate for finished products	7.5%
Interest rate or cost of money	10%

Annual FTZ Savings

A. Dutiable inventory cost of money
(annual imports/inventory turn over X avg. parts' duty rate X interest rate)
($75,000,000 x 4 x 10% x 10%) = $187,500

B. Obsolete and surplus (OS) = 5%
(annual imports X OS percentage X avg. parts' duty rate)
($75,000,000 x 5% x 10%) = $375,000

C. Waste and scrap (WS) = 5%
(annual imports X WS percentage X avg. parts' duty rate)
($75,000,000 x 5% x 10%) = $375,000

D. Exports = 15%
(annual imports X re-export percentage X avg. parts' duty rate)
($75,000,000 x 15% x 10%) = $1,125,000

E. International returns = 2%
(annual imports X return percentage x avg. parts' duty rate)
($75,000,000 x 2% x 10%) = $150,000

F. Zone-to-zone transfer = 10%
(annual imports X transfer percentage X avg. parts' duty rate)
($75,000,000 x 10% x 10%) = $750,000

G. Inverted duty
(annual imports X [100% - OS percentage – WS percentage – Export percentage – International returns percentage – Zone transfer percentage] X difference
between avg. parts' duty rate and average finished products' duty rate)
($75,000,000 x [100$ - 5% - 5% - 15% - 2% - 10%] x [10% - 7.5%]) = $1,181,250

Gross Savings (sum A through G) $4,143,750

 Annual FTZ Expenses

Annual fees, personnel, inventory system, bond, etc. $95,000

Net Annual FTZ Savings

(gross savings – expenses) $4,048,750

Please see accompanying CD-ROM for a blank template of this form.

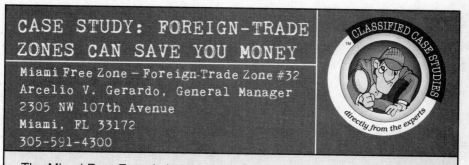

CASE STUDY: FOREIGN-TRADE ZONES CAN SAVE YOU MONEY

Miami Free Zone — Foreign-Trade Zone #32
Arcelio V. Gerardo, General Manager
2305 NW 107th Avenue
Miami, FL 33172
305-591-4300

The Miami Free Zone is located in the International Epicenter for Trade and Commerce of the Americas, just a few minutes from the Miami International Airport. The zone comprises over 850,000 square feet of mixed-use office, showroom, and warehouse space. It houses more than 80 international companies involved in the import and export of wholesale and duty-free distribution activities. Some of the companies housed in the Miami Free Zone include Bulgari, Richemont Latin America (parent company of Cartier, Dunhill, and Mont Blanc), Lenox, Brightstar Corporation, NSK, Sysco Food Services, Apex USA (U.S. distribution center for the government of Brazil), and government agencies such as U.S. Customs and Border Protection.

The zone is owned and managed by CV Miami, LLC, a partnership managed by the New York company Cargo Ventures. FTZ World Services, however, is the private operator of the zone, providing technology services and operations consulting, in compliance with Customs regulations, to its tenants. The operator also provides the zone's tenants with the tools, on an Internet-based platform, to manage the required documentation for their operations as well as their inventory.

General Manager Arcelio Gerardo cannot stress enough the advantages of operating in a foreign-trade zone. "There are significant savings by elimination and deferral in payment of Customs duties, fees, and taxes," he said. "FTZs offer companies financial benefits and increased convenience, efficiency, productivity, expedited cargo movement, and flexibility related to imported goods."

Another advantage, according to Gerardo, is that implementing heightened security measures, as required by Customs for foreign-trade zones, results in lower insurance costs and fewer incidents of loss of cargo imported into the zones. In addition, Gerardo said the main benefit offered by the FTZ is that merchandise may be admitted into an FTZ without going through formal Customs entry procedures, and the ability to defer, reduce, or even eliminate Customs duties on products admitted to the Zone.

The Miami Free Zone has been witness to many success stories of companies of all sizes starting operations in the zone and experiencing tremendous growth. The zone provides an incubator environment for small businesses that want to grow and compete in the international market with medium and large companies. "The deferment, reduction, and elimination of Customs duties, merchandise-processing fees, federal excise taxes, and Customs brokerage fees are prime examples of why the Miami Free Zone is an intelligent business location," Gerardo said.

Using Customs Bonded Warehouses to Your Advantage

Bonded warehouses are facilities that operate under a Customs bond. Goods can be brought into these warehouses and the payment of duty is deferred until such time that the goods enter U.S. Customs territory. Authority to establish bonded warehouses is provided in Title 19, Code of Federal Regulations, Section 1555. As an importer, you can apply to Customs for authorization to establish a bonded warehouse on your own premises. You can also take advantage of the benefits of operating in a bonded warehouse by utilizing the services of bonded public warehouses (warehouses where multiple users lease space). A Customs bond must be secured in order to guarantee payment of the duty that would be owned on that merchandise in case the merchandise is purposely or accidentally entered into U.S. commerce. The bond is secured through the completion of Customs Form 301, "Customs Bond."

In a bonded warehouse facility, goods are brought in and stored for up to five years, at which time goods must either be re-exported or entered in to the U.S. commerce for consumption. If they are withdrawn and entered into the U.S. commerce, duty will be paid on the current value of the goods rather than the duty that would have been owed at the time of admission into the bonded warehouse. Goods in a bonded warehouse can be marked, re-labeled, manipulated, sorted, or repackaged. Any form of manipulation of this sort is allowed, but unlike foreign-trade zones, manufacturing of any kind is prohibited.

Classes of bonded warehouses

There are 11 different classes of bonded warehouses as authorized by Title 19, Code of Federal Regulations, Section 19.1 (19 CFR 19.1). Class 10 warehouse is "Reserved," meaning that a classification has not yet been defined under this class.

Class 1: Facilities that are owned or leased by the government to store goods that are being inspected by Customs are under seizure, or those that are awaiting final release.

Class 2: Private bonded warehouses that are owned and operated by the importer, used solely to store goods that are consigned to or owned by the proprietor.

Class 3: Public bonded warehouses that are used exclusively to store imported goods.

Class 4: Bonded yards or sheds used to store merchandise that is too heavy and bulky to store in a conventional warehouse facility. This classification also includes corrals and stables used to shelter imported animals and tanks used to store liquid product imported in bulk.

Class 5: Bonded bins or parts of buildings used to store grain. These portions of the building that are bonded need to be separated from the rest of the building to secure the integrity of the goods stored under bond.

Class 6: Bonded warehouses used for manufacturing in-bond, or products made wholly or partially of imported components or components that are subject to internal revenue tax. In addition, these facilities can be used to manufacture cigars made from imported tobacco.

Class 7: Bonded warehouses used for smelting and refinishing imported metal-bearing materials, which will be either exported or admitted for domestic consumption.

Class 8: Bonded warehouses established for the sole purpose of cleaning, repackaging, sorting, or changing the condition of imported goods. There is absolutely no manufacturing allowed in this class of bonded warehouses.

Class 9: These are the bonded warehouses known as "duty-free stores" where duty-free merchandise is sold outside Customs territory. Merchandise from these warehouses is sold in places such as airports where the buyer of the products is departing from U.S. Customs territory.

Class 10: Reserved.

Class 11: Bonded warehouses established for the purpose of storing and disposing general order merchandise, exclusively. General order merchandise, as described in Title 19, Section 127.1 of the Code of Federal Regulations (19 CFR 127.1), is merchandise that has not been claimed or entered for 15 days after it arrived in the U.S. or final destination for in-bond shipments. These bonded warehouses are also known as "general order warehouses."

Applying to Establish a Bonded Warehouse

The application process to establish a Customs bonded warehouse is much simpler than the application and approval process to establish a foreign-trade zone. To establish a bonded warehouse, the importer must submit an application to the U.S. Customs and Border Protection district director for the area where you are considering establishing the bonded warehouse. The application package must include the following information:

- An application letter stating the physical address of the proposed facility, as well as specifying the type of bonded warehouse you anticipate operating. In addition, the application must include a general description of the merchandise that will be brought into the warehouse, the estimated amount of duties and taxes that could become due at any one given time, and whether the warehouse will be used for private storage or as a public warehouse.

- A blueprint of the building or facility that will be under bond.

- A certificate of fire insurance coverage for the facility.

- Certification by the warehouse owner that the inventory control and recordkeeping system that will be used in the warehouse meets Customs requirements.

- Application fee.

- At least a $5,000 bond on the facility — this amount will vary depending on the type of bonded warehouse for which the application is being submitted.

- If the warehouse to be bonded is a tank, all pipelines, outlets, and inlets must be identified in the blueprint. In addition, a gauge table, certified by the tank owner as accurate, must also be included showing the capacity of the tank in gallons per inch of height.

- When the entire facility is not to be used as a bonded warehouse, the application package must also include a detailed description of the materials used in the construction of the partitions to separate the bonded merchandise from the rest of the merchandise being stored in that facility.

- Applications for Class 11 warehouses (general order warehouses) must demonstrate that the proposed site will meet the minimum space requirements, as directed by the port director, to accommodate the storage of such merchandise.

As part of the application process, the Customs port director may request a set of fingerprints and a list containing the names and addresses of all the company principals, officers, and employees. He or she may also assign a Customs officer to conduct an inquiry as to the qualifications, character, and experience of the individual requesting approval to operate a bonded warehouse. The inquiry would include information such as credit and personal references, personal history, and financial and business data. Also, before approval is granted, the port director will conduct a security inspection to ensure that the physical security of the facility meets Customs requirements.

Once the application has been reviewed and processed by Customs, the port director notifies the applicant in writing as to his decision. If the application has been denied, the letter will state the reasons for the denial. If the application to establish a bonded warehouse is approved, a bond must be executed on Customs Form 301.

U.S. Customs and Border Protection Form CF 301 — Customs Bond

DEPARTMENT OF HOMELAND SECURITY
U.S. Customs and Border Protection

CUSTOMS BOND

19 CFR Part 113

OMB No. 1651-0050 Exp. 12-31-2010

| CBP USE ONLY | BOND NUMBER 1 (Assigned by CBP) |
| | FILE REFERENCE |

In order to secure payment of any duty, tax or charge and compliance with law or regulation as a result of activity covered by any condition referenced below, we, the below named principal(s) and surety(ies), bind ourselves to the United States in the amount or amounts, as set forth below.

Execution Date

SECTION I--Select Single Transaction OR Continuous Bond (not both) and fill in the applicable blank spaces.

| ☐ **SINGLE TRANSACTION BOND** | Identification of transaction secured by this bond (e.g., entry no., seizure no., etc.) | | Date of transaction | Port code |
| ☐ **CONTINUOUS BOND** | Effective date | This bond remains in force for one year beginning with the effective date and for each succeeding annual period, or until terminated. This bond constitutes a separate bond for each period in the amounts listed below for liabilities that accrue in each period. The intention to terminate this bond must be conveyed within the period and manner prescribed in the Customs Regulations. | | |

SECTION II-- This bond includes the following conditions, except that, 1a may be checked independently or with 1, and 3a may be checked independently or with 3. Line out all other parts of this section that are not used.

Activity Code	Activity Name and Customs Regulations in which conditions codified	Limit of Liability	Activity Code	Activity Name and Customs Regulations in which conditions codified	Limit of Liability
☐ 1	Importer or broker 113.62		☐ 5	Public Gauger. 113.67	
☐ 1a	Drawback Payments Refunds 113.65		☐ 6	Wool & Fur Products Labeling Acts Importation (Single Entry Only) 113.68	
☐ 2	Custodian of bonded merchandise. . . . . 113.63 (Includes bonded carriers, freight forwarders, cartmen and lightermen, all classes of warehouse, container station operators)		☐ 7	Bill of Lading (Single Entry Only) 113.69	
☐ 3	International Carrier. 113.64		☐ 8	Detention of Copyrighted Material (Single Entry Only). 113.70	
☐ 3a	Instruments of International Traffic 113.66		☐ 9	Neutrality (Single Entry Only) 113.71	
☐ 4	Foreign Trade Zone Operator. 113.73		☐ 10	Court Costs for Condemned Goods (Single Entry Only) 113.72	

SECTION III-- List below all tradenames or unincorporated divisions that will be permitted to obligate this bond in the principal's name including their CBP identification Number(s). 3 (If more space is needed, use Section III (Continuation) on back of form.)

Importer Number	Importer Name	Importer Number	Importer Name
		Total number of importer names listed in Section III:	

Principal and surety agree that any charge against the bond under any of the listed names is as though it was made by the principal(s).

Principal and surety agree that they are bound to the same extent as if they executed a separate bond covering each set of conditions incorporated by reference to the Customs Regulations into this bond.

If the surety fails to appoint an agent under Title 6, United States Code, Section 7, surety consents to service on the Clerk of any United States District Court or the U.S. Court of International Trade, where suit is brought on this bond. That clerk is to send notice of the service to the surety at:

Mailing Address Requested by the Surety

	Name and Address	Importer No. 3	
PRINCIPAL 4		SIGNATURE 5	SEAL
PRINCIPAL 4	Name and Address	Importer No. 3	
		SIGNATURE 5	SEAL
SURETY 4, 6	Name and Address 6	Surety No. 7	
		SIGNATURE 5	SEAL
SURETY 4, 6	Name and Address 6	Surety No. 7	
		SIGNATURE 5	SEAL
SURETY AGENTS	Name 8	Identification No. 9	Name 8	Identification No. 9

PART 1 - CBP, PART 2 - SURETY, PART 3 - PRINCIPAL

CBP Form 301 (05/98)

Bonded Warehouse Operations

Goods are entered into a bonded warehouse by making a warehouse entry using the Entry Summary Form — CF 7501, marked with the appropriate type of code applicable for warehouse entries and specifying the bonded warehouse in which the goods will be stored. Making this type of entry eliminates the need to pay estimated duties, thus paying the correct amount of duty at the time the merchandise is removed from the bonded warehouse for domestic consumption. Imported goods may be maintained in a Customs bonded warehouse for up to five years from the date of importation.

Although security and recordkeeping requirements are strictly regulated by Customs, operating a bonded warehouse is not that much different from operating a regular warehouse distribution facility. Another aspect to keep in mind about a bonded warehouse operation is that a strict inventory control system must be established, and adhered to, at all times. Merchandise in a bonded warehouse must always be accounted for, and bonded merchandise must be kept separate and not commingled with domestic goods. Bonded warehouses are closely supervised by U.S. Customs, and as part of normal operating procedures, Customs may supervise any transaction at any time. For instance, the owner of the warehouse is required to take a physical annual inventory of all the products within the bonded warehouse. When such inventory is scheduled to take place, Customs must be notified in case they want to be present during the inventory process. In addition, Customs may conduct periodic audits of the owner's records, inventory the merchandise, and spot check random warehouse transactions.

One of the most successful bonded warehouse applications is that of distribution. Merchandise can be imported into a bonded warehouse, where it is repackaged, labeled, and prepared for shipping for multiple companies. Looking at it from the small importer's point of view, there are significant savings in taking advantage of such operations. The importer will be saving money by not having to invest a large amount of money to set up a distribution center if the influx of merchandise is not large enough to justify it.

Due to the nature of a bonded warehouse operation, where goods are being imported without paying duties at that time, there is going to be a paper trail to keep track of the merchandise to ensure the timely and payment of duties when due. There are forms to be completed and filed with Customs at the time entry of the goods is made, as well as forms that must be completed when merchandise is transferred from one bonded warehouse to another, exported, or entered into Customs territory for domestic consumption. For example, within 45 calendar days from the end of the business's fiscal year, the owner of the warehouse must prepare Customs Form 300 — Bonded Warehouse Proprietor's Submission — and keep it on file for five years from the end of the fiscal year. The form itself is not submitted to Customs; rather, the warehouse's owner must submit a letter to Customs within ten days from the preparation of CF 300, notifying Customs that the form has been prepared, that it is accurate, and that it is available for their review. When in doubt about any rules, regulations, or procedures related to the operation or use of a bonded warehouse, the best thing to do is to review the specific section in the Code of Federal Regulations that address that particular issue. The penalties assessed by Customs for infractions conducted in the operation of a bonded warehouse can be quite significant.

U.S. Customs Form CF 300: Bonded Warehouse Proprietor's Submission

DEPARTMENT OF HOMELAND SECURITY U.S. Customs and Border Protection									OMB No. 1651-0033 Expires 08/31/2012
BONDED WAREHOUSE PROPRIETOR'S SUBMISSION 19 CFR 19.12 (a)(5)								1. IRS Identification No.	
2. Name of Warehouse Facility		3. Address			4. Name of Contact Person			5. Telephone No.	
A. Entry No. and Date of Importation	B. Description of Merchandise	QUANTITY		BREAKAGE		G. Beginning Inventory Quantity	H. Ending Inventory Quantity	I. Date Entry Closed and Forwarded to CBP	
		C. Per Entry	D. Over/Short on Receipt	E. Upon Receipt Quantity	F. In Warehouse Quantity				
	'								
6. Total Number of Entries Reported	CERTIFICATION								
	I hereby certify that the information contained in this submission completely and accurately represents all entry transactions as well as beginning and ending inventories of _____ warehouse facility for the year ending _____. (Name)								
7. Signature	8. Title		9. Name of Company				10. Date		

(Paperwork Reduction Notice and Instructions on reverse)   CBP Form 300 (08/09)

Advantages of a bonded warehouse

The main advantage of operating your import export business in a bonded warehouse setting is the deferral of duty payment. If you are definitely interested in some form of duty-payment deferral program, you might want to consider the advantages of establishing a bonded warehouse. For instance, bonded warehouses can be established on the user's facility with much more ease than a foreign-trade zone. In addition, the costs associated with establishing and operating a bonded warehouse are much less than the costs associated with that of a foreign-trade zone. Goods stored in bonded warehouses may be transferred, with some exceptions, from one bonded warehouse to another.

As it is the case with foreign-trade zones, bonded warehouses can also be used to store certain quota merchandise, and the duty owed on merchandise that has been manipulated in a bonded warehouse is determined at the time of withdrawal from the warehouse. Another advantage of operating or keeping your goods in a bonded warehouse is that should the anticipated buyer of the imported goods back out, you can always sell your merchandise abroad and never pay duties on those goods.

Disadvantages of a bonded warehouse

Operating your import export business using a bonded warehouse also has some disadvantages. The most evident disadvantage is the limitation on the type of manipulation allowed on imported goods. Goods may be cleaned, relabeled, and repackaged; however, manufacturing is not allowed. In addition, there is also a time limit as to how long you can keep your merchandise in the bonded warehouse, which is only five years. Another disadvantage is that there is no duty relief on waste and damaged merchandise — duty is owed on the entire shipment brought into the bonded warehouse. Lastly, in a bonded warehouse situation, there is the constant need to secure a bond — each time an entry is made into the warehouse, some type of bond must be secured.

CASE STUDY: SUCCESSFUL FAMILY-OWNED AND OPERATED IMPORT EXPORT BUSINESS

Carlos Manresa, Former Owner
International Consolidated
and Freight Forwarders
Miami, FL

"Operating International Consolidated and Freight Forwarders as a family-owned and operated import export business was the most rewarding business venture I ever entered into in my professional life," said Carlos Manresa, owner of an import and export business. Manresa started the business in a small, 200-square-foot warehouse in Miami, Florida, exporting goods to a few countries in Latin America. As he became more familiar and knowledgeable about the international trade industry, he was able to expand his facility and operations to an 18,000-square-foot facility, where they processed between ten to 14 cargo containers and 30 to 40 air shipments a week.

Service to his customers became the No. 1 goal; meeting the needs of the customers while meeting Customs rules and regulations were key to the business's success. Looking back at his business, Manresa feels that operating a bonded warehouse for eight years certainly had its challenges, but it also turned into a great opportunity to expand their services. Throughout the life of the business, he strived to maintain a positive working relationship with the Customs agents in the corresponding port of entry, looking at them more as partners in his import export business rather than just a regulatory agency. He also found it important to stay on top of changes in the industry and was member of several international trade organizations, such as the Air International Transportation Association (AITA), which provided excellent benefits to its members.

International Consolidated and Freight Forwarders was licensed to operate as a U.S. Customs Freight Station, Non-Vessel Operators Common Carrier (NVOCC), and as a bonded warehouse. "As a bonded warehouse, the advantages of being able to bring in multiple bonded containers at a time and then having the capability of making withdrawals as needed was advantageous," Manresa said. However, he feels it is important to remember that when you have such a large operation and work with imports from all over the world, you run the risk of having illegal cargo infiltrated within the legal cargo that was expected to come in. Nevertheless, being mindful of that and trusting your intuition if something does not look or feel right, the best thing to do is contact the authorities immediately.

After 28 years of operations, Manresa was forced to close the business due to health reasons, but said that if he had the opportunity, he would do it all over again. "I loved the international trade business — it was challenging and very rewarding at the end of the day."

Carlos Manresa is now retired in Daytona Beach, Florida.

Chapter 11

Marketing and Advertising

Marketing is described as the activities or efforts taken to move your products and services from the producers or manufacturers to the consumers so that their needs and wants are met. To accomplish this, you must implement a strong marketing mix, or follow the famous four Ps of marketing: product, price, promotion, and place.

The word "product" is all-encompassing, including the product itself and its characteristics, such as its label and packaging. In this case, you must examine your business as a whole rather than one product in particular. "Price" involves all aspects of the pricing strategy. "Promotion" includes public relations and advertising. It is getting the word out, to the right audience, that you have an import export business, that you provide certain services, and that you are involved in a particular line of products of importation, exportation, or both. Lastly, "place" has to do with the distribution system of the product — where the consumer can obtain the product or service. In this case, "consumer" does not have to be the ultimate consumer of your products, but could be a distributor abroad or a local supplier.

Marketing and advertising can make or break your business. Effective marketing — spending your marketing dollars wisely to suit your business needs — will make your business. However, marketing your business to the wrong audience can break your business, as you will be literally wasting your marketing dollars without getting anything in return. In a business, it is all about making the right decisions as to how to spend your money wisely to see the biggest return on your investment. The industry standard for marketing and advertising for startup or small- to medium-sized companies is between 15 to 20 percent of the company's revenues. For your first year of operation, the amount that you set aside for marketing will more than likely be a good guess than anything else, but do not hold back.

With the importance of marketing your business in the first year of operation in mind, the best way to ensure that your marketing and advertising dollars are going to be spent where you will get the most in return is to prepare a strong marketing plan that will meet your specific business's needs. Once you have that in place, the rest of your marketing efforts will unfold from there, creating quite an effective all-encompassing marketing program for your business.

The Marketing Plan

Although marketing strategies were briefly discussed as part of the business plan in Chapter 4, the actual marketing plan will be addressed in depth in the pages that follow. Marketing plans are as diverse and flexible as business plans, and they can be just as complex and lengthy as business plans, or they can be simple and easy to follow. But a good marketing plan must be size-appropriate. In other words, if you have a small- to medium-sized import export company, it would not make any sense to prepare a marketing plan patterned after a plan that was developed for a large company. There are various marketing plan formats available, but the marketing plan you choose to follow has to be molded to suit your particular business needs; otherwise, it will not work.

In essence, the marketing plan is simply putting everything in writing (so that it can be followed) — the process, or the steps that you must take to reach your target audience and persuade them to acquire your products or services. As a plan, you should try to adhere to it as much as possible, but you should always be prepared to deviate from it to accommodate unforeseen situations that may occur entirely out of your control, such as changes in the economy, both domestically and internationally. You can use the following basic marketing plan, which contains the basic information of a plan, as your guide. This can be easily adjusted to fit your business's needs:

I.   Objectives

This section of the plan should be to-the-point and straightforward. What is it that you ultimately want to accomplish? State what type of revenue you anticipate achieving as a result of your marketing efforts, and whether you foresee expanding your services and products to certain countries through aggressive marketing efforts.

II.   Situation Analysis

The exercise of preparing this section of the marketing plan is a powerful tool in itself because it forces you to take a hard look at your current business status. This section addresses your current business situation, which provides you with an excellent benchmark to work from as you shape your marketing plan. Begin by drafting a brief but concise description of your current products or services. Discuss possible external influences that could affect your business in the next 12-month period. Influences such as changes in free trade agreements, quotas, or even embargoes that could either have a detrimental effect in your business or a positive one, depending on the action taken. Address the marketing advantages and disadvantages of your business or products, including any potential threats by your competition.

III.   Goals

Discuss your business's marketing goals for the next 12-month period. These goals must be specific in nature, as well as realistic and measurable, allowing you the opportunity to reach them and later evaluate how well you did. Goals such as "penetrate new markets" are too vague and difficult to measure, but if you state "penetrate the Latin American market in the Caribbean," it would be a lot easier to measure whether that goal was reached.

IV.   Target Audience

Whom are you trying to reach with your marketing efforts? Are you trying to reach suppliers, manufacturers, distributors, governmental agencies in foreign countries, or all of the above? Try to be as specific as possible, as quite often your target audience will dictate how you proceed with your marketing efforts. Not all audiences are reached in the same manner. This is also an excellent opportunity to forecast future markets you want to reach, thus including them in your target audience list.

V.   Action Plan

This will be the longest section of your marketing plan. It will get to the specifics as to the actions you anticipate taking to meet your marketing objectives.

A. Strategies and tactics

List and describe the strategies you plan to undertake — including the tactics you will use to implement them — that will result in your accomplishing your marketing goals. Tactics should include things such as direct mail-outs, special promotions, trade shows, and public relations activities. For example, with your goal of penetrating the Latin American market in the Caribbean, you may want to develop a strategy that involves personally promoting your products and services to this segment of the market, and one of your tactics is to attend international trade shows hosted in these countries.

B. *Schedule of activities*

You have set your goals, you have outlined your strategies, and you have set your tactics. Now you need to list the specific activities or actions you will take to achieve those goals. For example, include a list of upcoming trade missions and trade shows of interest to you — complete with dates, location, and duration of the show. Also include a list of potential suppliers, distributors, or manufacturers you want to meet with during the following 12 months. Include their address, phone number, and other contact information, along with possible dates and locations where to meet.

VI.   Budget

The budget is the last element of the marketing plan. This section should include a breakdown of all the costs associated with implementing the marketing plan. Try to be as detailed and accurate as possible so that you will not run into a shortage toward the end of your budget year. Take into account every possible expense, and pay particular attention to any travel abroad that you may schedule, as you will incur additional expenses than if you were to travel domestically. Another issue to take into consideration when budgeting for foreign travel is the rate for currency exchange.

Remember that you want this document to be a "live" document in that you can go back from time to time and make necessary changes, such as in the budget section. For instance, as you become aware of any changes that may impact your budget, you should make the appropriate changes to reflect the adjustment so that you have a pretty solid idea of what your marketing budget actually looks like.

A template to of this marketing plan is available in the accompanying CD-ROM for your use.

Using the Internet

The Internet has become the No. 1 source of reference for most business people today. Whether you are looking for specific information on a product or looking for a distributor of such product in your area, nine times out of ten, the Internet will be used as the source. Although there are several ways of getting your company's name to your target market's attention, having a presence on the Internet will guarantee the most exposure.

Securing a domain name

The first step to achieving that exposure is to secure and register a domain name. A domain name is an identification label for a realm or authority on the Internet. Although securing a domain name does not afford you legal ownership of that name, it does provide you with the exclusive right to use that name. To register your domain name, you must obtain the services of one of many accredited domain name registrars. For a list of accredited registrars, visit the ICANN's Web site at **www.icann.org**. ICANN — Internet Corporation for Assigned Names and Numbers — is the agency responsible for certifying companies as domain name registrars.

The cost to register your domain name includes an annual fee and varies from registrar to registrar. There are laws that regulate domain name registration such as registering a copyrighted name. Also, you can register your domain name for a minimum of a year, but no longer than ten without renewing the domain name registration contract.

Developing a Web site

Basically, a Web site is a global portal to your business. Due to great advances in technology and the role the Internet plays in today's marketplace, the international trade industry has come to rely heavily on the Internet to obtain and conduct business. Because of that, it is essential that you have a well-designed, attractive, and functional Web site for your business. Your Web site should be user-friendly, informative, visually appealing and, most of all, current. In addition to using your Web site primarily to promote your products and services, your Web site can also become the backbone to your company's operation.

There is a wide variety of software programs available — too many to mention — that will guide you through the process of developing your own Web site. These programs can be purchased in department stores, office supply stores and, of course, online. However, unless you are knowledgeable and experienced in Web site development, you may want to leave this task to the experts. A great Web site is one of the most crucial elements for the success of your business, so this is not the place to cut corners. When you contract with a Web designer to develop your Web site, there are a number of elements you want to make sure are addressed. For instance, you want a layout that makes it easy to navigate and that displays your products and services clearly. If you are selling your products or services via that Web site, make sure the checkout process is simple. Also, provide the customer with a phone number where they can contact your company for questions and product inquiries. This will demonstrate that there is a solid business behind the Web site. Other elements to keep in mind during the development of your Web site are:

- Being in the international trade business, it is essential that you have your information available in a couple of different languages, giving you the capability of reaching the greatest number of people in foreign countries.

- Use the home page to clearly state the purpose of your Web site and create an image of your company you want site visitors to get.

- Title each page clearly, and make them easy to navigate.

- Do not overcrowd the site with too many graphics that will delay downloading your page.

- Make sure the text is concise and easy to read. If you get too wordy, you may lose the reader's interest, and they may miss the one piece of information that would make the sale. Also, the color of the text is important — sometimes the color of the text makes it difficult to read against the background.

- Pay particular attention to the photos you use to illustrate your products or services. The photos should be large enough to see the product clearly while highlighting key features.

- Keep your worldwide audience in mind. Develop a Web site that portrays a professional image of your company, and avoid using any material that could be offensive to other cultures.

Once your Web site is done, the next most important step is to promote the site to generate traffic. One of the main traffic generators is to register the site with several search engines. You should also promote your site in all your advertising, company literature, and your company's promotional materials. Lastly, visit your own Web site regularly for maintenance purposes, such as checking your links to make sure they work properly.

Advertising

Advertising your import export business needs to be handled differently from advertising a business that provides services locally, such as law firms or car dealerships. Being such a specialized industry, it will require that your advertising target those who work within the international trade industry. Your target market, more than likely, will not be found locally, but rather widely spread out. Thus, your method of advertising should be through widespread channels such as the Internet. You must think outside the box and use alternative forms of advertising, such as joining chat groups and networking sites as a means of getting the information out, thereby advertising your goods and services.

There are numerous networking sites online, but your best option is to join business networking sites such as LinkedIn® and chat groups, such as the international trade chat groups sponsored by Yahoo!® LinkedIn is a networking site connecting professionals of some 170 different industries, representing some 200 countries from around the world. Joining a networking site like this can prove to be quite rewarding, not only because of the contacts you can make, but also because of its potential to generate new customers. Likewise, some of Yahoo!'s international trade-related chat groups are great places to make connections. These include **World-Export-Import** at **yahoogroups.com**, **Export-Import-Club** at **yahoogroups.com**, and **World-Trade-Groups** at **yahoogroups.com**. These chat groups' membership comprises export companies, suppliers, import companies, distributors, producers, and brokers. Members post queries for goods or services they are looking for, as well as post what products or services they have available in search of a trading partner.

Another form of Internet-based advertising is including your name in the various international trade directories available online. For example, the Directory for International Trade — Import Export Internet Advertising is a directory where you can advertise your business at no cost. The Web site, **www.importers-exporters.com**, allows you to establish a link from their site to your Web page and thereby promote your business worldwide. Some other sites include **www.trademama.com** — an international trade directory of wholesalers, suppliers, and manufacturers; **http://us.kompass. com** — a business-to-business import and export directory that serves as a venue to promote your company in the global marketplace; and **www. traderscity.com** — a site that contains free access to trade leads worldwide. The number of Web sites containing business directories of companies involved in international trade are too numerous to mention; however, the sites mentioned above are good sites to begin with, giving you an idea as to what is available. Conducting a search under "international trade directories," "import export business directories," or "global business trade directories" will result in a large number of possible sites to explore.

In addition to Internet-based advertising, another excellent venue to advertise is in print media, placing ads or articles in business magazines and periodicals, such as *Business Week*, *Forbes*, and *Entrepreneur*. Although advertising rates in these magazines may be somewhat on the expensive side, the returns may be worth the investment. There are also magazines published by various organizations, such as the *Florida Small Business* magazine published by Enterprise Florida (discussed earlier in the book), that have a more limited area of circulation, but can still directly reach your target market. There are also several magazines geared specifically toward the import export industry. Some of these magazines include *Air Cargo World*, *The Journal of Commerce*, *World Trade*, and *Latin Trade* (English and Spanish).

Direct Mail Marketing

There is nothing wrong with direct mail marketing, especially when you are new to the industry. Mailing a short letter introducing your business and the services provided to your target market can prove to be a successful endeavor, as well as cost-effective. Obtaining quality international business lists is very inexpensive (sometimes lists are free) and relatively easy to accomplish. Start by contacting international trade associations and requesting a copy of their membership list. Membership lists are not always available, but are worth the effort. In addition, these associations host trade shows and conferences on a regular basis; you might also want to request a copy of their attendance list.

Another avenue for obtaining business lists is by contacting major multinational publishing houses. The publishing industry penetrated the foreign market many years ago and continues to remain strong in those markets. These companies often have separate databases for the different countries they service, thus making it easier to choose the right lists for the countries you want to target, including the domestic market. Some of the leading sources for these international subscribers' lists are *Newsweek, Time, Fortune, International Herald Tribune, Harvard Business Review, The Wall Street Journal,* and *Business Week.* There is a charge, however, for obtaining these lists, and prices vary according to the publishing house.

One last suggestion for obtaining names and addresses for prospective business leads is the good old phone book, which is often overlooked, but valuable. As you get more involved in international trade, you will find that there are certain areas in each country that are a Mecca for international trade activity — those are the phone books you want to get. Generally, for a nominal fee, the telephone company of the region will provide you with a copy of the phone book you wish to obtain.

International Trade Shows

Trade shows are popular venues used by all industries as a means of bringing together businesses and consumers of certain goods and services. When you are in the import and export business, there are many trade shows that you can attend, both domestically and abroad, that will effectively serve your purpose of promoting your goods and services. Trade shows can be part of annual conventions and conferences hosted by professional organizations, such as the annual Central Europe-U.S. Airport Issues Conference & Exhibit. This annual conference, held every year in different countries throughout Europe or the U.S., is an event where multiple seminars, round-table discussions, and meetings take place relating to international aviation issues. However, running concurrent with the conference is a trade fair showcasing airport- and aviation-related products and services, thereby providing companies involved in this industry an opportunity to make contacts with potential customers or secure new suppliers for their products.

In addition to conference-related trade shows, trade shows and fairs can also be stand-alone events designed to bring together businesses from a particular industry sector. For example, every year Colombia hosts a trade show specifically geared toward the telecommunications industry. The trade show, ANDICOM Congress, is the most prominent telecommunications trade show in Colombia, and it is well-attended by U.S. companies that exhibit and promote their products and services in the telecommunications industry. Events like this are excellent ways to introduce your business abroad. Not only will you be able to showcase your products and services, but you will also have an opportunity to assess the competition.

You will also be able to identify new products you may be interested in importing or exporting, as well as build sales for your existing products. When preparing to attend a trade show, there are several details you must keep in mind:

- Make sure you take enough business cards and promotional literature to last you through the show.

- Have some of your literature available in the native language of the country you are visiting.

- Go over the displays you normally take to trade shows and make sure there is nothing offensive or inappropriate for that particular country.

- If you already have customers, or potential customers, whom you have been working with in that area, let them know ahead of time that you will be there. It will be a great opportunity to personally meet with them and finalize some sales.

One way you can learn about upcoming trade shows and fairs is by contacting professional trade organizations such as the National Association of Foreign-Trade zones, the Organization of Women in International Trade, and the American Association of Exporters and Importers, to name a few. Also, the U.S. Department of Commerce Office of Export Promotion Services, through the Export.gov Web site, maintains an up-to-date list of events worldwide, such as trade shows, for the U.S. importer and exporter. You can search trade show locations by country, industry, and dates at **www. export.gov/tradeevents/index.asp**. Another excellent source of information as to trade show events is the Federation of International Trade Associations' Web site, **www.fita.org/conferences.html**, which contains links to various sites that contain information about upcoming trade shows and fairs worldwide.

Trade Missions

Trade missions are quite different from trade shows. A trade mission is when a group of individuals travels abroad with the purpose of meeting with potential trading partners. Trade missions are generally organized by state, local governments, or public private partnerships such as Enterprise Florida (discussed earlier in the book) for the sole purpose of promoting international trade. The benefit of participating in trade missions is that not only are the meetings prearranged with foreign business owners, but you also receive assistance from these agencies prior and during the trip.

The U.S. Department of Commerce International Trade Administration is also responsible for organizing trade missions to various different countries throughout the year. Department of Commerce employees travel with independent business owners that have been recruited and selected by the Department of Commerce from the private business community. The Department establishes the selection for the participants based on the mission's objective and the mission's specific written criteria. A complete list of scheduled trade missions (including its objectives and criteria that must be met) is available on the U.S. Department of Commerce Trade Mission Calendar Web page at **www.trade.gov/doctm/tmcal.html**. A list of trade missions is also available on the Export.gov Web site and the Federation of International Trade Associations' Web site, both listed above.

Typically, trade missions result in successful business transactions because when you attend a trade mission, you know you will be meeting with individuals who are looking for the products and services you have available or who are manufacturers and suppliers of goods you are interested in importing into the U.S.

Important Things to Remember When Traveling Abroad

Before traveling abroad for a trade show, trade mission, or to visit a trading partner, there are a number of issues that must be addressed prior to your trip.

Passports

Passports are mandatory when traveling to a foreign country. Because it can take up to six weeks from the time you apply for a passport to the time you actually receive it, it is essential that you plan ahead. If you get into a bind and need it quickly, they can expedite the process and get your passport shipped within two weeks, but it will be quite expensive. Passports are issued through the U.S. Department of State and can be obtained through a number of passport agencies located throughout your state. To locate a passport agency near you, visit the National Passport Information Center, under the U.S. Department of State, Bureau of Consular Affairs Web site at **www.travel.state.gov/passport**.

Visas

Visas are permits required by some foreign countries that allow you to enter that country. Visa requirements vary from country to country, and some countries do not even require a visa to enter. However, those countries that do require visas have systems in place that may take several weeks, if not months, to grant you a visa to enter. The U.S. Department of State Bureau of Consular Affairs Web site has a page with country-specific travel information, which is an excellent source to determine if a visa is required from the country you are interested in visiting. Again, planning ahead is vital.

Registering with U.S. Embassies in foreign countries

If you are traveling abroad to attend a trade show or to meet with a prospective supplier or buyer, it is a good idea that you register with the U.S. Embassy in that country. By registering, your presence and your whereabouts will be known should there be an emergency or natural disaster. In such instances, it will be easier for the American Embassy in that country to locate you and provide assistance. Registration with the U.S. Embassy is recommended especially if the country you are traveling to does not have a politically stable environment or there is civil unrest.

Vaccinations

Vaccinations are regulated by the Centers for Disease Control and Prevention (CDC). The CDC has divided vaccination for traveling into three categories: routine, recommended, and required. Their Web site has a list of the vaccines required by the International Health Regulation according to the country to which you will be traveling. The CDC's Traveler's Health Web site address is **www.cdc.gov/travel/content/vaccinations**.

Any time you are planning to travel abroad, you should visit the Bureau of Consular Affairs Web site's International Travel page for up-to-date information on the state of any country at any given time. The site contains country-specific information, travel warnings, and travel alerts on any country around the world. Their Web site is at **www.travel.state.gov/travel/travel_1744.html**.

Globalizing Your Marketing Plan

When you are dealing with people from different parts of the world, you will most notice great differences in their cultures. Culture, according to the Merriam-Webster Dictionary, is "the integrated pattern of human knowledge, belief, and behavior that depends upon the capacity for learning and transmitting knowledge to succeeding generations; the customary beliefs, social forms, and material traits of a racial, religious, or social group." For the purpose of interacting in a different culture when marketing your products and services, it is important to realize that culture influences a great deal of the way people raise their children; purchase their food, clothing, and other consumables; and are motivated to work and ultimately make decisions in purchasing certain products.

What may be appropriate and acceptable in one country may be totally unacceptable in another. Sometimes something as simple as a comment or a gesture may have totally different meanings in different cultures.

Consequently, it may be helpful to gain some general insight into the culture, traditions, language, and common business practices of those countries with which you will be dealing. Being aware of these cultural differences will be helpful in avoiding embarrassing situations and possible disastrous outcomes.

Every culture has its own ways of doing business. For instance, it is common for the U.S. business person to be highly time-conscious, individualistic, and goal-oriented. However, in many European and Asian countries, it is the opposite. Another issue of considerable importance is to understand how executives from different countries perceive power and authority. For example, in the U.S. it is accepted to have women in positions of authority, such as business owners and managers of businesses. But that is not the case in a number of countries across the globe, making it difficult to conduct business. If the owner of the import export business is a woman, or the international sales manager is a woman, closing a deal with business representatives from these countries can be quite challenging, although it is not impossible.

Differences in national and religious holidays also play a key role when marketing your products or services in foreign countries. Religion can often be a dominant influence in the consumers' buying practices. Religious holidays are strong determinants of buying and consumption patterns. To avoid wasting time and resources in marketing campaigns that will be totally off-track, make sure you are aware when these holidays take place in countries where you are establishing trading relationships. The same holds true when planning to travel to these foreign countries. For example, during the celebration of the Chinese New Year it is not a good idea to try to conduct business in China, as there are numerous manufacturing plant and business office closures throughout the country during that time.

The issue of language barriers, although it seems relatively easy to overcome, can be disastrous if you are not careful. In a technologically advanced world, there are numerous translation software programs available that make it relatively easy to transform simple documents into different languages. However, keep in mind that the intent of what is being said often gets lost in translation. When preparing marketing materials for countries abroad, if at all possible, it will be a great investment to have someone native to that country help you with the translation and production of those documents. Not only are you going to be sure that there will not be any misunderstandings, but you will also make a much better impression with the local business people with whom you are trying to conduct business. Along the same line of language issues, as you travel to different countries to meet with suppliers or customers, it is always a good idea to secure an interpreter if both parties do not speak a common language. Money invested on an interpreter is money well invested. In the long run, it will cost you more to resolve issues that may result from miscommunication than what the services of an interpreter may cost.

Chapter 12

Government Regulations, Free Trade Agreements, and Other International Trade Issues

The legal structure of international trade business is based on the fundamental principles of contract law. There are numerous regulations affecting import and export activities, as well as trading restrictions on certain countries imposed due to national interest issues, human rights violation issues, or abuse of international laws. Therefore, it is essential to have a thorough understanding of all the governmental requirements regulating international commerce.

U.S. Government Regulations

There are several government regulations affecting international trade, and all have been established with the intent of protecting the interests of the U.S. international trade business owner. Some of these laws are pretty recent, while others have been in place for a long time, undergoing amendments from time to time to accommodate changes in the industry. The most commonly referred-to laws and regulations are discussed as follows; however, keeping up with the enactment of new laws and changes in these existing regulations is critical.

Foreign Corrupt Practices Act (FCPA)

The Foreign Corrupt Practices Act, enacted in 1977, makes it illegal for companies, individuals, and direct foreign subsidiaries of U.S. companies from offering or compensating in any way any government official with the purpose of obtaining or retaining business. The FCPA is applicable to all U.S. international marketers, and your company is considered to be liable even when using independent contractors, agents, or distributors. Under FCPA regulations, you are required and expected to know how and where your company's funds are being allocated in order to avoid misuse of funds. Enforced by the Department of Justice, violations under the FCPA can result in penalties of up to $2 million dollars, as well as possible imprisonment.

U.S. anti-boycott laws

In order to keep U.S. citizens from participating in other countries' economic boycotts and embargoes not sanctioned by the United Sates, two laws were enacted in late 1976 and 1977. The 1977 amendment to the Export Administration Act (EAA) and the Ribicoff Amendment to the 1976 Tax Reform Act (TRA) were enacted to prevent U.S. companies from being used to put into action other countries' foreign policies that oppose U.S. policy. The anti-boycott stipulations are applicable to the activities of U.S. corporations, companies, and individuals involved in international trade, both in the United States and abroad. Penalties for the violation of such laws include fines of up to $10,000 per violation, or even losing export rights.

U.S. Environmental Protection Agency (EPA) regulations

The EPA requires exporters of hazardous waste materials to notify the agency of their exporting activities. Through the Office of Enforcement and Compliance Assurance, the Import-Export Program (IEP) is responsible for overseeing the international trade activities of hazardous waste that involve the United States. For more information as to the EPA's involvement in the importation and exportation of hazardous waste, visit **www. epa.gov/epawaste/hazard/international/imp-exp.htm**. The Web site breaks down the international and domestic requirements and procedures applicable to exports and imports of hazardous waste.

Antidumping and countervailing duties (ADCVD)

Antidumping and countervailing duties regulations are a big part of the U.S. trade policy, based on fighting unfair trade imports. These regulations have been put into place to provide relief to the domestic manufacturers who are unfavorably affected by imports of subsidized products — products that have benefited from government subsidies in the country of origin and are "dumped" at extremely low prices in the domestic market. Antidumping duties are duties assessed on imported goods that are sold to importers or buyers in the United States at prices less than what the goods would be sold for in the manufacturer's country. Countervailing duties are duties assessed on certain imported goods to offset the effect of subsidies that are provided by foreign governments to their manufacturers on products that are to be exported to the United States. The problem with these subsidies is that when that foreign government provides financial assistance to the manufacturer, it reduces their manufacturing cost, thus creating an artificially lower price and making difficult, if not impossible, for the U.S. manufacturer to compete. When imported goods are subject to either antidumping or countervailing duties regulations, the total amount of Customs duties — payable by the importer — tends to be much higher than on normal importations. In such instances, Customs does not allow the foreign supplier to reimburse the U.S. importer for those duties and further requires the importer to sign a certificate (under penalty of perjury) that he or she has not entered into an agreement with the supplier for the reimbursement of such duties.

Import quotas

Import quotas were originally established by the U.S. government to protect the interests of domestic industries from lower-priced competition by foreign manufacturers. An import quota limits the quantity of goods producers abroad can import into the United States during a determined time, which is usually a year. Because the amount of product — subject to quotas — that can be imported is limited, manufacturing jobs are preserved as a means of meeting the market's demand for that particular product. However, at times the result can be higher prices for those goods in the domestic market, as the quality of cheaper foreign manufactured products is reduced and the competition for domestic manufacturers is pretty much eliminated. Nevertheless, there is a down side to import quotas, even to domestic industries. Many of the manufacturing companies in the United States also have manufacturing plants outside the U.S., and the establishment of quotas, at times, does not allow them to bring their own products back into the U.S. Import quotas can also be tariff rate quotas, which means that a certain amount of a particular product can be imported at a specified duty rate and, once the specified quantity has been exceeded (allowed quota) for the United States as a whole, not a particular importer, the tariff duty rate for that particular product increases.

The United States is not the only country to have established import quotas. Other countries have established them to protect their own domestic industries from excessive import of U.S. made products. Import quotas imposed in other countries have been known to adversely impact U.S. industries and, ultimately, the U.S. economy, by limiting the volume of products that they can import into those countries. For example, several European countries currently have established import quotas on U.S.-made films in an effort to promote and encourage the growth and development of the European film industry.

Although originally designed to protect the nation's domestic industries, import quotas' harmful effect on other industries caused the issue to be addressed during the 1995 renegotiation of GATT — the General Agreement on Tariffs and Trade (discussed at length later in this chapter). The renegotiation resulted in the limitation of quotas that could be imposed by any one country, such as the elimination of temporary quotas established by countries to offset outpours of imports of a specific product from markets overseas.

Foreign Government Regulations

Just as the United States has laws and regulations in place to protect the interests of companies in the States, other governments also have in place laws that have been implemented to protect their domestic commerce from too much foreign competition. These laws also seek to limit potentially environmentally damaging issues and sometimes even prevent what they would consider being or unacceptable cultural influences. For example, U.S. companies that wish to establish sales operations in Brazil must first form a joint venture with a local Brazilian firm. Another example is Saudi Arabia, where it is required that marketing activities of foreign-based companies be conducted by locals. Therefore, when conducting business abroad, it is essential that you research and be aware of such country-specific laws that may affect your business transactions. The following Web sites are excellent resources of information on country-specific international trade rules and regulations:

- **www.ucblibraries.colorado.edu/govpubs/for/foreigngovt.htm** — A Web site developed by the University of Colorado at Boulder that includes information on foreign governments, including the country's profile and other information such as health-related issues.

- **www.library.northwestern.edu/govinfo/resource/internat/
  stats.html** — This Web site, compiled by the Government Publications Department of Northwestern University, contains a collection of direct links to foreign government's Web sites with international trade information.

International Free Trade Agreements —
Established to Help You

When you are involved in international trade, it is essential to stay abreast of changes in the industry such as the establishment of free trade agreements, which will more than likely have a significant impact on your import and export operations. International free trade agreements are an important element in the overall expansion and well-being of the U.S. economy. These agreements, entered into with other countries, have the potential of creating new employment and business opportunities for entrepreneurs in the United States. International trade agreements are entered into by members of the World Trade Organization (WTO) in an effort to promote trade among its members and thus enhance the countries' financial stability. The United States is one of the 154 members of the WTO and, as of the writing of this book, it has free trade agreements in effect with 17 countries throughout the world. In the United States, these free trade agreements are administered by the Office of the United States Trade Representative (USTR), which is an Executive Office of the President. It is the trade representative's responsibility to negotiate and sign proposed trade agreements that complement U.S. trade policy. In addition, the trade representative is responsible for monitoring the implementation of the trade agreements by U.S. trading partners as well as enforcing the United States' rights under those established agreements.

Free trade agreements can be bilateral agreements between two countries or multilateral agreements among several countries, such as the well-known North American Free Trade Agreement, better known as NAFTA. As of the writing of this book, the following bilateral free trade agreements were in place:

North American Free Trade Agreement (NAFTA)

Effective as of January 1994, the North American Free Trade Agreement between the United States, Canada, and Mexico resulted in the world's largest free-trade area, producing over 17 trillion dollars worth of products and services. According to the Office of the United States Trade Representative's Web site, in 2008 U.S. exports to NAFTA countries were up 190 percent from 1993 — the year prior to NAFTA coming to effect — with the exports of agricultural products alone totaling 2.3 billion dollars. NAFTA's economic impact on the U.S. importer and exporter has been extraordinary, especially in the electrical machinery, vehicles, plastic, and mineral fuel and oil sectors.

United States-Dominican Republic-Central America FTA (CAFTA-DR)

In August 2004, the United States signed a free trade agreement with the Dominican Republic and five Central American countries — Costa Rica, Honduras, El Salvador, Guatemala, and Nicaragua — establishing what is known as CAFTA-DR. This became the first free trade agreement the United States entered into with a group of smaller developing countries, which happens to represent the third-largest export market in Latin America for the U.S. The agreement has not only facilitated trade among the countries involved, but has also been conducive to new opportunities by opening new markets, eliminating tariffs, and promoting overall trade activity.

United States-Australia FTA

As of the inception of this agreement in January 2005, both countries have experienced a remarkable increase in the trade of goods and services. Under this agreement, 99 percent of all U.S.-manufactured products are exported into Australia duty-free.

United States-Bahrain FTA

Entered into in August 2006, this free trade agreement has resulted in a 100 percent bilateral trade of consumer and industrial products entirely duty-free. Thus, encouraging new trade opportunities for goods such as fiber, yarn, and fabric, as well as the manufacturing of apparel.

United States-Chile FTA

Established in January 2004, this FTA eliminates tariffs on 87 percent of all bilateral trade between the U.S. and Chile, with stipulations to establish totally duty-free trade in all goods within the next 12 years. This free trade agreement is of immense benefit to the U.S. importer because even though Chile has one of the most liberal trade systems, with a uniform 6 percent tariff for most goods, normally importers would still have to pay a 19 percent value-added tax, based on the Customs valued plus the import tariff.

United States-Israel Free Trade Area Agreement

The free trade agreement with Israel was established in 1985, and it took ten years to fully implement the phased tariff reductions planned under this program with the total elimination of duties by 1995. Since then, several modifications or additions have been made to this agreement to accommodate agricultural goods trade issues. One of the modifications, the Agreement on Trade in Agricultural Products, established a program of measured market access for agricultural products and food, effective through December 2001. The value of this agreement to the U.S. importer and exporter is that it provides for annual increases in the importation quota quantity under the tariff-rate quotas. In addition, it permits the exportation of U.S. food and agricultural products into Israel under unlimited duty-free access, preferential tariffs, or duty-free tariff-rate quotas, which are at least 10 percent below Israel's Most Favored Nation rates.

United States-Jordan FTA

Entered into in December 2001, the agreement consisted of reducing tariffs in phases, completing the tariff reduction program by 2010.

United States-Morocco FTA

This agreement, which went into effect in January 2006, eliminates duties on more than 95 percent of all products and services traded. One of the agreement's most fundamental elements is that Morocco has committed to greater regulatory transparency in order to promote trade, as well as the protection of intellectual property rights. The result of this agreement was achieving immediate duty-free access by key U.S. export segments into the Moroccan market.

United States-Oman FTA

As of the writing of this book, the free trade agreement with Oman is one of the two most recent free trade agreement entered into by the United States, coming into effect in January 2009. This agreement immediately made most of all industrial and consumer products in its tariff schedule available duty-free. The remaining products will be phased in duty-free within the next ten years. In addition, 87 percent of U.S. agricultural products in the tariff lines became duty-free immediately upon its becoming effective.

United States-Peru Trade Promotion Agreement (PTPA)

Approved in December 2007 and entered into force on February 2009, the PTPA right away removed most of its tariffs on U.S. exports. The remainder tariffs that were not eliminated immediately upon enactment will be phased out over a specified period. The PTPA covers a wide range of branches of international trade, such as telecommunications, intellectual property rights, electronic commerce, and environmental protection and labor issues.

United States-Singapore FTA

Coming into effect in January 2004, this free trade agreement has contributed to the increase in exports to Singapore by 73 percent. After its enactment, the most significant increase in exports has been in the area of construction equipment, machinery, and medical services.

Pending FTAs

As of the writing of this book, there were several free trade agreements still pending congressional approval, all of which will be of immense significance to U.S. importers and exporters as well as to the overall U.S. economy. Pending free trade agreements include:

United States-Colombia Free Trade Agreement — The approval of this agreement with Colombia will have a serious impact on the trade community, especially in the sectors of government procurement, telecommunications, investment, intellectual property rights, electronic commerce, and environmental and labor protection. This program will allow U.S. companies to have better access to service industries in Colombia than other members of the World Trade Organization.

United States-Korea Free Trade Agreement — If approved by Congress, this agreement will become the most notable free trade agreement in over 16 years for the United States. Under this free trade agreement, 95 percent of bilateral trade in industrial and consumer products would become duty-free within the first three years, with most of the remaining tariffs being eliminated within ten years from the time the agreements is approved. The agreement will also significantly impact the service industry, financial services sector, trade of agricultural products, and provide the U.S. exporter with better access to the procurement market of the Korean government.

United States-Panama Trade Promotion Agreement — This agreement has been in the works since June 2007, and although Panama approved it a month later, as of the writing of this book the United States had not yet approved it. The agreement will facilitate trading in the areas of government procurement, telecommunications, investment, intellectual property rights, and other similar areas of trade. It will provide U.S. companies with better access to the service sector in Panama. In addition, it will try to resolve existing issues that are currently affecting the successful trade of agricultural products such as poultry, dairy, and rice.

Free trade agreements can also be Trade and Investment Framework Agreements (TIFA). These agreements provide the framework for countries to come together, discuss, and settle any trade and investment issues before they escalate. In addition, the United States has Bilateral Investment Treaties (BIT's), which are established to assist in protecting private investments in the U.S. as well as promoting U.S. exports and developing market-oriented policies in affiliate countries.

Free trade agreements have an extraordinary economic impact in the U.S. economy and are a powerful tool for importers and exporters to increase their trading capabilities. Carefully evaluating the provisions of the various free trade agreements will be helpful when making a decision as to where you may want to take your business for higher profitability in future transactions.

Other International Trade Issues

Although it would be impossible within the context of this book to cover all of the existing international trade issues, there are some major trade issues of global relevance with which you should be familiar. Knowing that they exist, their relevance to your international trade activities, and their ramifications as they extend to other trade issues is fundamental to your success. As you become more involved in the import and export activities of your business, you will encounter various other issues that will be relevant to your services or products. However, having the basic understanding of these key topics will give you the knowledge you need to be able to research and evaluate other trade-related issues as they arise while operating your import export business.

Generalized System of Preferences

The Generalized System of Preferences is a program enacted by the United States in the Trade Act of 1974 for the purpose of encouraging the economic growth in developing countries and territories. Through the Generalized System of Preferences, certain commodities from these developing countries and territories are provided with duty-free status, which encourages their trade worldwide. Goods eligible under the Generalized System of Preferences are identified as such by the Tariff Classification Code found in the Harmonized Tariff Schedule of the United States discussed in previous chapters.

GATT — General Agreement on Tariffs and Trade and The World Trade Organization (WTO)

Effective January 1, 1948, GATT became the leading international multilateral agreement regulating world trade. Rules governing GATT are set forth in the Protocol of Provisions Application of the General Agreement on Tariffs and Trades, which is signed by all GATT members. Terms under GATT have been renegotiated seven times since its origination, with the most recent round — the Uruguay Round — becoming effective July 1, 1995, where the World Trade Organization (WTO) was created. Rounds are called when GATT nations come together to negotiate international trade issues such as import duties. During these rounds, member countries also entered into trade agreements and even decided which countries would receive preferential treatment, such as the Generalized System of Preferences as discussed under the Harmonized Tariff Schedule. In addition, GATT also provided a forum in which member countries could discuss and resolve international trade disputes.

GATT's creation of the World Trade Organization with its 123 initial member countries became the entity that replaced GATT, thereby becoming the primary agency of the United Nations, responsible for the discussion and resolution of international trade issues. The WTO currently consists of 153 member nations whose primary goal is to promote international trade by helping manufacturers, importers, and exporters conduct business effectively in the international trade arena. The WTO's Web site at **www.wto.org** is an abundant source of information on international trade issues, containing information on the latest events in international trade, up-to-date information on rules and regulations affecting trading activities in the world, and links to several sites relating to international trade.

Intellectual property rights

Intellectual property rights are the rights given to individuals over their own creations. The most common avenues used to protect intellectual property rights are through patents, trademarks, and copyrights. Intellectual property rights give the creator the exclusive right over the use of his or her creation for a determined time.

Intellectual property rights are generally divided into two focal areas — copyright and industrial property rights. Copyrights include the rights of literary and artistic authors such as books, musical compositions, computer programs, and paintings. By copyright, these rights are protected for a minimum of 50 years after the author's death. Industrial property rights include the protection of distinctive signs like trademarks and other signs such as those that identify goods as being from a specific geographic location, thereby giving the product its identity. The purpose of protecting these rights is to protect customers from misrepresented goods, thereby stimulating fair competition. Industrial property rights also include inventions, trade secrets, and industrial designs. The protection of these rights is for a fixed term — usually for 20 years, as it is in the case of patents.

Trademarks are considered to be words, symbols, pictures, or a combination thereof that is used to recognize a company's products or services from among others in the industry. In the United States, trademarks are valid for 15 years and can be renewed without limitation. However, in most foreign countries, the only way to obtain trademark rights is through registration of the trademark, and some countries even require the use of the registered mark locally to keep the registration. An excellent source of information on how to register trademarks abroad is a document posted on the Export America Web site — within the International Trade Administration's site — which discusses the basics of filing a trademark abroad. The site is **www.ita.doc.gov/exportamerica/TechnicalAdvice/ta_trademarks.htm**.

Although intellectual property rights are strongly protected in the United States, not all countries have such protective laws over one's creations, and U.S. intellectual property rights afford little or no protection of these rights in foreign countries. Consequently, to possibly avoid violating foreign requirements, you should familiarize yourself with international patent, trademark, and copyright laws that may apply to goods you are considering importing or exporting. To learn about intellectual property rights, laws, and regulations of individual countries, visit the World Intellectual Property Organization's Web site at **www.wipo.int/portal/index.html.en**.

There is, however, some protection of intellectual property rights internationally through treaties and other international agreements. Such is the case with copyrights, which are protected automatically without any formalities, in all WTO member countries. During the Uruguay Round, the World Trade Organization established what is commonly known as TRIPs — Trade-Related Aspects of Intellectual Property Rights, which is an agreement related to all aspects of intellectual property rights and sets the standards of protection for a wide range of intellectual property rights as well as provide for the enforcement of those standards. The TRIPs agreement is the first multilateral agreement pertaining to intellectual property rights that is enforceable between countries. The entire text of the TRIPs agreement can be found in the WTO's Web site.

Chapter 13

Managing an Ethical and Environmentally Responsible Business

A truly successful business is one that is not only thriving financially, but one that is being managed ethically and environmentally conscious. Although the common believe is that it would be difficult to have a financially successful business unless it is being properly managed, that is certainly not true. Unfortunately, there are companies that are thriving financially, but their managing methods leave a lot to be desired. To be truly successful, one must be conscious of its managing practices, maintaining the highest standards of ethics and responsibility if you are going to be truly successful.

Operating an import export business can be a one-person operation, in which case a great deal of the following information will not be applicable to you. However, in many instances, small, one-person import export business operations have grown to operations hiring multiple employees. That would be the case if your business grows to become a manufacturing facility involved in import and export, or a distribution center. If the latter is the case, then much of the information that follows will be of significant importance to your success.

Practicing Good Business Ethics

There is nothing wrong with wanting to be financially successful and making a lot of money in your business; however, you must never compromise your ethical or moral standards in order to accomplish this. Good ethics should be an integral part of every business. Conducting your business ethically is being able to generate a reasonable profit for your business while conducting business honestly. It is being aware of environmental and social issues, and providing a safe working environment for your employees. Remember that your company's greatest assets are your employees. Investing wisely in them and making them part of a team, rather than "just employees," will result in the employees' sense of belonging and commitment, thereby increasing productivity and, ultimately, revenues for the company. Investments can be rewarding your employees fairly and equitably for their performance with appraisals and reward systems. Another form of investment is making training available for your employees so that they can better themselves and have opportunities for advancement within the company.

Good business ethics not only applies to the way you manage your business alone, but also extends to the companies you do conduct business with overseas. Corrupt business practices are so common in foreign countries that in 1977, the Foreign Corrupt Practices Act was established by the United States government in order to curtail these activities. Requiring you to pay port officials or other government officials to allow your shipment to go through is not only morally wrong, but illegal — it is called bribery. Ultimately, it will be in your best interest to stay away from doing business with individuals and companies abroad that regularly engage in this type of activity.

Keep in mind that the success of your business cannot be attributed to internal forces alone; it influences and it is influenced every day by outside forces such as your suppliers and your customers, as well as the community where you are located, thereby making it part of a whole. The effects of the decisions you make will permeate all facets of the communities, societies, and nations in which you conduct business. In a larger scale, it is part of the global trading community, and at a smaller scale, it is part of the community where your company is located. Your business is directly contributing to that community by hiring local residents as employees. Those employees are buying houses, buying from local stores, sending their children to local schools, and ultimately paying taxes that help support the community, which is then able to grow and provide better services to its constituents — including your business. In a larger scale, you are contributing to the global economy, making goods and services available to consumers across the world. Conducting your business ethically will have a ripple effect on all those you come in contact with on your everyday business operations.

Labor and Employment Issues

Manufacturing as well as warehousing and distribution operations are common types of ventures associated with the import and export industry. Due to the nature of these operations, they often lend themselves to unfair labor practices. Nevertheless, meeting every aspect of established fair labor laws is not only conducting business in a lawful manner, but it is also the right thing to do. The United States Department of Labor has information readily available to employers regarding the various laws and regulations affecting employment practices. These laws and regulations are too many and too complex to explore within the scope of this book, but before you expand your business to the point where you must hire employees, you should become familiar with these laws. The penalties associated with failure to comply with these laws are quite steep and may even result in your having to shut down your operations.

Fair labor laws address issues such as:

- Equal employment opportunity
- Wages

- Work hours
- Workers' compensation
- Work safety and health
- Unemployment
- Workers with disabilities

All the information you need regarding these laws can be found on the U.S. Department of Labor Web site at **www.dol.gov/index.htm**.

Labor and employment issues are not limited to your operations only. They also extend to those companies you are doing business with abroad. As a conscientious import export business owner, you may be particularly conscious of running a first-class operation, meeting established fair labor laws and looking out for your employees well being. However, your responsibility should not end there. In the import export business, it is common to encounter manufacturing operations in foreign countries that run sweat shops or employ child labor because there may not be laws to protect these individuals. Low wages, long hours, and unsafe work environments are commonplace in many of the third-world countries' manufacturing plants. Although you cannot control how these facilities operate, you can do your part in not condoning unfair labor practices, taking a morally and ethically correct position on the issue, and avoiding conducting business with such companies.

Imported Product Safety

The safety of products being imported has become a great concern as the number of products being imported into the U.S. that do not meet consumer safety standards continues to increase. It is essential that you take diligent care in researching and carefully evaluating products that you are considering importing to avoid products such as contaminated foods or toys that pose a safety hazard. The United States has well-established regulations that must be met before products are exported to ensure they meet adequate safety standards. However, there are foreign countries that do not have such standards, thus posing a threat to the consumers' well-being. The importation of defective or unsafe products can be detrimental to the success of your business, as you will be losing a lot of money from these types of importations. In November 2007, the Interagency Working Group on Import Safety submitted a report to the President of the United States, outlining a proposed action plan to reduce and eliminate the importation of unsafe products into the United States. This report will provide you with some insight as to current import safety issues. The report can be accessed online at **www.importsafety.gov/report/actionplan.pdf**.

CASE STUDY: GLOBAL SOURCING AND AWARENESS OF CONSUMER PRODUCT SAFETY

Eddith G. Tolchin, owner, EGT Global Trading, New York
Co-author of Sourcing Smarts: Keeping it Simple with China Sourcing and Manufacturing
www.egtglobaltrading.com
(845) 321-2362

CLASSIFIED CASE STUDIES
directly from the experts

EGT Global Trading has been successfully operating since 1997, when owner Eddith G. Tolchin decided it was time to open a business of her own. Working in the international trade industry since 1973, Tolchin's experience is quite versatile, having dealt with the import and export of products such as waxes, chemicals, twine, imported nuts, silk garments, and baby products. In her business, Tolchin provides sourcing, prototyping, quality control, manufacturing, production testing, and importing services for investors and entrepreneurs with new products.

During the many years of sourcing in China, there has only been one single incident where she faced the problem of having contracted with a company that gave her problems. The manufacturing plant she had contracted with for the production of a product destined to be imported into the U.S. shut down in the middle of production. Fortunately, she was able to resume production with another nearby manufacturing facility. Her recommendation to avoid such issues is to work with companies that have been recommended to her by her "existing network of factories" as well as checking references, and once you find manufacturing companies that work to your satisfaction, stay with them.

Recently, Tolchin co-authored a book titled *Sourcing Smarts: Keeping it Simple with China Sourcing and Manufacturing*, an all-inclusive guide about sourcing, manufacturing, packaging, production testing, quality control, product safety, and importing safely and legally into the U.S. She said that all importers should be fully versed in the Consumer Product Safety Commission's (CPSC) new Consumer Product Safety Improvement Act. As required by this law, most consumer products and all children's products require a General Conformity Certificate (GCC), which certifies that the product meets the required safety standards.

Tolchin said she truly enjoys her lifetime career in international trade. In regard to new importers in the international trade industry, she feels strongly about the importance of being knowledgeable about the Consumer and Product Safety Improvement Act, as well as being familiar with the Customs and Border Protection and the Federal Trade Commission's Web sites. She also recommends reading her book, being an all-inclusive guide to sourcing and importing from China. Lastly, this veteran of imports and exports said she has learned the importance of having someone there to help you in the beginning stages of your business: "Use a sourcing consultant or import consultant for the very first import transaction so the start-up importer can learn the ropes from someone who has the specific experience they require," she said.

Environmental Concerns

Concern for the environment should not just be a local or national concern; it should be a global concern. As you manage your business operation, be aware of the potential environmental impacts of your business locally and globally. After all, operating an import export business makes you part of a much larger community — a global community. Thus, smart business management would involve taking responsible steps, even if it is not as cost-effective as other means, to minimize adverse effects on the environment. At times, in an attempt to reduce operational costs and run an environmentally friendly operation domestically, the environment is compromised somewhere else. For example, the practice of trucking waste to Mexico has become quite common for U.S. companies because it reduces their waste disposal cost. However, the waste is being dumped legally in Mexico — in the Rio Grande. Although the dumping is polluting the river on the Mexican side, with the increase in dumping, the effects are now also felt in the United States side. In the end, nothing is being accomplished with this operation because regardless of location, the environment is compromised anyway.

As we become more aware of the lasting negative effects environmentally irresponsible operations have in our environment, advancements are constantly being made to correct this situation. Gradually investing to adopt cleaner manufacturing operations will position your company to continue competing globally as the demand from the larger companies to conduct business with only environmentally friendly suppliers and manufacturers continues increase. To assist companies of all sizes in running more environmentally friendly operations, The Green Suppliers Network will evaluate your operations and provide you with a report on how to run a more "green" operation. The Network is a consortium of private industry leaders, the U.S. Environmental Protection Agency, and the U.S. Department of Commerce's National Institute of Standards and Technology's Manufacturing Extension Partnership. Representatives from the Network will conduct a two to three-day visit to your manufacturing plant. During that visit, they will evaluate your current operations and teach you about "lean and clean" manufacturing practices that will help you enhance energy efficiency, pinpoint cost-saving opportunities, and optimize what you have available to eliminate waste. For more information on The Green Suppliers Network and how they can help your business, visit their Web site at **www.epa.gov/greensuppliers**.

Chapter 14

Working with Industry Experts for Assistance

There is a great deal that you can do for yourself when running an import export company, especially when it is a small enterprise. However, even with a small operation there are times when you will be better off contracting with experts in the industry to help you with the tremendous amount of paperwork involved. In addition, the laws and regulations that you must comply with are many because it is not just U.S. laws and regulations, but also laws from the countries with which you doing business with that will regulate your activities. As we discussed previously in the book, it is critical to abide by all the applicable laws to avoid any possible penalties as well as delay or a lost shipment. In this chapter, you will be introduced to the various trades, businesses, and agencies that are experts in the various fields associated with international trade.

Customs Brokers

Customs brokers are professional licensed individuals who act as agents for importers. They prepare and process the appropriate paperwork to safely clear through Customs shipments of merchandise imported into the United States. Brokers gather the appropriate information on the products being imported to make sure you meet Customs requirements and process the required Customs documentation. The broker acts as the middle person between the importer and U.S. Customs, preparing and submitting the necessary information — electronically or in paper form — on the various forms provided by Customs. They make it easier for individual importers and exporters, as well as the large businesses involved in international trade, to comply with complex government regulations affecting the importation and exportation of merchandise. Customs brokers will calculate the appropriate amount of taxes and duties owed to Customs. Brokers also prepare and submit the necessary documentation required to obtain clearance from other governmental agencies involved in any import or export transaction. A Customs broker can also help with advice on issues such as country of origin, marking requirements and issues related to products subject to quotas.

The location of Customs brokers is not critical. Although helpful, they do not necessarily have to be located next to a port of entry where there is international traffic; they can have offices anywhere in the United States. Brokers can be an individual, partnership, or corporation. They are subject to strict reporting and recordkeeping requirements by Customs, such as submitting regular status reports of their activities to Customs. Customs brokers are well versed on the Harmonized Tariff Schedule (HTS) and are always up to date with any changes to the HTS. They are also extremely knowledgeable about regulations and any updates thereto affecting importations and exportations as outlined in the Code of Federal Regulations. Their assistance and knowledge can be critical in avoiding costly delays in shipment and delivery, assessment of penalties, or even the seizure of the cargo. The Customs broker's involvement in the shipment does not always end upon arrival at the port, but it can also continue through the delivery of the merchandise to its final destination, working with domestic trucking companies that pick up the merchandise at the port of entry upon arrival.

To be a Customs broker, the individual must pass a background check, be at least 21 years of age, be a U.S. citizen, and be licensed by the U.S. Customs and Border Protection. The license is obtained by passing a comprehensive and exhaustive examination which covers all areas of importation and exportation, including laws, regulations, duty rates, and such. The exam is only offered certain times of the year and at specific locations throughout the United States. Although most brokers process every possible type of entry available, some brokers actually specialize in certain areas of trade such as textiles, petroleum products, or perishables, to name a few.

There are several reliable sources that can help you locate Customs brokers near you. One is the International Federation of Customs Brokers Association's Web site that contains a list of all member Customs brokers in the nation. The Web site address is **www.ifcba.org**. Another excellent source is the Web site for the National Customs Brokers and Forwarders Association of America. They also have a list of member brokers, which you can research to locate brokers in your area. That Web site address is **www.ncbfaa.org**.

Freight Forwarders

Using the services of a freight forwarder for the movement of your goods is one of the best investments you will ever make in the import export business. They play a significant role in the commerce of the United States as well as in the expansion of international trade. Freight forwarders work on behalf of the importers and exporters, facilitating the movement of cargo to and from foreign destinations as well as providing many other services such as providing warehousing arrangements, packing, and tracking of shipments, which save their customers both time and money. They handle entire ship-loads of cargo as well as individual shipments of all different sizes. Often, these smaller shipments are consolidated with cargo from other clients to make shipments more cost-effective for their clients.

The freight forwarders' involvement in the shipment of goods starts even before the goods are ready to be shipped. Their expertise in the transportation industry is of great assistance, as they can advise you on the most economical methods of transportation for each shipment. In addition, they can provide you with advice regarding the most efficient and cost-effective ways to pack and ship your merchandise. Freight forwarder's services also include making ocean, land, or air freight transportation arrangements (or a combination thereof) for your cargo, all the way from pick up to delivery of the goods to the final destination. Because of their ability to purchase space on airlines and vessels at wholesale prices, they are better able to negotiate with the carriers better rates for their customers.

The freight forwarders' function is not only limited to shipping the goods; they are also responsible for making sure that the goods being shipped are properly classified and that such classification is consistent with the description of the goods provided on the bill of lading, commercial invoice, and other pertinent documents. Freight forwarders must also ensure that all merchandise be properly packed and labeled, as well as check that that each shipment meets the proper documentation requirements to clear the goods at the port of destination. In cases when there is a letter of credit involved in the shipment, the freight forwarder is responsible for making sure that the terms of the letter of credit are met so that the exporter is then able to collect payment for the goods.

Like Customs brokers, freight forwarders are also required to maintain financial and service records for up to five years from the document's origination date. Freight forwarders are licensed by the Federal Maritime Commission (FMC). To obtain a license, the applicant must have at least three years of experience with ocean freight forwarding activities in the United States and obtain a valid surety bond with the FMC. Employees of freight forwarding companies, however, are not required to be licensed — they can operate under the employing company's license.

Freight forwarders also have professional organizations, which serve as excellent sources to locate reputable, well-established freight forwarders.

One of those organizations is the National Customs Brokers and Forwarders Association, which has a list of its member freight forwarders on their Web site at **www.ncbfaa.org**. You may search the membership listing by city, state, or member name. In addition, conducting a general search on the Internet under "freight forwarders" will produce an extensive list of freight-forwarding companies available.

CASE STUDY: MORE THAN
50 YEARS MEETING
LOGISTICS NEEDS

Salvatore J. Stile, II, CHB, President
Alba Wheels Up International, Inc.
150-30 132nd Avenue, Suite 208
Jamaica, NY 11434
(718) 276-3000
www.albawheelsup.com

Incorporated in 1949 in lower Manhattan, Alba Wheels Up International, Inc. has gone through many changes since that time, adapting to the ever-changing world of international trade. For more than 50 years, the company has been providing Customs brokerage and freight forwarding services to importers and exporters in the U.S. Salvatore Stile, II, president of the company, said importers and exporters should always seek to find a reliable forwarder. "It is important for the small business to focus on the core requirements of starting a new business," Stile said. "Some of these requirements are establishing a customer base, improving sales, and building up its internal and external networks."

When it comes to shipping costs, Stile said freight forwarders are able to provide better negotiated rates to the importer and exporter because they can consolidate many shipments and provide the service at a lower cost. Forwarders will also know what is happening with different modes of transportation around the world. For instance, you have a shipment ultimately destined for New York, so you bring it through the port of Los Angeles to be carried by rail to its final destination, as that is the uickest route. However, if you bring the goods in yourself, not using a freight forwarder, the chances are that you would not know of any possible delays at the port, such as strikes by port employees that would cause your goods to sit at the port for weeks while negotiations take place.

Another example of how using the expertise of a freight forwarder can make your shipping experience smoother is in cases of shipping high-value goods such as jewelry — which requires a secure supply chain — race horses, and large machinery. For example, according to Stile, moving a generator from Iowa to South America will require moving the generator on rail, by boat, and by special flat beds to its final destination. The forwarder will have to deal with local government agencies to shut down roads so the generator can be moved.

Often, the start-up importer or exporter does not realize that multiple agencies or individuals will be interacting with their freight during the shipping process and, according to Stile, the risk of delays and errors associated with doing your own paperwork are not worth the costs of having a freight forwarder do the documentation. Thus, acting as the agent for the importer or exporter, the freight forwarder can more easily determine what the requirements are for any specific shipment. In addition, freight forwarders can use their expertise and established contacts throughout each step of the shipping process to handle any problems that may arise, thereby ensuring the shipments flow smoothly from beginning to end.

International Insurance Brokers

International insurance brokers generally specialize in marine, cargo, and surety insurance. They also provide seamless coverage for businesses involved in international trade or transportation of goods across the borders. Insurance coverage and surety bonds required to conduct international trade operations are acquired through international insurance brokers. Surety bonds provided by international insurance brokers include:

- U.S. Customs importer bonds, which are required when importing goods into the United States to guarantee the payment of taxes, fees, duties, and compliance with Customs laws and regulations.

- International carrier bonds, which protect all activities related to the entry of vessels, aircraft, or on-land carriers.

- Custodial bonds, which protect the obligations of common carriers, centralized examination stations, bonded warehouses, and container freight stations.

- Temporary importation bonds.

- Foreign-trade zone bonds, which are required of operators for all general purpose zones and subzones.

Other insurance services provided by international insurance brokers include:

- International coverage insurance, which provides you coverage for legal defense should a lawsuit be filed against you by suppliers or customers outside the United States.

- Warehouse legal liability insurance, which provides coverage for damage to cargo or loss of cargo while stored in warehouses leased or owned by you.

- Cargo legal liability insurance, which provides coverage for the loss of cargo or damage caused to cargo for which you are responsible under your bill of lading or air waybill.

It is important that you feel comfortable with the company you contract with to meet your international insurance needs. Word of mouth is the best form of advertising, and contacting fellow importers and exporters to seek their counsel in this matter is highly recommended. However, you can also find international insurance brokers by conducting a general search online under "international insurance brokers."

International Trade Consultants

International trade consulting services can be obtained from large consulting companies, specializing in all types of international trade issues or from individual consultants. These would be individuals who have been involved in international trade in one form or another for a number of years and are experts in certain fields of the industry. International trade consultants are generally not required for your common import and export operations. However, in instances where you want to establish a bonded warehouse operation, a foreign-trade zone, or even as you prepare to enter into a new market or venture, the advice and counseling of these experts is well worth the investment. Consultants can charge a flat fee per project or charge by the hour, depending on the service requested.

Not having available a single organization specifically established for international trade consultants, these companies and individuals typically become members of organizations where the members would have a need for their services. Therefore, searching the Web sites for Customs brokers and freight forwarders professional organizations, as well as the National Association of Foreign-trade Zones, will provide you with excellent results in locating international trade consultants.

International Trade and Customs Law Attorneys

From time to time during your import export business operations, you may need to secure the services of attorneys who specialize in the international trade industry. Because they specialize in this field, these attorneys are up-to-date with all rules and regulations, and any changes thereto, in the import and export industry. Their knowledge and understanding of Customs regulations can be absolutely invaluable when trying to resolve disputed issues with Customs. These law firms, or individuals, can also serve as consultants, providing you with guidance in all aspects of the structuring, development, and management of foreign-trade zones as well as in other import export business-related matters.

As it is the case with the international trade consultants, international trade and Customs law attorneys do not have a professional association of their own, but they can be located through the same previously mentioned professional organizations.

Chapter 15

Monitoring Changes in the Industry

Staying current with changes in the import export industry is vital to your success. Fortunately, staying on top of what is happening in the industry is an easy goal to achieve if you have the right resources at hand.

General International Trade-related Resources

Information is always available at your fingertips by tapping into the Internet. It is an endless source of information from import and export e-magazines to directories of services, products and suppliers, to definitions of not-so-common terms. It is just about the ultimate source, always available at your convenience. All the sources of information available are too numerous to mention, but the following three are worth tapping into right away as they contain links to just about any area of interest to you related to importing and exporting:

Export.gov at **www. export.gov**: A Web site created to provide services to U.S. businesses and those businesses abroad that interact with the U.S. federal government on international trade issues. Export.gov is managed by the U.S. Department of Commerce's International Trade Administration, along with 19 other federal agencies that provide export-related assistance programs and services to businesses involved in international trade.

The Federation of International Trade Associations at **www.fita.org**: The Web site for the Federation of International Trade Associations is a major international business portal containing information on international import and export trade leads. It also features links to over 8,000 international trade-related Web sites.

The National Trade Data Bank at **www.stat-usa.gov/tradtest.nsf**: The National Trade Data Bank's Web site contains trade leads, worldwide exchange rates, a comprehensive database of market contacts, and country-specific research databases.

Agencies You Need to Know

Get to know the private and public agencies that are involved in economic development efforts, as well as those directly related to the import and export business. As you have been reading through the book, you have been introduced to a number of agencies that play key roles in the import and export business. The following are agencies that, although they have been briefly addressed throughout the book, are worth revisiting from a different perspective. Become familiar with their staff (if local) and the services they provide. These agencies usually have a wealth of information and services available, mostly free of charge:

U.S. Customs and Border Protection (www.cbp.gov)

Customs and Border Protection is the No. 1 agency you must be familiar with when involved in importing and exporting. Every transaction you make, whether it is importing or exporting, will be impacted by Customs' rules and regulations. Their regulations are many, and enforcement is strict. Therefore, getting to know your local Customs office and its staff (if you have one locally) will be a great investment. Having a close working relationship with your local Customs officials is invaluable.

U.S. Small Business Administration (www.sba.gov)

The Small Business Administration is a Federal government agency dedicated to helping small- to medium-sized businesses establish their operations. In addition to providing low interest loans to businesses and different forms of counseling, they also have an International Trade division that provides the importer exporter with a great deal of international trade information and business leads.

International Trade Administration (www.trade.gov)

The International Trade Administration is a division of the Department of Commerce dedicated to promoting trade. The agency's Web site has a wealth of up-to-date information on international trade issues and regulations. The site also contains a great deal of information on upcoming trade missions and events, trade leads, and helpful trade statistics.

Economic development public-private partnerships

Public-private partnerships are common throughout the United States. These are agencies operated by the private sector in conjunction with public agencies. An example of this agency is Enterprise Florida, which has an entire staff dedicated to promoting and educating business owners about importing and exporting. They maintain a database of trade leads and conduct trade missions abroad on a regular basis.

CASE STUDY: ASSISTANCE
THROUGH PUBLIC-PRIVATE
PARTNERSHIP AGENCIES

Janet Jainarain, Director of
International Marketing & Research
Enterprise Florida
800 Magnolia Avenue, Suite 1100
Orlando, FL 32803
www.eflorida.com/export
(407) 956-5618

Enterprise Florida is a classic example of what public-private partnership agencies can do to help businesses grow and expand. The agency is a partnership between some of Florida's private sector businesses and the State of Florida, funded by both sectors. Enterprise Florida works with local businesses and a statewide network of economic development partners to help attract and create businesses in high-growth industries. In addition, through its award-winning **www.eflorida.com** Web site they make available a network of service providers from around the state who are geared toward small and start-up businesses, working directly with them and providing the assistance they need. The agency has received numerous awards for their efforts such as the Gold Award from *Export Magazine,* award for the Best Statewide Export Development Program, the President's "E" Award for Export Services, and the International Achievement Certificate from the U.S. Commercial Service.

One of the efforts of Enterprise Florida is its International Trade and Business Development Division, which provides a variety of services to Florida's exporters. Some of the programs available through this division include export counseling, qualified trade leads, overseas trade missions, and export finance. Janet Jainarain, director of International Marketing & Research, said the services are provided free of charge to the clients with the exception of some local in-state events, such as training workshops for which a small fee is charged. In addition, for overseas trade missions and trade shows, there are participation fees, and the client is responsible for his or her own travel expenses.

The staff at Enterprise Florida's International Trade and Business Development Division recommends that the company develop a business plan, including an international marking plan that clearly identifies the products/services to import/export and has the know-how and financing in place to execute business deals. In addition, they advise the starting-up entrepreneur to seek out countries that have purchasing power and products/services that sell. Look for new and innovative, in-demand products/services, and lean toward items with higher margins.

Enterprise Florida's Tampa Field Office began working with a Tampa-based manufacturer's representative of appliances, lighting, plumbing, and electrical products in 2005. They started as a manufacturer's representative for General Electric (GE), selling appliance packages to developers in Roatan, Honduras. They came to Enterprise Florida in 2005 for export consulting.

With the encouragement of our staff, the company participated in Enterprise Florida's Export Sales Mission to Central America in 2005 and our Export Sales Mission to Panama and Costa Rica in 2007. Both of the missions include one-on-one appointments with potential business partners in the countries visited. In early 2009, they were selected as the exclusive agent for Progress Lighting — one of the largest residential lighting manufacturers in the U.S. — in selected markets in Central America and the Caribbean. Most recently, Enterprise Florida provided detailed trade statistics to the company to help them determine which products would be most suitable in various markets. The company now represents Progress Lighting, Delta, and Moen in addition to GE, and offers packages to residential and commercial developers with projects in Central America and the Caribbean.

Local economic development corporations (administrations)

Most medium- to large-sized communities have a local economic development corporation (or administration). These agencies are in place to work toward attracting new business to the community, retaining already existing businesses, and providing workforce initiatives. Your local economic development corporation will be an excellent source to tap into as you commence your operations.

Professional Organizations Available

Joining trade-related professional organizations is also a great way to stay informed. Professional organizations host educational seminars and conferences where members are provided with information as to the latest changes in the industry, as well as with educational tools that will help you succeed. Most of all, they provide you with excellent networking opportunities where you can meet other members of the international trade community whom you can always turn to for advice and guidance. There are numerous professional trade organizations related to the import and export business. The following list is not all-inclusive by any means. However, it is a good list to begin with, and through these organizations, you will be able to learn of other organizations that might also be of interest to you:

American Importers Association (AIA)
(www.americanimporters.org)

The AIA is headquartered in Tampa, Florida, and its mission is to bring foreign companies who are interested in exporting into the U.S. together with U.S. importers. They maintain a data base of suppliers, vendors, and importers that all parties can access to find prospective business partners.

American Association of Exporters and Importers (AAEI)
(www.aaei.org)

AAEI is made up of companies from the U.S. who import, export, or both, as well as companies or individuals who are involved in one way or another in the international trade industry. The organization's main drive is to serve as the industry's "voice" in Washington, representing its members on Capitol Hill. The AAEI holds regular training sessions for its members to keep them up-to-date on international trade issues.

National Association of Foreign-trade Zones (NAFTZ) (www.naftz.org)

The NAFTZ is a professional organization comprising members of the international industry who participate in the foreign-trade zone program in one way or another. Some of the main objectives of the organization include promoting the use of FTZs, educating the public regarding what FTZs are all about, and constantly maintaining its members of changes and updates in regulations affecting FTZs. The NAFTZ also conducts educational seminars throughout the year to further educate its members on issues related to foreign-trade zones. The NAFTZ is also a very active voice in Washington, keeping the communication channels open between law makers and foreign-trade zone users and participants.

Professional Association of Exporters and Importers (PAEI) (www.paei.org)

The PAEI is comprised of professionals in the import and export industry. The association is very active in promoting the role of those involved in international trade through education and active participation in ongoing international trade issues and policies discussions. The association provides its members with a number of networking opportunities throughout the year as well as maintaining an informative Web site.

Local Chamber of Commerce

It is always a good idea to join your local chamber of commerce. They provide you, as a new business, with the support and the networking opportunities you need to get your business off the ground. Membership also provides you with excellent networking opportunities with other businesses in the area. Although your import export business is of a global nature, you are still part of the community where your business is located.

Becoming a Certified Global Business Professional (CGBP)

Not all industries have professional certifications available for those involved. However, when such a certification is available, it is in your best interest to take advantage of it. Becoming certified as a professional in your field will always give you an edge over all those that do not have the certification. This can be attributed to all the knowledge and benefits that are naturally a part of that, as well as the perceived prestige associated with such certifications. For the international trade industry, one of those certifications is becoming a Certified Global Business Professional.

The certification is achieved by completing a series of courses and examinations in various subjects such as global marketing, international business management, international trade finance, and several other relevant courses. Obtaining a CGBP certification is equivalent to receiving a CPA credential. The courses are offered by NASBITE International, a professional organization under the auspices of Cleveland State University, which is also responsible for awarding the certification. The organization is made up of international business educators at educational institutions and trade specialists from federal, state, and local trade assistance organizations. NASBITE's Web site, **www.nasbite.org**, provides information on how to become CGBP-certified.

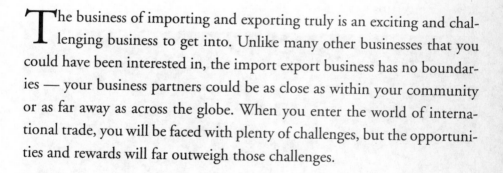

Conclusion

The business of importing and exporting truly is an exciting and challenging business to get into. Unlike many other businesses that you could have been interested in, the import export business has no boundaries — your business partners could be as close as within your community or as far away as across the globe. When you enter the world of international trade, you will be faced with plenty of challenges, but the opportunities and rewards will far outweigh those challenges.

A lot has been covered in this book, beginning with the first and most basic steps to take when you start up a business, to covering a vast amount of information specifically related to importing and exporting. Rules and regulations affecting this industry are directly affected by changes in the global economy, as well as the political climate in the U.S. and across the globe. Review and carefully evaluate all the information that has been provided to you as you go through the motions of establishing and operating your import export business, but also stay on top of changes in the industry. In the puzzle of success, your key to succeeding is not just one piece of that puzzle; it is a combination of those pieces wisely put together, such as establishing a solid operation, having a clear understanding of the rules and regulations affecting the industry, and knowing which programs are available to you that can help your business. Also, it is the smart marketing of your products and services, getting to know all the private and governmental agencies that take part in the industry, and managing your business ethically and environmentally friendly.

The goal is not only to provide you with the information you need to establish an import export business, but also to provide you with the tools and knowledge you need to continue to operate this business successfully for as long as you wish to own the business. Starting a business is not an easy task, and at the beginning, we may not see when or where the rewards will come from. But keep forging ahead, confident that the final key to your operating a financially successful import export business is right here at your fingertips.

# Glossary

Air waybill — A bill of lading for air transportation.

Bill of lading — The contractual agreement between the supplier and the carrier who will be transporting the goods.

Bonded warehouse — A facility that operates under a Customs bond where goods can be brought in for storage and the payment of duty is deferred until such time that the goods enter U.S. Customs territory.

Customs broker — An individual or company that represents the importer when conducting business with Customs.

Customs ruling — Customs' determination as to what duty rate applies to a particular product.

Domestic market — U.S. market.

Dumping duties — The sale of goods at less than the normal price.

Intellectual property rights — Rights given to individuals over their own creations, such as through patents, trademarks, and copyrights, where the creator is given the exclusive right over the use of his or her creation for a determined time.

Foreign-trade zones (FTZ) — Enclosed, secured areas located in or close to a port of entry where imported merchandise can be stored, manipulated, and re-exported without paying Customs duties.

Freight forwarders — Individuals or companies who work out the logistics of shipping merchandise, making sure the shipment reaches its destination safely, on time, and in the most cost-effective manner.

Letters of credit — Used by financial institutions to guarantee payments on behalf of its customers.

Line of credit — An arrangement through a financial institution whereby the bank extends a specified amount of unsecured credit to the borrower.

Loan proposal — A condensed version of the business plan and used by businesses to request financing.

Logistics — Logistics refers to the storage and movement of goods from its original location to its final destination.

Private-public partnership agencies — Private agencies that receive government funding and sometimes partnered with government agencies for the day-to-day operations.

Return on investment (ROI) — A return ratio that compares the net benefits of your products and services, versus their total cost.

Shareholders — Shareholders are owners of the corporation through the ownership of shares, or stocks, which represent a financial interest in the company and gives them voting rights.

Shipper's export declaration (SED) — Is a form required by the U.S. Census Bureau to control all U.S. exports and gather trade statistics.

Temporary Importation under Bond (TIB) — This is a procedure whereby certain items may be entered into U.S. Customs territory for a limited time and under certain conditions, duty-free.

Title to goods — Having ownership of the goods.

Trade mission — When a group of individuals travels abroad with the purpose of meeting with potential trading partners.

Trade publications — Industry-specific publications such as magazines and other periodicals.

Trade shows — Exhibitions organized with the purpose of providing a venue where companies involved in international trade can showcase their products and services.

Bibliography

Capela, John J., *Import/Export For Dummies*, Wiley Publishing, Inc., New Jersey, 2008.

Markheim, Daniella, "America's Free Trade Agenda: The State of Bilateral and Multilateral Trade Negotiations," Backgrounder by The Heritage Foundation, Washington, D.C., November 2, 2005.

Nelson, Dr. Carl A., *Import/Export: How to Take Your Business Across Borders, Fourth Edition*, McGraw Hill, New York, 2009.

Seyoum, Belay, *Export-Import Theory, Practices, and Procedures, Second Edition*, Routledge, New York, 2009.

Weiss, Kenneth D., *Building An Import/Export Business, Fourth Edition*, John Wiley & Sons, Inc., New Jersey, 2008.

Internet References

About.com, Small business information
www.sbinformation.about.com

American Importers Association, U.S. Import Requirement
www.americanimorters.org

American Society of International Law
www.asil.org/iel1.cfm

Articles of incorporation
www.lawdepot.com

Asmara USA, Inc., International Trade Compliance
Management Consultancy
www.asmara.com/drawback.htm

Export.gov
www.export.gov

Export-Import Bank of the United States
www.exim.gov

The Federation of International Trade Associations
www.fita.org/conferences.html

FindLaw, Import
http://library.findlaw.com

Foreign-Trade Zone Corporation: Foreign-trade zone resource center
www.foreign-trade-zone.com

International Trade Administration
www.trade.gov

Multilateral and bilateral free trade agreements
www.upiasia.com/Economics/2008/01/28/multilateral

NASBITE, Certified Global Business Professional
www.nasbitecgbp.org

National Association of Foreign-trade Zones
www.naftz.org

The National Law Center for Inter-American Free Trade
www.natlaw.com/about.htm

Office of the United States Trade Representative
www.ustr.gov/trade-agreements/free-trade-agreements

Small Business Administration
www.sba.gov

Small Business Notes: Information and resources for small
business owners
www.smallbusinessnotes.com

Tuttle Law Trade Library
www.tuttlelaw.com

U.S. Customs and Border Protection
www.cbp.gov

U.S. Department of Agriculture, Foreign Agricultural Services
www.fas.usda.gov

U.S. Department of Commerce, "A Basic Guide to Exporting,"
1998 Edition
www.unzco.com/basicguide

U.S. Department of Commerce, Bureau of Industry and Security
www.bis.doc.gov/licensing

United States Foreign-trade Zones Board
www.ia.ita.doc.gov/ftzpage/index.html

United States International Trade Commission
www.usitc.gov

Web Marketing Today
www.wilsonweb.com/articles/checklist.htm

World Trade Organization
www.wto.org

Author Biography

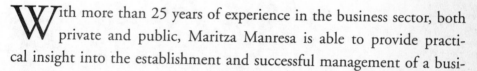

With more than 25 years of experience in the business sector, both private and public, Maritza Manresa is able to provide practical insight into the establishment and successful management of a business. While in the public sector, Manresa was responsible for the development, submittal, and ultimately the activation of a foreign-trade zone in Ocala, Florida, which she managed for almost 10 years. In addition to the foreign-trade zone, Manresa was also instrumental in establishing a U.S. Customs user-fee operation at the local airport, changing its designation to an "international airport," thereby opening a new world of trade opportunities — internationally — for the local business community.

As a Saint Leo University magna cum laude graduate, Manresa holds a bachelor's degree in business administration. Her involvement in international trade from the public sector's end, as well as from the private sector's perspective, gives this author the unique capability to present readers with in-depth, must-know information to help them successfully establish and operate an import export business. After 20 years of employment in the public sector, Manresa owns and manages a business with her husband, Manny, and her children, Wesley and Monica, and also works as a freelance writer.

Index